Lab Manual for
A+ Guide to Hardware
Third Edition

Jean Andrews, Ph.D.

THOMSON
COURSE TECHNOLOGY

D0082265

Australia • Canada • Mexico • Singapore • Spain • United Kingdom • United States

THOMSON
™
COURSE TECHNOLOGY

Lab Manual for A+ Guide to Hardware, Third Edition
is published by Course Technology.

Managing Editor:
Will Pitkin III

Product Manager:
Manya Chylinski

Associate Product Manager:
Sarah Santoro

Editorial Assistant:
Jennifer Smith

Senior Marketing Manager:
Brian Berkeley

Development Editor:
Jill Batistick

Production Editor:
Philippa Lehar

Executive Editor:
Bob Woodbury

Composition:
GEX Publishing Services

Text Designer:
GEX Publishing Services

Manuscript Quality Engineer:
Marianne Snow

Manufacturing:
Melissa Hulse

Cover Designer:
Abby Scholz

Disclaimer:
Course Technology reserves the right to revise this publication and make changes from time to time in its content without notice.

ISBN-13: 978-1-4188-3564-4
ISBN-10: 1-4188-3564-1

TABLE OF Contents

Preface

This Lab Manual is designed to be the very best tool on the market to enable you to get the hands-on practical experience needed to learn how to troubleshoot and repair personal computers and operating systems. It contains 82 labs, each of which targets a very practical problem you are likely to face in the "real world" when troubleshooting PCs. We have made every attempt to write labs that allow you to use generic hardware devices. A specific hardware configuration is not necessary to complete the labs. In learning to install, support, and troubleshoot operating systems, you will learn to use the command prompt and learn to support Windows 98, Windows NT Professional, Windows 2000 Professional, and Windows XP Professional. Each chapter contains labs that are designed to provide the structure needed by the novice, as well as labs that challenge the experienced and inquisitive student.

This book helps prepare you for the revised A+ Core Hardware Certification exam offered through the Computer Technology Industry Association (CompTIA). Because the popularity of this certification credential is quickly growing among employers, obtaining certification increases your ability to gain employment, improve your salary, and enhance your career. To find more information about A+ Certification and its sponsoring organization, CompTIA, go to the CompTIA Web site at *www.comptia.org*.

Whether your goal is to become an A+ certified technician or to become a PC support technician, the *Lab Manual for A+ Guide to Hardware, Third Edition*, along with Jean Andrews' textbooks, will take you there!

Features

To ensure a successful experience for both instructors and students, this book includes the following pedagogical features:

- **Objectives**—Every lab opens with learning objectives that set the stage for students to absorb the lessons of the lab.

- **Materials Required**—This feature outlines all the materials students need to complete the lab successfully.

- **Activity Background**—A brief discussion at the beginning of each lab provides important background information.

- **Estimated Completion Time**—To help students plan their work, each lab includes an estimate of the total amount of time required to complete the activity.

Activity—Detailed, numbered steps walk students through the lab. These steps are divided into manageable sections, with explanatory material between each section.

- **Figures**—Where appropriate, photographs of hardware or screenshots of software are provided to increase student mastery of the lab topic.
- **Review Questions**—Exercises at the end of each lab help students test their understanding of the lab material.
- **Web Site**—For updates to this book and information about other A+ and PC Repair products, go to *www.course.com/pcrepair*.

ACKNOWLEDGMENTS

I would like to give special thanks to Jill Batistick, for her patience and her undying commitment to excellence throughout this entire project.

I would also like to extend my sincere appreciation to Manya Chylinski, Philippa Lehar, and all the Course Technology staff for their instrumental roles in the development of this Lab Manual.

Many thanks to Nadine Schreiter of Lakeshore Technical College and Michael Lehrfeld of Brevard Community College, who served as technical editors of previous editions of the manual and still had an impact on this edition. Thank you to Scott Johns for your invaluable experience and for help in developing many of the labs. And I especially want to thank Jill West whose patience, support, and careful attention to detail made my life so much easier. This book is dedicated to the covenant of God with man on the earth.

—Jean Andrews, Ph.D.

CLASSROOM SETUP

Lab activities have been designed to explore many different hardware setup and troubleshooting problems while attempting to keep the requirements for specific hardware to a minimum. Other lab activities have been designed to progressively explore several operating systems so that you can install and use Windows 98, followed by Windows NT Professional, Windows 2000 Professional, and Windows XP.

Most labs take 30 to 45 minutes; a few may take a little longer. For several of the labs, your classroom should be networked and provide access to the Internet. When access to the Windows setup files is required, these files can be provided on the Windows installation CD or on a network drive made available to the PC.

When the particular OS is not of concern, the minimum hardware requirements are:

- 90 MHz or better Pentium-compatible computer
- 24 MB of RAM
- 540-MB hard drive
- A PC toolkit with ground bracelet (ESD strap)

The minimum hardware requirements for Windows 98 are:

- 90 MHz or better Pentium-compatible computer
- 24 MB of RAM
- 195-MB hard drive

The minimum hardware requirements for Windows NT Workstation are:

- 90 MHz or better Pentium-compatible computer
- 16 MB of RAM
- 125-MB hard drive

Additional setup notes on Windows NT Workstation:

- Install Windows NT Workstation on a FAT partition and provide an additional NTFS partition for data
- You will need a user account with administrative privileges

The minimum hardware requirements for Windows 2000 Professional are:

- 133 MHz or better Pentium-compatible computer
- 64 MB of RAM
- 2-GB hard drive

Additional setup notes on Windows 2000 Professional:

- You will need a user account with administrative privileges
- An NTFS partition that might be the partition where Windows 2000 is installed

The minimum hardware requirements for Windows XP are:

- 233 MHz or better Pentium-compatible computer (300 MHz preferred)
- 64 MB of RAM (128 MB preferred)
- 1.5-GB hard drive (2-GB preferred)

Additional setup notes on Windows XP Professional:

- You will need a user account with administrative privileges

A few of the labs focus on special hardware. For example, one lab requires that a CD-ROM drive, sound card, and speakers be installed, and another lab uses a PC camera, a sound card, microphone, and speakers. Two labs require a multimeter. Also, one lab requires a modem and a working phone line, and another lab requires a parallel cable.

LAB SETUP INSTRUCTIONS

Configuration Type and Operating Systems

Each lab begins with a list of required materials. Before beginning a lab activity, verify that each student workgroup or individual has access to the needed materials. Then, make sure that the proper operating system is installed and in good health. Note that in some cases, it is not necessary that an operating system be installed. When needed, the Windows setup files can be provided on the Windows CD, on a network drive, or, in some cases, on the local hard drive. In some labs, device drivers are needed. Students will be able to work more efficiently if these drivers are available on floppy disk or on a network drive prior to beginning the lab.

Protect Data

In several labs, it is possible that data on the hard drive might get lost or corrupted. For this reason, it is important that valuable data stored on the hard drive is backed up to another media.

Access to the Internet

Several labs require access to the Internet. In these labs, if necessary, you can use one computer to search the Internet to download software or documentation and another computer for performing the lab procedures. If the lab does not have Internet access, you can download the needed software or documentation prior to lab and bring the files to lab stored on floppy disk.

THE TECHNICIAN'S WORK AREA

When opening a computer case, it is important to have the proper tools and be properly grounded to ensure that you don't cause more damage than you repair. Now, let's take a look at the components of an ideal technician's work area:

- Grounding mat (with grounding wire properly grounded)
- Grounding wrist strap (attached to the grounding mat)
- Non-carpet flooring
- A clean work area (no clutter)
- A set of screwdrivers
- ¼" Torx bit screwdriver

- ⅛" Torx bit screwdriver
- Needle-nose pliers
- A PLCC (Plastic Leadless Chip Carrier)
- Pen light (flashlight)
- Several new antistatic bags (for transporting and storing hardware)

At minimum, you must have at least two key items. The first is a ground strap. If a grounding mat isn't available, you can attach the ground strap to the computer's chassis and, in most cases, provide sufficient grounding for handling hardware components inside the computer case. The second key item is, of course, a screwdriver. You won't be able to open most chassis without some type of screwdriver.

PROTECT YOURSELF, YOUR HARDWARE, AND YOUR SOFTWARE

When you work on a computer, it is possible to harm both the computer and yourself. The most common accident that happens when attempting to fix a computer problem is erasing software or data. Experimenting without knowing what you are doing can cause damage. To prevent these sorts of accidents, as well as the physically dangerous ones, take a few safety precautions. The following text describes the potential sources of damage to computers and how to protect against them.

Power to the Computer

To protect both yourself and the equipment when working inside a computer, turn off the power, unplug the computer, and always use a grounding bracelet. Consider the monitor and the power supply to be "black boxes." Never remove the cover or put your hands inside this equipment unless you know about the hazards of charged capacitors. Both the power supply and the monitor can hold a dangerous level of electricity even after they are turned off and disconnected from a power source.

STATIC ELECTRICITY, OR ESD

Electrostatic discharge (ESD), commonly known as static electricity, is an electrical charge at rest. A static charge can build up on the surface of a nongrounded conductor and on non-conductive surfaces such as clothing or plastic. When two objects with dissimilar electrical charges touch, static electricity passes between them until the dissimilar charges are made equal. To see how this works, turn off the lights in a room, scuff your feet on the carpet, and touch another person. Occasionally you may see and feel the charge in your fingers. If you can feel the charge, then you discharged at least 3,000 volts of static electricity. If you hear the discharge, then you released at least 6,000 volts. If you see the discharge, then you released at least 8,000 volts of ESD. A charge of less than 3,000 volts can damage most electronic components. You can touch a chip on an expansion card or system board and damage the chip with ESD and never feel, hear, or see the discharge.

ESD can cause two types of damage in an electronic component: catastrophic failures and upset failures. A catastrophic failure destroys the component beyond use. An upset failure damages the component so that it does not perform well, even though it may still function to some degree. Upset failures are the most difficult to detect because they are not easily observed.

Protect Against ESD

To protect the computer against ESD, always ground yourself before touching electronic components, including the hard drive, system board, expansion cards, processors, and memory modules. Ground yourself and the computer parts, using one or more of the following static control devices or methods:

- *Ground bracelet or static strap:* A ground bracelet is a strap you wear around your wrist. The other end is attached to a grounded conductor such as the computer case or a ground mat, or it can plug into a wall outlet. (Only the ground prong makes a connection!)

- *Grounding mats:* Ground mats can come equipped with a cord to plug into a wall outlet to provide a grounded surface on which to work. Remember, if you lift the component off the mat, it is no longer grounded and is susceptible to ESD.

- *Static shielding bags:* New components come shipped in static shielding bags. Save the bags to store other devices that are not currently installed in a PC.

The best way to protect against ESD is to use a ground bracelet together with a ground mat. Consider a ground bracelet to be essential equipment when working on a computer. However, if you find yourself in a situation where you must work without one, touch the computer case before you touch a component. When passing a chip to another person, ground yourself. Leave components inside their protective bags until ready to use. Work on hard floors, not carpet, or use antistatic spray on the carpets.

Besides using a grounding mat, you can also create a ground for the computer case by leaving the power cord to the case plugged into the wall outlet. This is safe enough because the power is turned off when you work inside the case. However, if you happen to touch an exposed area of the power switch inside the case, it is possible to get a shock. Because of this risk, in this book, you are directed to unplug the power cord to the PC before you work inside the case.

There is an exception to the ground-yourself rule. Inside a monitor case, the electricity stored in capacitors poses a substantial danger. When working inside a monitor, you *don't* want to be grounded, as you would provide a conduit for the voltage to discharge through your body. In this situation, be careful *not* to ground yourself.

When handling system boards and expansion cards, don't touch the chips on the boards. Don't stack boards on top of each other, which could accidentally dislodge a chip. Hold cards by the edges, but don't touch the edge connections on the card.

After you unpack a new device or software that has been wrapped in cellophane, remove the cellophane from the work area quickly. Don't allow anyone who is not properly grounded to touch components. Do not store expansion cards within one foot of a monitor, because the monitor can discharge as much as 29,000 volts of ESD onto the screen.

Hold an expansion card by the edges. Don't touch any of the soldered components on a card. If you need to put an electronic device down, place it on a grounded mat or on a static shielding bag. Keep components away from your hair and clothing.

Protect Hard Drives and Disks

Always turn off a computer before moving it to protect the hard drive, which is always spinning when the computer is turned on (unless the drive has a sleep mode). Never jar a computer while the hard disk is running. Avoid placing a PC on the floor, where the user can accidentally kick it.

Follow the usual precautions to protect disks. Keep them away from magnetic fields, heat, and extreme cold. Don't open the floppy shuttle window or touch the surface of the disk inside the housing. Treat disks with care and they'll generally last for years.

HOW COMPUTERS WORK

Labs included in this chapter

➤ Lab 1.1 Gather and Record System Information

➤ Lab 1.2 Identify Computer Parts

➤ Lab 1.3 Use Shareware to Examine a Computer

➤ Lab 1.4 Compare Costs

➤ Lab 1.5 Plan an Ideal System

LAB 1.1 GATHER AND RECORD SYSTEM INFORMATION

Objectives

The goal of this lab is to use a system's physical characteristics and other sources to determine how the system is configured. After completing this lab, you will be able to:

➤ Gather system information by observing a system

➤ Use available tools to access specific system information

Materials Required

This lab will require the following:

➤ Windows 98, Windows 2000, or Windows XP

➤ Workgroup of 2–4 students

Activity Background

When working with a computer system, it is a good idea to know what components are installed on the system. This lab will help you identify some of these components as you gather information by observing the system and by using system tools.

Estimated completion time: **15 minutes**

ACTIVITY

Observe the physical characteristics of your system and answer the following questions:

1. Does the system have any identification on it indicating manufacturer, model, or component information? If so, list them.

   _____

   _____

2. How many floppy drives does your system have?

   _____

3. Describe the shape of the connection used by your mouse. How many pins does the connection have?

   _____

4. Does your system have CD or DVD drives? If so, how many?

_____

5. How many internal hard drives does your system have? Explain how you got your answer.

_____

_____

_____

Like other versions of Windows, Windows XP can be customized by the user to behave and to display information to that user's taste. Windows XP also has the ability to mimic the way previous versions of Windows presented menus and settings for users who are more comfortable with those methods. To help ensure that the step-by-step instructions for Windows XP exercises are easy for you to follow, complete these steps to restore Windows XP defaults to your system.

1. Boot your system and log in if necessary, then select **Control Panel** from the Start menu. The Control Panel window will open.

2. Under the Control Panel section on the left side of the Control Panel window, click **Switch to Category View** if Classic View has been enabled. See Figure 1-1.

Figure 1-1 Windows XP Control Panel in Classic View

3. With the Category View of Control Panel enabled, click the **Appearance and Themes** category. The Appearance and Themes window appears.

4. From the Appearance and Themes window, select the **Folder Options Control Panel** icon. The Folder Options dialog box appears.

5. On the General tab of the Folder Options dialog box, click the **Restore Defaults** button, then click **Apply**, as shown in Figure 1-2.

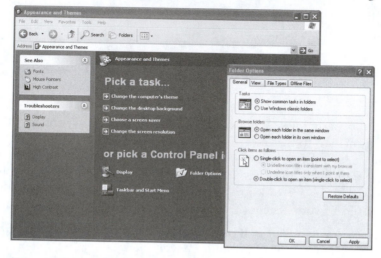

Figure 1-2   Use the Folder Options dialog box to restore Windows XP defaults to a folder

6. Select the **View** tab in the Folder Options dialog box. On the View tab, click the **Restore Defaults** button, then click **OK** to apply the settings and close the dialog box. See Figure 1-3.

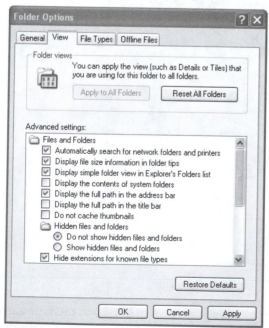

Figure 1-3   View tab of the Folder Options dialog box

7. From the Appearance and Themes window, select the **Taskbar and Start Menu** icon. The Taskbar and Start Menu dialog box appears.

8. On the Taskbar tab of the Taskbar and Start Menu dialog box, verify that all boxes are checked except for Auto-hide the taskbar and Show Quick Launch boxes under the Taskbar appearance section. Click **Apply** if any changes were made. See Figure 1-4.

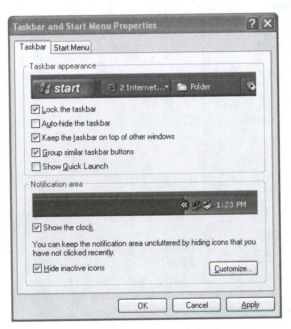

Figure 1-4   Use the Taskbar and Start Menu Properties dialog box to control how the taskbar appears and functions

9. Select the **Start Menu** tab in the Taskbar and Start Menu dialog box. On the Start Menu tab, verify that the radio button next to Start Menu is selected, then click **OK** to apply the settings and close the dialog box. See Figure 1-5. Close the Appearance and Themes window.

Figure 1-5   The Start Menu tab of the Taskbar and Start Menu Properties dialog box

From the Start menu, open the Control Panel. From the Control Panel, click the **Performance and Maintenance** category and the Performance and Maintenance window will appear. From the Performance and Maintenance window, click the **System** icon to open the System Properties dialog box. With the General tab visible as shown in Figure 1-6, record the following:

1. Which OS is installed?

_____

2. What is the version number of your operating system?

_____

3. Who is the system registered to?

_____

4. What type of CPU is your system built around?

_____

1

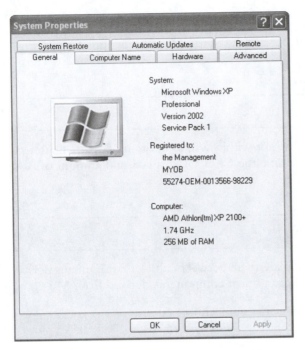

Figure 1-6   The System Properties dialog box

5. How much RAM is installed in your system?

_____

Close the System applet. Close the Performance and Maintenance window.

From the Start menu, open My Computer and locate the following information:

1. How many floppy disk drives appear and which drive letters are assigned to them?

_____

2. How many other local drives appear and which drive letters are assigned to them?

_____

3. How many network drives appear and what are their names?

_____

4. What System Tasks are listed in the left of the My Computer window?

_____

_____

_____

Review Questions

1. List two other ways to get to the System Properties applet besides using the Control Panel.

   _____

   _____

2. What is one other place, not within Windows or any documentation, where you would be able to determine the CPU, CPU speed, and amount of RAM installed on your system?

   _____

   _____

3. What differences, if any, are there between a list of components derived from a physical inspection versus a list of components derived from My Computer and System Properties?

   _____

   _____

4. How might a user, unfamiliar with how Windows XP presents menus and maintenance utilities, improve their ease and efficiency while using Windows XP?

   _____

   _____

LAB 1.2 IDENTIFY COMPUTER PARTS

Objectives

The goal of this lab is to examine your computer to identify the parts inside and outside the case. After completing this lab, you will be able to:

➤ Identify computer components outside the case

➤ Identify computer components inside the case

Materials Required

This lab will require the following:

➤ Working computer

➤ Phillips head screwdriver

➤ Anti-static bracelet

➤ Workgroup of 2–4 students

➤ A display of four or more unknown computer parts prepared by the instructor

Activity Background

When working with a computer system, you must be able to identify the hardware components, both inside and outside the case. Components are not always adequately labeled, especially those inside the case. This lab helps you learn to recognize these components.

Estimated completion time: **30 minutes**

ACTIVITY

Observe the physical characteristics of your system and answer the following questions:

1. What size monitor do you have? Measure the diagonal on the monitor screen.

   _____

2. How many keys are on your keyboard?

   _____

3. Are there any switches on the sides or bottom of the keyboard? If so, how are these switches labeled?

   _____

4. What other external components does your PC have (speakers, printer, and so forth)? Describe each component with as much detail as you can.

   _____

   _____

   _____

5. Look at the back of your PC and list all cables and cords connected to ports and other connections. Fill in the following table:

Describe the port or connector the cable or cord is connected to	Purpose of the cable or cord
1.	
2.	
3.	
4.	
5.	
6.	

6. What other ports on the PC are not being used? List them here:

_____

_____

_____

_____

Now you will open the PC case and examine the components inside. As you work, it is very important that you *not* touch anything inside the case unless you are wearing an anti-static bracelet. Follow these directions:

To remove the cover from a desktop PC, follow these steps:

1. Power down the PC and unplug it. Next, unplug the monitor, printer, and any other device that has its own external power supply. Do not disconnect any cables or cords connected to the back of the PC case.

2. Locate and remove the screws on the back of the case. Look for the screws in each corner and one in the top, as shown in Figure 1-7. Be careful that you don't unscrew any other screws besides these. (These other screws probably are holding the power supply in place, as illustrated in Figure 1-8.)

Figure 1-7   Locate the screws that hold the cover in place

Power supply
mounting screws

Figure 1-8   Power supply mounting screws

3. After you remove the cover screws, slide the cover forward and up to remove it from the case, as shown in Figure 1-9.

Remove screws   Pull cover back, then up, to remove

Figure 1-9   Removing a desktop cover

To remove the cover from a tower PC, follow these steps:

1. Power down the PC and unplug it from its power outlet. Next, unplug from the power outlet the monitor and any other device that has an external power source.

2. Look for screws in all four corners and down the sides. Remove the screws and then slide the cover back slightly before lifting it up to remove it. See Figure 1-10. Some tower cases have panels on either side of the case held in place with screws on the back of the case. Remove the screws and slide each panel toward the rear and then lift it off the case.

First, remove the screws holding the cover in place

Then carefully pull the cover toward the back

Figure 1-10   Removing a tower cover

With the cover removed, you are ready to look for some components. As you complete the following, refer to drawings in Chapters 3 and 4 of the textbook *A+ Guide to Hardware* or in Chapters 4 and 5 of the textbook *A+ Guide to Managing and Maintaining Your PC*, as necessary.

1. Put on your anti-static bracelet and connect the clip to the side of the computer case.

2. Identify and describe the following major components. List any other components found inside the case. Fill in the table:

Component	Description (include size, location, what it connects to, and what is connected to it in the system)
Power supply	
Floppy disk drive	
Hard drive	
Motherboard	
CPU	
Cooling fan (not inside the power supply)	
CD-ROM drive	
Video card	
Network card	
Sound card	

1

Challenge Activity

If your instructor has prepared the display of four assorted computer parts, fill in the following table:

Identify the part	Describe how you determined your answer
1.	
2.	
3.	
4.	

Review Questions

1. Describe how you determined which expansion card was the video card.

   _____

2. If your system has a CD-ROM drive, describe how you determined which drive was the CD-ROM drive.

   _____

3. Describe how you identified the type of CPU you have.

   _____

4. How did you know that you were or were not connected to a network?

   _____

5. Does your system have much room for adding new components? Explain your answer.

   _____

6. If you were adding one other component to the inside of the computer case, what would it be and where would you install it?

   _____

Lab 1.3 Use Shareware to Examine a Computer

Objectives

The goal of this lab is to use SANDRA, Standard version to examine your system. After completing this lab, you will be able to:

> ➤ Download a file from the Internet

> ➤ Install SANDRA

> ➤ Use SANDRA to examine your system

Materials Required

This lab will require the following:

> ➤ Windows 98, Windows 2000, or Windows XP

> ➤ Internet access

> ➤ If using Windows 98 or Windows 2000, software such as WinZip to uncompress a zipped file

Activity Background

Good PC support people are always good investigators. This lab is designed to help you learn how to conduct an investigation via the Internet. As you will see, the Internet offers a wealth of resources to those who take the time to search, download, and investigate the possible uses of software available there. This exercise is designed to help you learn to be such an investigator. Follow these directions to find and download a shareware utility that you can use to diagnose PC problems. Then you will print a report from the downloaded software about the hardware and software on your computer.

Estimated completion time: **30 minutes**

Activity

1. Open your browser and go to *www.sisoftware.co.uk*.

2. Click the **Downloads** link.

3. Follow one of the links pointing to a location that offers the SANDRA download.

4. Follow the instructions on the site that you selected to begin the download process.

5. When the File Download dialog box appears, save the file to your PC desktop. You can then disconnect from the Internet. What is the name of the downloaded file?

1

Note that if the Sisoft Web site is unavailable, you can use a search engine to locate the shareware.

Next, you can install SANDRA on your PC. Follow these steps:

1. If the file has a .zip file extension, double-click it to uncompress the SANDRA zip file and extract the setup file.

2. Run the setup program by double-clicking the executable file, which has an .exe file extension. (This might be the downloaded file or the extracted file.) Within the installation wizard, use English as the language selection, accept the EULA, and accept the default settings throughout. The SANDRA installation creates a new program in your Program Group and adds an icon to your desktop.

3. When you finish the installation, SANDRA will launch. Read the Tip of the Day, clear the checkbox next to Show Tips on Start-up, and then click **OK** to close. If you are using Windows XP, you should see a screen similar to the one shown in Figure 1-11.

Figure 1-11 SiSoftware Sandra main window installed under Windows XP

The screens for Windows 98 and Windows 2000 look similar, but, as shown in Figure 1-12, they do not group the icons under headings.

Figure 1-12   SiSoft Sandra main window installed under Windows 2000 or Windows 98

You can execute each of the utilities, in turn, by double-clicking the icons, or you can create a composite report of the results of each selection. To learn more, complete the following:

1. Double-click the **System Summary** icon. The System Summary utility launches and gathers information about your system before displaying it in a format similar to Device Manager, with devices listed by type.

2. Click the red X at the bottom of the System Summary utility or press Esc on your keyboard to close the System Summary utility.

3. Open the **Windows Information** utility. Scroll down and note the information types that are listed. According to this utility, which version of Windows are you using?

_____

4. What is the path to the Temporary Folder on your system?

_____

5. Click the red X at the bottom of the Windows Information utility or press Esc on your keyboard to close the Windows Information utility.

6. Open the **Drives Information** utility. The utility begins to gather information regarding your drives. Do not move the mouse or touch the keyboard while this is in progress. How much Total Space does the hard drive contain? How much Free Space does the hard drive contain? What type of File System does the hard drive use?

_____

_____

7. Click the red X at the bottom of the Drives Information utility or press Esc on your keyboard to close the Drives Information utility.

8. Open the **DMA Settings** utility. Why are you unable to view the DMA Settings information?

_____

_____

9. Close the DMA Settings utility.

You can create a composite report of your system using SANDRA. To learn more, follow these steps:

1. From the SiSoft SANDRA menu bar, click **File** and then click **Create a Report Wizard...**.

2. In the wizard introduction window, click **Next** (right-pointing arrow in a green circle).

3. In the Step 1 of 9 window, accept the default **Make choices and generate report** from the drop-down menu. Click **Next** to continue.

4. In the Step 2 of 9 window, click the **Clear All** (red X over a box) button. Check the boxes next to both Mainboard Information and Windows Memory Information, and then click **Next** to continue.

5. In the Step 3 of 9 window, click the **Clear All** button and then click **Next** to continue.

6. In the Step 4 of 9 window, click the **Clear All** button and then click **Next** to continue.

7. In the Step 5 of 9 window, click **Next** to continue.

8. In the Step 6 of 9 window, add any comments that you desire and click **Next** to continue.

9. In the Step 7 of 9 window, select the **Print or Fax** option from the drop-down menu and then click Next to continue.

10. In the Print dialog box, click **OK** for Windows 98 or **Print** for Windows 2000 or Windows XP. Click the **Exit** (red X) to close the wizard and then collect your report from the printer.

11. Continue to explore each utility in SANDRA, and then close SANDRA. You will use SANDRA again in later chapters, so don't uninstall it.

In this lab, you downloaded SANDRA from the SiSoft Web site. But many popular utilities are available from multiple sources on the Internet. To see for yourself, follow these steps:

1. Attempt to find SANDRA at www.zdnet.com.

2. Is the program available through this avenue as well? Print the Web page or pages to support your answer.

Review Questions

1. What URL can you use to find a link to download SANDRA?

2. Is SANDRA capable of hardware diagnostics only?

3. Which two of the four system resources are you *not* able to view with the version of SANDRA you downloaded and why?

4. What type of software is SANDRA?

LAB 1.4 COMPARE COSTS

Objectives

The objective of this lab is to compare a pre-assembled system and the components that could be assembled to build a comparable system. After completing this lab, you will be able to:

➤ Identify the key components of a pre-assembled system

➤ Locate prices for components needed to assemble a comparable system

➤ Compare the cost of a pre-assembled system and a self-assembled system

Materials Required

This lab will require the following:

➤ Internet access and/or access to a computer publication such as *Computer Shopper*

Activity Background

In this lab you will compare the cost of a brand name system with the cost of a system with the same specifications assembled from individual components. If you can't find an exact match for components, find the closest possible substitute. Use the Internet and available computer-related publications as your sources for information.

Estimated completion time: **45 minutes**

ACTIVITY

1. Find an advertisement for a complete, pre-assembled system similar to the one shown in Figure 1-13.

Figure 1-13   Complete, pre-assembled system

2. Study the advertisement and list the following specifications:

■ Processor/MHz:————————————————————

■ RAM:————————————————————————

■ OS:——————————————————————————

■ HDD capacity:—————————————————————

- Monitor: _____
- Sound/Speakers: _____
- Other Drives: _____
- Bonus Items: _____
- Bundled Software: _____
- Total Price: _____

3. Find advertisements similar to those shown in Figure 1-14. Notice that the items are grouped by component type.

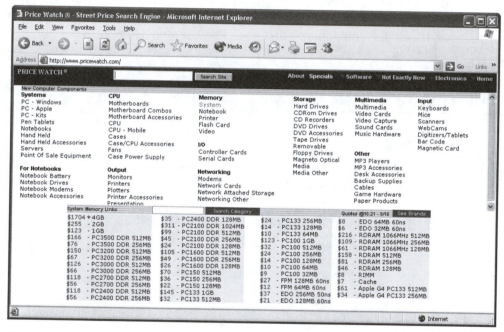

Figure 1-14   Components for sale

Using the following table, list and describe the comparable components, their individual prices, and the source of your information. You may wish to check several sources to find the best price. Remember, most mail order or online purchases have shipping costs associated with them. If you can determine an exact shipping price for each particular component, include this as part of the component's price. If you cannot find the exact shipping price, include a 10 percent fee as part of the price for each shipped component. You might have to include tax, depending on the state-to-state taxing laws that apply. Sometimes the shipping cost is offset by not having to pay state sales taxes on an item.

Component	Description	Source	Price
Processor/MHz			
Motherboard			
RAM			
Case and power supply			
OS			
HDD capacity			
Monitor			
Sound/speakers			
CD-ROM drive			
Other drives			
Bonus items			
Bundled software			
TOTAL SYSTEM PRICE			

Review Questions

1. Which approach to acquiring a system seems to be less expensive?

   _____

   _____

2. What is the single most expensive component of a system built from individual components?

   _____

3. What was the estimated cost of shipping (if any) associated with the component-built system?

   _____

4. What are some potential pitfalls of building your own PC? Rewards?

   _____

   _____

Note: As you continue with this course, you will be better able to answer this last question based on your own experiences in the course.

LAB 1.5 PLAN AN IDEAL SYSTEM

Objectives

The objective of this lab is to plan and price your own ideal system within a budget. After completing this lab, you will be able to:

➤ Describe what you want your system to be able to do

➤ Pick components that best meet your goal

➤ Stay within a budget

Materials Required

This lab will require the following:

➤ Internet access and/or access to a computer publication such as *Computer Shopper*

Activity Background

In the future you may be in a position to build a system to your specifications from individual components. Within a budget of $1200, what system would you put together? In this activity, you determine the answer based on your current knowledge and experience. Expect that your opinions will most likely change as you continue in this course.

Estimated completion time: **30 minutes**

ACTIVITY

1. On a separate piece of paper, make a table similar to the one used in Lab 1.4. Use the table to list the components that you would like to include in your system, the cost of each component, and the source for each component. To begin, list everything you want and do not worry about price.

2. Once you have determined the total price of all the components you want to include in your ideal system, add up the prices and see if you are within your $1200 budget.

3. If you are under budget, consider including additional components in your system or better versions of components you are already including. If you are over budget, determine what components you need to exclude or whether you need to use less expensive versions of some components. Either way, record what components you choose. Also, note how you altered your ideal system to meet your budget.

Review Questions

1. What is the goal of your system? In other words, how do you plan to use your system? Explain your choices for components.

   _____

   _____

   _____

2. How would you change your choices if you were to use this computer at a corporate office as a business workstation?

   _____

   _____

   _____

3. What single change would you make if you had an extra $200 in the budget?

   _____

   _____

4. How might you change your design if your budget was only $1000?

   _____

   _____

Keep your responses to this lab for later reference. As you learn more about PCs in this course, you can look back at these responses and see where you might change your mind based on new information you have learned.

How Hardware and Software Work Together

Labs included in this chapter

➤ Lab 2.1 Examine System Resources with Device Manager

➤ Lab 2.2 Create and Examine a Windows 98 Startup Disk

➤ Lab 2.3 Use Microsoft Diagnostics with Windows

➤ Lab 2.4 Observe the Boot Process

➤ Lab 2.5 Modify Configuration Files and Observe the Results

LAB 2.1 EXAMINE SYSTEM RESOURCES WITH DEVICE MANAGER

Objectives

In this lab, you will learn about Device Manager. After completing this lab, you will be able to use Device Manager to:

➤ Determine what components are installed on a system

➤ Examine system resource allocation

➤ Print a system summary

Materials Required

This lab will require the following:

➤ Windows 98, Windows 2000, or Windows XP

Activity Background

Windows 98, Windows 2000, and Windows XP provide a powerful configuration tool called Device Manager, which you can use to view and print a system's hardware configuration. Windows NT does not have Device Manager. Device Manager is more powerful than MSD, but not quite as good as some third-party utilities. (You examined one of these third-party utilities in Lab 1.3.) Note that Windows 98 and Windows 2000/XP offer slightly different Device Managers, so as you complete this lab be sure to follow the directions for your version.

> Estimated completion time: **30 minutes**

ACTIVITY

To access Device Manager in Windows 98, follow these steps:

1. Click the **Start** button on the taskbar, point to **Settings**, and then click **Control Panel**. The Control Panel window opens.

2. Double-click the **System** icon.

3. In the System Properties dialog box, click the **Device Manager** tab.

To access Device Manager in Windows 2000, follow these steps:

1. Click the **Start** button on the taskbar, click **Settings**, and then click **Control Panel**. The Control Panel window opens.

2. Double-click the **System** icon.

3. In the System Properties dialog box, click the **Hardware** tab, and then click the **Device Manager** button.

4. Device Manager opens. If a message dialog box appears, read and close it. According to this message, what must you do in order to actually make changes in Device Manager?

To access Device Manager in Windows XP, follow these steps:

1. Click the **Start** button on the taskbar and then click **Control Panel**. The Control Panel window opens. Click **Performance and Maintenance**.

2. Click the **System** Control Panel icon. The System Properties dialog box appears.

3. In the System Properties dialog box select the **Hardware** tab.

4. In the Device Manager section of the System Properties dialog box, click the **Device Manager** button. The Device Manager window appears.

5. If a message dialog box appears, click **OK** to continue. Why did you receive the prompt?

In both Windows 2000 and Windows XP, Device Manager appears similar to Figure 2-1. You can right-click an item in the list and then select Properties from the shortcut menu to view information about that item, or you can view the item's Properties by double-clicking the item. When you click the + sign to the left of an item, a list of the installed devices for that item appears beneath the item. To see how this works, follow these steps:

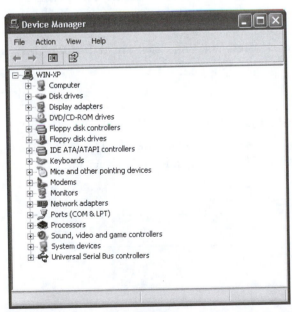

Figure 2-1   Windows 2000 and Windows XP Device manager can be accessed from the System Properties window

1. Click the **plus sign** next to Network adapters.

2. Double-click a device listed under Network adapters. A Properties dialog box opens.

3. Click the **Resources** tab. This tab shows all resources used by the selected device.

Use the Resources tab in the Properties dialog box to complete the following:

1. What IRQ is assigned to the network adapter?

   _____

2. What is the I/O range of the network adapter?

   _____

3. What Memory Addresses are available to the network adapter?

   _____

4. Close the Properties window.

Device Manager in Windows 2000 and Windows XP hides some resources from initial view. To view hidden devices in Windows 2000 and Windows XP:

1. List the device types that are currently displayed.

   _____

   _____

   _____

2. From the menu bar, click **View** and then click **Show hidden devices**.

3. How many additional devices appeared?

   _____

4. Expand **Non-Plug and Play Drivers**.

5. Explore the properties of several drivers and note some of the differences between the Driver tabs of Non-Plug and Play Drivers and non-hidden devices.

   _____

   _____

Device Manager also enables you to view resources in other ways.

To view resources in Windows 98:

1. In Device Manager, click the **View resources by connection** option button and observe that the groupings change.

2. Click the **plus sign** next to Plug and Play BIOS to view the devices managed by the Plug and Play BIOS.

To view resources in Windows XP:

1. Click **View** on the Device Manager menu bar and then click **Resources by type**. Note that information is now grouped into four categories.

2. Click the **plus sign** next to Interrupt request (IRQ) to see which device is assigned to each IRQ line.

Device Manager enables you to print information about individual devices or device categories. You can also print a system summary. To print a system summary, follow the directions for your version of Windows.

To print a system summary for Windows 98:

1. Click the **Print** button.

2. Click the **System summary** option button and click **OK**.

To print a system summary for Windows 2000:

1. Click **View** on the Device Manager menu bar and then click **Print**.

2. Click the **System summary** option button and then click **Print**.

To print a system summary for Windows XP:

1. Click the **Print** button.

2. Click the **System summary** option button and then click **Print**.

Review Questions

1. For each entry below, list the tab on a device's Properties box in Device Manager where you would be able to perform the action or find the information.

- Start a troubleshooting wizard: _____
- Determine the IRQ setting: _____
- Disable or enable the device: _____
- Allow the device to bring the system out of standby: _____
- Find conflict information: _____

2. How do you display individual devices under the group headings?

_____

3. What are two ways to access a device Properties box in Device Manager?

_____

_____

4. What types of additional devices appeared when you chose to display hidden devices?

_____

_____

5. What three options are available for printing in Device Manager?

_____

_____

_____

LAB 2.2 CREATE AND EXAMINE A WINDOWS 98 STARTUP DISK

Objectives

The objective of this lab is to learn how a Windows 98 startup disk is made and used. After completing this lab, you will be able to:

➤ Create a Windows 98 startup disk

➤ Describe the steps in booting from a startup disk

Materials Required

This lab will require the following:

➤ Windows 98 operating system

➤ Blank floppy disk

➤ Workgroup of 2–4 students

Activity Background

From within Windows 98, you can create a startup disk, which is a great tool for troubleshooting and setup. A startup disk is a bootable disk that also contains several helpful utilities and drivers. In this activity, you will create and experiment with a startup disk.

Estimated completion time: **30 minutes**

ACTIVITY

1. Open the Control Panel and double-click the **Add/Remove Programs** icon.

2. In the Add/Remove Programs applet, click the **Startup Disk** tab.

3. In the Startup Disk tab, click the **Create Disk** button and follow the prompts to create the startup disk.

4. When the process is complete, close the Add/Remove Programs applet.

Answer the following questions about the startup disk:

1. What two files on the startup disk end in the ".bat" extension?

   _____

2. What are the purposes of these files?

   _____

   _____

3. What kind of information is provided in the README.TXT file?

   _____

   _____

With the startup disk in the drive, reboot your computer and answer these questions:

1. What prompt do you see while the system boots?

   _____

2. What type of drive is set up during the boot process?

   _____

3. Why do you think this drive is set up?

   _____

To continue exploring the startup disk, follow these steps:

1. Using the command prompt provided by the startup disk, access the hard drive by entering the following command: **C:**

2. Your prompt should now be the C prompt. Write the prompt here.

   _____

3. Use the DIR command to view the contents of the root directory of the **C** drive.

4. Keeping in mind that filenames usually describe the file's function, record the names of the files listed as a result of the DIR command. Explain what you think the purpose of each file is.

   _____

   _____

   _____

Keep your startup disk to use in later labs.

Review Questions

1. Why might you want to use a startup disk?

   _____

   _____

2. What icon in the Control Panel do you use to create a startup disk?

   _____

3. Why would you need CD-ROM support when using the startup disk?

   _____

   _____

4. If you wanted to examine the files on the CD-ROM drive, what command(s) would you execute at the command prompt?

   _____

5. What three files must be on the startup disk to make the disk bootable?

   _____

LAB 2.3 USE MICROSOFT DIAGNOSTICS WITH WINDOWS

2

Objectives

The goal of this lab is to observe the boot process. After completing this lab, you will be able to:

➤ Use the Microsoft Diagnostics (MSD) utility to examine your system

➤ Compare results of MSD using real mode and protected mode

Materials Required

This lab will require the following:

➤ Windows 98 operating system

➤ Bootable floppy disk from Lab 2.2 or startup disk from Lab 2.2

➤ Path to Windows 98 setup files as provided by your instructor

Activity Background

The Microsoft Diagnostics (MSD) utility, which is included with both DOS and all versions of Windows, examines your system and displays useful information about ports, devices, memory, and the like. The program file for Microsoft Diagnostics, MSD.EXE, is located in the Tools/OldMSDOS directory on your Windows 98 installation CD. In this lab you will install and use MSD.

Estimated completion time: **30 minutes**

ACTIVITY

Before you can begin using MSD, you need to copy the program file to your hard disk.

1. Insert the Windows 98 installation CD into your CD-ROM drive or access the setup files at the location provided by your instructor.

2. Copy the file **MSD.EXE** from the Windows 98 Tools/OldMSDOS directory to your hard drive, storing it in a folder named **\Tools**.

Now that you have copied the necessary program file to your hard disk, you can launch MSD. Follow these steps to use MSD in a real mode environment:

1. Reboot your computer using the bootable floppy disk from Lab 2.2 or a Windows 98 startup disk from Lab 2.2, which will boot your PC into real mode and provide a command prompt. Or you can point to Start, click Shut Down, and then click "Restart Computer in MS-DOS mode."

2. At the command prompt, type **C:\TOOLS\MSD.EXE** and then press **Enter**. Note that this is a way to execute a program file located in a different directory from the one you are working in. You told the computer the exact path, called an absolute path, to the file you wanted to execute. At this point, your screen should look similar to Figure 2-2.

Figure 2-2   The MSD utility

Study all the MSD menu options and answer the following questions about your system:

1. What categories of information are available in MSD?

2. What version of the operating system are you running?

3. What COM ports are available on the system?

4. What IRQ and Port Address are associated with COM1?

5. How far does the MEMORY map extend?

6. What is the Address Range at 1024K?

Save the information you noted so that you can compare it with the information you will obtain from MSD in the next set of steps. Now you are ready to close MSD.

1. Click **File** on the MSD menu bar and then click **Exit**.

2. Remove the floppy disk and reboot your PC to the Windows desktop.

3. Using Windows Explorer, double-click the **MSD.EXE** file to start it again.

With MSD open, answer the following questions again:

1. What categories of information are available in MSD?

_____

_____

2. What version of the operating system are you running?

_____

3. What COM ports are available on the system?

_____

4. What IRQ and Port Address are associated with COM1?

_____

5. How far does the MEMORY map extend?

_____

6. What is the Address Range at 1024K?

_____

Compare the information obtained the first time you used MSD with the information you obtained the second time, and then answer these questions:

1. How does your first set of answers compare to your second set of answers?

_____

_____

2. How do you explain the differences?

_____

_____

3. What key can you press to exit MSD?

_____

You are finished with MSD now, so you can close it.

Review Questions

1. In what categories would you look to find information on COM ports?

_____

2. What message did you see when you started MSD from within Windows?

_____

3. Which category gives information on the type of network installed?

_____

4. What is an advantage of saving MSD.EXE to the hard drive?

_____

5. What is the absolute path to MSD.EXE on the Windows 98 setup CD?

_____

6. What Windows tool is similar to MSD?

_____

7. As a PC repair technician, when would you use MSD?

_____

_____

2

LAB 2.4 OBSERVE THE BOOT PROCESS

Objectives

In this lab you will observe the sequence of events in a PC's boot process. After completing this lab, you will be able to:

➤ Describe the boot process in detail

➤ Halt the boot process

➤ Diagnose problems in the boot process

Materials Required

This lab will require the following:

➤ Lab PC designated for disassembly

➤ Windows 9x or Windows 2000/XP operating system

➤ Blank floppy disk

➤ Workgroup of 2–4 students

Activity Background

This lab will familiarize you with the boot process and give you some practice recognizing when the boot process halts and observing the resulting information displayed on the monitor. Working in teams, you will begin by observing a PC booting up and noting every step, from turning on the power to the appearance of the Windows desktop. Once you are familiar with all the steps in the boot process, your workgroup will intentionally introduce problems that will cause the boot process to fail on your PC and observe the results. Then you will introduce one problem on your PC and your workgroup will switch PCs with another workgroup's PC and attempt to figure out why that workgroup's PC failed to boot.

Estimated completion time: **30 minutes**

ACTIVITY

1. Boot your team's PC and then, using the information displayed on the monitor as a guide, record every step in the process. (List this information on a separate piece of paper.) For example, you are looking for RAM initialization, display of CPU speed, a list of devices that are detected, what happens when the screen turns from black to another color, and other similar events. You may have to boot the PC several times in order to record all of the steps.

Perform each of the following steps to introduce a problem in the boot process of your team's PC. For each problem, boot the PC and describe the problem as a user unfamiliar with PC technology might describe it. List any error messages that you see.

1. Insert a blank floppy disk into the floppy drive.
   - Describe the problem as a user sees it, including error messages.

   _____

   _____

2. Unplug the keyboard.
   - Describe the problem. Does the computer still boot into Windows?

   _____

   _____

3. Unplug the mouse.
   - Describe the problem. Does the computer still boot into Windows?

   _____

   _____

4. Unplug the monitor.
   - Describe the problem.

   _____

5. After a minute, plug the monitor in. Did the system boot correctly?

   _____

6. Now cause one problem in the list above and switch places with another team. Do not tell the other team what problem you caused.

7. Detect, diagnose, and remedy the problem on the other team's PC.

Review Questions

1. What is the first message displayed on the monitor after you turn on the power?

   _____

   _____

2. What devices are detected during the boot process?

   _____

   _____

3. Of all the problems you studied during the activity, which halts the boot process earliest in the process?

_____

_____

4. Which problem results in messages about the operating system not being present?

_____

_____

5. Why do you think it is useful to be familiar with all the different steps in the boot process?

_____

_____

LAB 2.5 MODIFY CONFIGURATION FILES AND OBSERVE THE RESULTS

Objectives

The objective of this lab is to learn to use configuration files that affect the MS-DOS command-line environment. Specifically, you will load drivers that make it possible to use a mouse in the command-line environment. You will also learn to use utilities executed at the commandline. After completing this lab, you will be able to:

> ➤ Create a bootable floppy disk

> ➤ Copy files to a floppy disk

> ➤ Modify configuration files

Materials Required

This lab will require the following:

> ➤ Windows 9x operating system

> ➤ File provided by your instructor needed to load a 16-bit generic mouse driver (for example, Mouse.com or Mouse.sys)

> ➤ Location provided by your instructor of the Windows and DOS utility programs Msd.exe and Edit.com.

> ➤ Blank floppy disk

Activity Background

In this lab you will boot to a command prompt by using a bootable floppy disk. As you will see, normally a command prompt environment does not allow you to use the mouse. Once the PC is booted, you will use Microsoft Diagnostics utility (MSD), a program that displays information about the hardware environment, to verify that the PC does not provide mouse support. Then you will add mouse support by adding to your system a configuration file that loads a mouse driver. The mouse driver file normally comes on a floppy disk bundled with a mouse, but your instructor might provide an alternate location. Finally, you will reboot the PC, run MSD again, and verify that mouse support has indeed been enabled.

Estimated completion time: **30 minutes**

ACTIVITY

Follow these steps on a Windows 9x PC to create a bootable floppy disk and to copy a file to the disk.

1. Click **Start** on the taskbar, point to **Programs**, and then click **MS-DOS Prompt**.

2. Insert a blank floppy disk.

3. Type **FORMAT A: /S** and press **Enter**.

4. The following prompt appears: "Insert new diskette for drive A: and press Enter when ready." Press **Enter** to start formatting the disk.

5. Watch as the floppy disk is formatted and the system files are transferred to the floppy disk.

6. When prompted, type a volume name if you wish and press **Enter** (or simply press **Enter** to bypass this step entirely).

7. When asked if you want to format another disk, type **N** and then press **Enter**. (Note that if your disk was already formatted, you could have used the SYS A: command to copy system files to the disk.)

Now that you have created a boot disk, follow these steps to copy some configuration files to the boot disk.

1. Insert the Windows 9x CD into the CD drive, type **Copy D:\tools\ oldmsdos\msd.exe A:**, and then press **Enter**. (If you don't have access to the Windows 9x CD, your instructor might give you an alternate location for the file. If your CD has a drive letter other than D, substitute the appropriate drive letter.)

2. Repeat Step 1 for the mouse driver file and the text editor, Edit.com, in the location specified by your instructor. The mouse driver file will be named Mouse.com, Mouse.sys or a similar name.

3. Close the Command Prompt window and shut down the system.

At this stage, the boot disk contains the necessary configuration files. Next, you will boot the PC using the boot disk and verify that the mouse is not available.

1. With the floppy disk still in the drive, boot the system. An A prompt displays on your screen.

2. To use the Microsoft Diagnostic Utility, at the command prompt, type **MSD.EXE** and then press **Enter**.

3. Move the mouse around. Does the mouse work as you would expect?

_____

4. Press **F3** to exit MSD.

You will now use the Edit program to create and edit an Autoexec.bat file.

1. At the A prompt, type **Edit Autoexec.bat**. The Edit window opens and the Autoexec.bat file is created.

2. Enter the command to load the mouse driver, using the filename of the driver, such as Mouse.com.

3. To exit the editor and save your changes, press the **Alt** key, and use your arrow keys to select **Exit** from the Exit menu.

4. When asked if you want to save your changes to the file, select **Yes**.

Now you will test your floppy disk to see if it provides mouse support.

1. With the boot disk still in the floppy drive, reboot.

2. Run the MSD program. Did you observe any change when you moved the mouse?

_____

3. Click **Exit** from the **File** menu to close MSD. Remove the floppy disk and reboot the PC.

Review Questions

1. When formatting a disk, what command can you use to make the floppy disk a boot disk?

_____

2. If you have a formatted floppy, what command other than **Format a: /s** can you use to transfer the system files to the floppy disk?

_____

3. Which configuration file did you modify to cause the mouse to be automatically supported?

_____

4. Did you notice a difference in the boot process after you changed a configuration file?

_____

5. When booting from a floppy disk, how would you automatically load a program to provide support for your CD-ROM drive?

_____

_____

ELECTRICITY AND POWER SUPPLIES

Labs included in this chapter

➤ Lab 3.1 Take a Computer Apart and Put It Back Together

➤ Lab 3.2 Find Documentation on the Internet

➤ Lab 3.3 Learn PC Power Supply Facts

➤ Lab 3.4 Measure the Output of Your Power Supply

➤ Lab 3.5 Replace a Power Supply

LAB 3.1 TAKE A COMPUTER APART AND PUT IT BACK TOGETHER

Objectives

The goal of this lab is to help you get comfortable working inside a computer case. After completing this lab, you will be able to:

➤ Take a computer apart

➤ Recognize components

➤ Reassemble the computer

Materials Required

This lab will require the following:

➤ Computer designated for disassembly

➤ PC toolkit

➤ Ground strap and static mat

Activity Background

If you follow directions and take your time, there is no reason to be intimidated by working inside a computer case. This lab will take you step by step through the process of disassembling and reassembling a PC. Follow your computer lab's posted safety procedures when disassembling and reassembling a PC and remember to always wear your ground strap. Also, never force a component to fit into its slot.

You will begin this lab by removing the cover of your PC. Then you will remove the components inside. Next you will reassemble the components and replace the cover. This lab includes steps for working with a desktop PC and a tower PC. Follow the steps that apply to your situation.

Also, in this lab, you are instructed to disassemble your PC in this order: remove the expansion cards, interior cables and cords, power supply, case fans, motherboard, and drives. Because some systems are designed so that the disassembly order should be different from the one above, your instructor might change this order. For example, you might not be able to get to the power supply to remove it until drives or the motherboard are out of the way. Be sure to follow any specific directions from your instructor.

Estimated completion time: **45 minutes**

ACTIVITY

Follow the procedure outlined below to remove the case cover and expansion cards. (If you are working with a tower case, lay it on its side so that the motherboard is on the bottom.)

3

1. Remove the cover from your desktop PC.

2. To make reassembly easier, take notes or make a sketch of the current placement of boards and cables and identify each board and each cable. You can mark the location of a cable on an expansion card with a marker if you like. Note the orientation of the cable on the card. Each cable for the floppy disk drive, hard drive, or CD-ROM drive has a colored marking on one side of the cable called the edge color. This color marks pin 1 of the cable. On the board, pin 1 is marked either with the number 1 or 2 beside the pin or with a square soldering pad on the back side of the board. (See Figure 3-1.) You might not be able to see this soldering pad now.

Pin 1 is shown by a stencil on the circuit board

Pin 1 is shown by square solder pads on the reverse side of the circuit board.

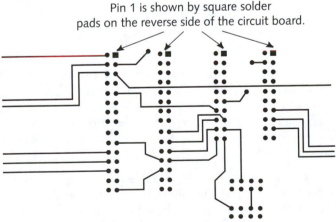

Figure 3-1   How to find pin 1 on an expansion card

3. Remove the cables from the expansion cards. There is no need to remove the other end of the cable from its component (floppy disk drive, hard drive, or CD-ROM drive). Lay the cable over the top of the component or case.

4. Remove the screw holding the card to the case. If for some reason you aren't wearing a ground strap, touch the case before you touch the card.

5. Grasp the card with both hands and remove it by lifting straight up and rocking the card from end to end (not side to side). Rocking the card from side to side might spread the slot opening and weaken the connection.

6. If the card had a cable attached, examine the card connector for the cable. Can you identify pin 1? Lay the card aside on a flat surface.

7. Remove any other expansion cards in the same way.

8. In some proprietary systems, an expansion card assembly attaches to the motherboard, with each card attached to the assembly. If your system has this arrangement, remove it now. It is probably held in place by screws or clips and may or may not have a rail guide that you can use to locate the assembly within the case.

9. To remove the power supply, first remove the power cables to the motherboard, case fans, other remaining components, and the power switch if necessary. Make notes about which cable attaches to what. Once the cables are removed, support the power supply with one hand and remove the screws attaching it to the case.

10. Remove any case fans.

In some systems, it is easier to remove the drives first and then the motherboard. In other systems, it is easier to remove the motherboard first. In these instructions, in order to not risk your dropping a drive on the motherboard when removing the drive, you are directed to first remove the motherboard and then the drives. Your instructor, however, might prefer you first remove the drives, then the motherboard.

1. Begin removing the motherboard by removing any power cables connected to any case or component fans. Be sure to make notes or label the cables so that you can reinstall them correctly.

2. Finish removing the motherboard by removing the screws holding the board to the stand-offs. Usually six to nine screws attach the motherboard to the case. Be careful not to gouge the board or otherwise damage components with the screwdriver. Because the screws on the motherboard are often located between components, they can be hard to reach. Be very careful not to damage the motherboard.

3. To remove drives, remove the ribbon cable if it is still attached. Many cases have a removable drive bay. The drives are attached to this bay and the bay may be removed with all the drives attached. This allows easier access to drive mounting screws than from inside the case. If your case has a removable drive bay, this is the preferred method of removal. Otherwise remove each drive separately. Be careful not to jar the drive as you remove it from the case.

3

4. If your system has a removable drive bay, it is likely that the floppy drive came out with the removable bay. If the floppy drive is still in the system, remove the screws holding the drive in place and slide the drive out of the case.

5. Remove any CD-ROM, DVD, or tape drives from the case. These drives are usually in the 5-inch drive bays and are held in place by four to eight screws. Once the screws are removed, the drive will slide out the front of the case.

6. Remove any other components.

Now that you have removed all the components, you are ready to reassemble the PC. Replace each component carefully. Take care to install each component firmly without over-tightening the screws. Do not force components to fit. If a component will not easily fit the way it should, look for some obstruction preventing it from falling into place. Look carefully for the reason the component will not fit correctly and make any small adjustments as necessary. The following steps outline the necessary procedure, which is essentially the reverse of the disassembly procedure:

1. Install the drives in their bays and then install the motherboard, unless your instructor prefers you install the motherboard first.

2. Place each card in its slot (it doesn't have to be the same slot, just the same bus) and replace the screw. Don't place a PCI or ISA video card near the power supply; otherwise, EMI from the power supply might affect the video picture.

3. Replace the cables, being sure to align the colored edge with pin 1. (In some cases it might work better to connect the cable to the card before you put the card in the expansion slot.)

4. Check to make sure that no cables are interfering with any fan's ability to turn. A common cause for an overheated system is a fan that can't move air because a cable is preventing it from spinning.

5. When all components are installed, you should have refitted all of the screws that you removed earlier. If some screws are missing, it is particularly important to turn the case upside down and *gently* shake the case to dislodge any wayward screws. Any screw lying on a board has the potential to short out that board when power is applied. Do not use a magnet to try and find missing screws in the case because you might damage the data on hard drives and floppy disks left in the floppy disk drives.

6. Plug in the keyboard, monitor, and mouse.

7. In a classroom environment, have the instructor check your work before you power up.

8. Turn on the power and check that the PC is working properly before you replace the cover. Don't touch the inside of the case while the power is on.

9. If all is well, turn off the PC and replace the cover and its screws. If the PC does not work, don't panic. Turn off the power and then go back and check each cable connection and each expansion card. You probably have not solidly seated a card in the slot. After you have double-checked everything, try again.

Review Questions

1. When removing the cover, why should you take care only to remove the screws that hold the cover on?

    _____

    _____

2. How should you rock a card to remove it from its slot? Why is it important to know how to properly rock a card?

    _____

    _____

    _____

3. What should you do to help you remember which components connect to which cables?

    _____

4. What marking on a ribbon cable identifies pin 1?

    _____

5. What component(s) defines the system's form factor?

    _____

    _____

6. What form factor does your PC use?

    _____

7. Why would a PC technician ever have to change out a computer's motherboard?

    _____

3

LAB 3.2 FIND DOCUMENTATION ON THE INTERNET

Objectives

The goal of this lab is to show you how to locate documentation on the Internet in order to determine how much power a component uses. After completing this lab, you will be able to:

➤ Find the manufacturer and model of a component

➤ Search for a product's documentation or manual

➤ Download and view a product manual

Materials Required

This lab will require the following:

➤ Computer designated for disassembly

➤ Internet access

➤ Adobe Acrobat Reader

➤ PC toolkit with ground strap

Activity Background

Often the power specifications for a component are not labeled on the component itself but are included in the documentation. When working with PCs, it is very common to encounter a component for which you have no documentation on hand. In this exercise, you will learn to find the make and model of a component and, if possible, find online documentation for it.

Estimated completion time: **30 minutes**

ACTIVITY

1. Open the PC's case and locate the component assigned to you by your instructor (or randomly select a component). If you are working with a team, each person on your team should be assigned a different component.

2. Examine the component until you find a sticker or stenciled label identifying its manufacturer and model number.

The manufacturer and model are not clearly marked on every component. If you're having trouble finding this information on a component, such as a video card, try researching according to the component's chipset. The information identifying the chip is usually stenciled on the chip. If you need to find out how much power an unlabeled component will use, it's sometimes helpful to consult the documentation for similar components.

3. Take your notes to a computer that has Internet access.

4. If you already know the manufacturer's URL, go to that site and try to find documentation in these locations:

   - The Support section of the site, as shown in Figure 3-2
   - The Downloads section
   - The Customer Service section

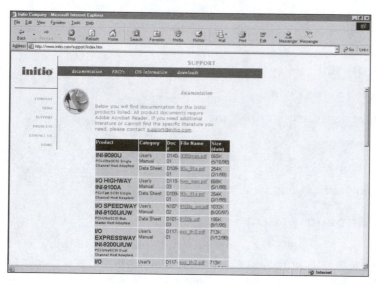

Figure 3-2   Manuals are available for download from the Support section of a manufacturer's Web site

If you are not sure of the manufacturer's URL, try searching for the manufacturer or model number using a good search engine. In fact, searching by model number will often get you to the information in the fewest steps. Keep in mind that most documentation is provided in PDF format, which means you may need Adobe Acrobat Reader or a browser plug-in to view the documentation.

5. Print out or save the documentation, and file it as a reference for when you need information about that component.

6. What CPU does your system use?

   _____

7. Go to the manufacturer's Web site and find and print the Web page showing the power consumption of your CPU expressed in watts.

Review Questions

1. How is a component commonly marked for identification?

_____

_____

2. In what sections of a Web site are manuals commonly found?

_____

3. In what format are manuals commonly provided?

_____

4. What software do you need to view a PDF document?

_____

5. Why would a PC repair technician need to know the power consumption of a peripheral?

_____

_____

_____

LAB 3.3 LEARN PC POWER SUPPLY FACTS

Objectives

The goal of this lab is to determine if a PC's power supply is adequate for the PC's components. After completing this lab, you will be able to:

➤ Examine documentation and estimate the peak power consumption (in watts) required by the system components

➤ Examine a power supply to determine if it meets the system's needs

Materials Required

This lab will require the following:

➤ Lab computer designated for disassembly

➤ Documentation for system components that includes information about electrical requirements

➤ Access to the Internet

➤ PC toolkit with ground strap

➤ Workgroup of 2-4 students

Activity Background

A power supply must be able to provide adequate power for all devices in a system at peak consumption. If the power supply's maximum rated wattage (peak wattage) is not greater than the sum of the peak consumption of all components, the system may crash or spontaneously reboot (or worse) during heavy use. Furthermore, an inadequate power supply might run well during light use, but then fail when the system is stressed. You can prevent such problems by using documentation to determine whether a power supply is adequate for the demands of a particular system. In this activity, you'll learn more about your system's power supply.

Estimated completion time: **30 minutes**

ACTIVITY

Remove the cover from your PC and answer the following questions:

1. How many watts are supplied by your power supply? (This information is usually printed on the label on the top of the power supply.)

   _____

2. How many cables are supplied by your power supply?

   _____

3. Where does each cable lead?

   _____

   _____

4. Does the power supply provide adequate power for the estimated peak consumption of the system? Fill in the following table:

Component	Wattage
Hard drive	
Floppy drive	
CD-ROM drive	
DVD drive	
Zip drive	
Other drive	
Motherboard	
CPU	

5. Determining the power consumption of the motherboard and CPU can be difficult without adequate documentation. If you were able to locate that documentation in the previous lab, calculate the total wattage requirements for the system. Otherwise, this might not be possible.

Total wattage requirements for all components: _____

3

6. Suppose your power supply stops working, and you must buy a replacement. Search the Internet for a comparable power supply. The cost of power supplies varies greatly. For example, a 400-watt power supply can cost from $15 to $75. The difference in quality can be judged partly by the weight of the power supply because, in general, the heavier it is, the more transistors and the more heavy duty the transistors are, which, in turn, makes for a better power supply. Print two Web pages showing a high-end and a low-end power supply that would meet your system's needs. Which power supply would you recommend be purchased for your system and why?

_____

Review Questions

1. Where can you usually find electrical information about your power supply?

_____

2. What can happen if the power supply does not meet the electrical demands of the system?

_____

_____

3. When would a system approach its peak power consumption?

_____

_____

4. How can you estimate a system's peak power consumption?

_____

_____

5. Will a system with an inadequate power supply always fail immediately when it is powered up? Why or why not?

_____

6. What is one way to determine if a power supply is of good quality or not of good quality?

_____

LAB 3.4 MEASURE THE OUTPUT OF YOUR POWER SUPPLY

Objectives

The goal of this lab is to use a multimeter to measure the various voltages supplied by a power supply. After completing this lab, you will be able to:

➤ Use a multimeter

➤ Measure voltage supplied by a power supply

Materials Required

This lab will require the following:

➤ Lab computer designated for this exercise

➤ PC toolkit with ground strap

➤ Multimeter

➤ Workgroup of 2-4 students

Activity Background

In most situations, if you suspect a problem with a power supply, you would simply exchange it for a known-good one. But in a few instances, you might want to measure the output of your power supply using a multimeter.

A multimeter is an electrical tool that performs multiple tests. It can typically measure continuity, resistance, amperage, and voltage. It may have a digital or analog meter that displays output. It will also have two leads used to contact the component you are testing. The various models of multimeters work slightly differently. Follow the appropriate procedure for your specific multimeter. In this lab you will measure the electrical voltage supplied to the motherboard and floppy drive. Follow your computer lab's posted safety procedures when completing this activity.

Estimated completion time: **30 minutes**

ACTIVITY

Caution: Be sure you have your multimeter set to measure voltage and not current (amps). If the multimeter is set to measure current, you might damage the power supply, the motherboard, or both.

Using your multimeter, measure the power output to your system's motherboard and to the floppy drive, and then fill in two of the three tables below. Note that the column headings "Red Lead" and "Black Lead" refer to the color of the probes.

Detailed directions for using a multimeter can be found in Chapter 3 of the textbook *A+ Guide to Hardware*. Be very careful as you work inside the computer case with the power on. Don't touch any components other than those described below. The following steps outline the basic procedure for using a multimeter:

1. Remove the cover from the computer case.

2. Set the multimeter to measure voltage in a range of 20 volts and set the AC/DC switch to DC. Insert the black probe into the meter's − jack and the red probe into the meter's + jack.

3. Turn on the multimeter and turn on the computer.

4. Measure each circuit by placing a red probe on the lead and a black probe on ground (see Figure 3-3). Use the leads listed in the table on the next page. Write the voltage measurement for each connection in the "Voltage Measure" column.

Figure 3-3   Multimeter measuring voltage on an AT motherboard

5. Turn off the PC and replace the cover.

Complete the following table for the AT motherboard:

Red Lead	Black Lead	Voltage Measure
3	5	
3	6	
3	7	
3	8	
4	Ground	
9	Ground	
10	Ground	
11	Ground	
12	Ground	

Complete the following table for the ATX motherboard:

Red Lead	Black Lead	Voltage Measure
10	7	
10	5	
10	3	
10	17	
10	16	
10	15	
10	13	
9	Ground	
6	Ground	
4	Ground	
2	Ground	
1	Ground	
20	Ground	
19	Ground	
18	Ground	
12	Ground	
11	Ground	

Complete the following table for the floppy drive:

Red Lead	Black Lead	Voltage Measure
1	3	
4	2	

Review Questions

1. What is the electrical voltage from the house outlet to the power supply?

_____

2. What voltages are supplied by the power supply on your system?

_____

3. What model of multimeter are you using?

_____

4. List the steps to set this multimeter to measure resistance.

_____

_____

_____

5. Besides voltage and resistance, what else can this multimeter measure?

_____

LAB 3.5 REPLACE A POWER SUPPLY

Objectives

The goal of this lab is to give you experience replacing a power supply. After completing this lab, you will be able to:

➤ Identify the power supply

➤ Remove the power supply from the case

➤ Install a new power supply and new cabling

Materials Required

This lab will require the following:

➤ Lab PC designated for this exercise

➤ PC toolkit with anti-static ground strap

➤ Workgroup of 2-4 students

Activity Background

This exercise will test your ability to remove and replace a power supply. Power supplies, as a rule, are considered Field Replaceable Units (FRU). This means that because of the danger of working inside power supplies and as a time saver, a PC technician does not repair them. If you find that a power supply is faulty, replace it with a compatible power supply, then send the original off to be reconditioned or recycled.

Estimated completion time: **30 minutes**

ACTIVITY

1. Disconnect the power and all peripherals and remove the case cover.

   _____

2. Examine the power supply and record the number and type of connectors needed, and estimate the peak power requirements for the system (which you learned how to do in Lab 3.3). If the components required more power than the power supply could provide, this could have contributed to its failure.

   _____

3. What type of power connector to the motherboard does the power supply provide?

   _____

4. What is the form factor of the power supply?

   _____

5. Remove the cabling and the power supply. Usually the power supply is held in place by four screws in the back of the case. Some proprietary systems may use other methods of securing the power supply.

6. Examine the power supply designated by your instructor, or swap your power supply with your neighbor's.

7. What is the form factor of this new power supply?

   _____

8. What is the power rating of this new power supply?

   _____

9. Will this new power supply satisfy the needs of your system?

   _____

10. Install the new power supply.

11. Close the case, reattach the peripherals, and test the system.

Review Questions

1. How many connectors linked your original power supply to the motherboard?

   _____

2. How many watts of peak power could the original power supply provide?

   _____

3. Why should you calculate the peak power required for all components?

   _____

   _____

4. What are two reasons that PC technicians do not usually repair a power supply?

   _____

   _____

5. What term is used to refer to components that are commonly replaced but not repaired?

   _____

6. What is the most efficient way to determine if your power supply is bad?

   _____

CHAPTER FOUR

THE MOTHERBOARD

Labs included in this chapter

➤ Lab 4.1 Examine and Adjust CMOS Settings

➤ Lab 4.2 Use a Motherboard Diagnostic Utility

➤ Lab 4.3 Identify a Motherboard and Find Documentation on the Internet

➤ Lab 4.4 Remove and Replace the Motherboard

➤ Lab 4.5 Identify Motherboard Components and Form Factors

LAB 4.1 EXAMINE AND ADJUST CMOS SETTINGS

Objectives

The goal of this lab is to help you explore and modify CMOS settings. After completing this lab, you will be able to:

➤ Enter the CMOS setup utility

➤ Navigate the CMOS setup utility

➤ Examine some setup options

➤ Save changes to setup options

Materials Required

This lab will require the following:

➤ Lab PC designated for this lab

➤ SANDRA, Standard version, installed in Lab 1.3

Activity Background

When a system is powered up, the startup process is managed by a set of instructions called the BIOS. The BIOS, in turn, relies on a set of configuration information stored in CMOS that is continuously refreshed by battery power when the system is off. You can access and modify the CMOS setup information via the CMOS setup utility included in the BIOS. In this lab, you will examine the CMOS setup utility, make some changes, and observe the effects of your changes.

Setup utilities vary slightly in appearance and function, depending on manufacturer and version. The steps in this activity are based on the common Award Modular design. You might have to perform different steps to access and use the CMOS utility on your computer.

> Estimated completion time: **30 minutes**

ACTIVITY

Before you access the BIOS on your computer, you will record the exact date and time as indicated by your computer's internal clock. (You will use this information later, to confirm that you have indeed changed some CMOS settings.) After you record the date and time, you will determine which version of the BIOS is installed on your computer. To do this, you will use the SANDRA utility, which you installed in Lab 1.3. Follow these steps:

1. Using Windows, double-click the clock on the taskbar and record the time and date.

_____

_____

2. Close the Date/Time Properties window.

3. Start **SANDRA**, and then double-click the **CPU & BIOS Information** icon.

4. Select **System BIOS** in the **Device** field.

5. Record the manufacturer and version information for your BIOS.

6. Close SANDRA.

Now that you know what BIOS your computer runs, you can determine how to enter the setup utility. In general, to start the setup utility, you need to press a key or key combination as the computer is booting up. To learn more about entering the setup utility on your particular computer, follow these steps:

1. Using the information recorded in Step 5, consult Table 4-1 to find out how to enter your system's setup utility. (Alternatively, when you first turn on the PC look for a message on your screen, which might read something like "Press F2 to access setup.")

Table 4-1　Methods for entering CMOS setup utilities, by BIOS

BIOS	Method for entering CMOS setup
AMI BIOS	Boot the computer, and then press the Delete key.
Award BIOS	Boot the computer, and then press the Delete key.
Older Phoenix BIOS	Boot the computer, and then press the Ctrl + Alt + Esc or Ctrl + Alt + S key combination.
Newer Phoenix BIOS	Boot the computer, and then press the F2 or F1 key.
Dell Computers with Phoenix BIOS	Boot the computer, and then press the Ctrl + Alt + Enter key combination.
Older Compaq computers like the Deskpro 286 or 386	Place the diagnostics disk in the drive, reboot the system, and choose Computer Setup from the menu.
Newer Compaq computers like the Prolinea, Deskpro, DeskproXL, Deskpro LE, or Presario	Boot the computer, wait for two beeps, then, when the cursor is in the upper-right corner of the screen, press the F10 key.
All other older computers	Use the setup program on the floppy disk that came with the PC. If the floppy disk is lost, contact the motherboard manufacturer to obtain a replacement.

Note: For Compaq computers, the CMOS setup program is stored on the hard drive in a small, non-DOS partition of about 3MB. If this partition becomes corrupted or the computer is an older model, you must run setup from a diagnostic disk. If you cannot run setup by pressing F10 at startup, it's likely that a damaged partition or a virus is taking up space in conventional memory.

Now you are ready to enter the CMOS setup utility included in your BIOS. Follow these steps:

1. If a floppy disk is necessary to enter the CMOS setup utility, insert it now.

2. Restart the computer.

3. When the system restarts, enter the setup utility using the correct method for your computer.

4. Notice that the CMOS utility groups settings by function. For example, all the power management features will be grouped together in a Power Management window.

5. The main screen usually has a Help section that describes how to make selections and exit the utility. Typically, you can use the arrow keys or Tab key to highlight options. Once you have highlighted your selection, you usually need to press the Enter key, Page Down key, or the spacebar. The main screen might display a short summary of the highlighted category. Look for and select a category called something like **Standard CMOS Setup**.

6. In the Standard CMOS Setup screen, you should see some or all of the following settings. List the current setting for each of the following:

   - Date: _____

   - Time: _____

   - For IDE hard drives, a table listing drive size and mode of operation, cylinder, head, and sector information:

     _____

     _____

   - Floppy drive setup information, including drive letter and type:

     _____

   - Halt on error setup (the type of error that will halt the boot process):

     _____

   - Memory summary (summary of system memory divisions):

     _____

   - Boot sequence (drives the BIOS searches for an OS):

     _____

7. Exit the Standard CMOS setup screen and return to the main page. Select a section called something like **Chipset Features Setup**.

8. Record settings for the following, as well as any other settings in this section:

   - RAM setup options:

     _____

     _____

- AGP setup options:

  _____

  _____

- CPU-specific setup options:

  _____

  _____

- Settings for serial and parallel ports:

  _____

  _____

- Provisions for enabling/disabling onboard drive controllers and other embedded devices:

  _____

  _____

  _____

  _____

  Note: Most of the CMOS settings never need changing, so it isn't necessary to understand every setting.

9. Exit to the CMOS setup main screen. You may see options for loading CMOS defaults (which restores factory settings and can be helpful in troubleshooting) as well as options for exiting with or without saving changes. There might be an option to set user and supervisor passwords as well as a utility to automatically detect IDE hard disk drives.

Now that you are familiar with the way the CMOS setup utility works, you will change the date and time settings. Then you will reboot the computer, confirm that the changes are reflected in the operating system, and return the CMOS date and time to the correct settings.

1. Return to the Standard CMOS setup screen.

2. Highlight the time field(s) and set the time ahead one hour.

3. Move to the date field(s) and set the date ahead one year.

4. Return to the main CMOS setup screen and select an option named something like **Save Settings and Exit**. If prompted, verify that you do wish to save the settings.

5. Wait while the system reboots. Allow Windows to load.

6. At the desktop, check the time and date. Are your CMOS setup changes reflected in Windows?

_____

7. Reboot the computer, return to CMOS setup, and set the correct time and date.

8. Verify that the changes are again reflected in Windows.

Critical Thinking (additional 30 minutes)

Working with your team, do the following to practice troubleshooting problems with CMOS.

1. Propose a change that you could make to CMOS setup that would prevent a computer from booting successfully. What change do you propose?

_____

2. Have your instructor approve the change, because some changes might cause information written to the hard drive to be lost, making it difficult to recover from the problem without reloading the hard drive. Did your instructor approve the change?

_____

3. Now go to another team's computer and make the change to CMOS setup while they make a change to your system.

4. Return to your computer and troubleshoot the problem. Describe the problem as a user would describe it.

_____

_____

5. What steps did you go through to discover the source of the problem and fix it?

_____

_____

6. If you were to encounter this same problem in the future, what might you do differently to troubleshoot it?

_____

_____

Review Questions

1. Do all systems use the same method to enter CMOS setup? Can you enter CMOS setup after the system has booted?

   _____

2. How are settings usually grouped in the CMOS setup utility?

   _____

3. In what section will you usually find time and date setup located in the CMOS setup utility?

   _____

   _____

4. What types of options are shown on the CMOS setup main screen?

   _____

5. What automatically happens after you exit CMOS setup?

   _____

6. What tool in SANDRA can you use to find information on your version of the BIOS?

   _____

   _____

7. Why does a computer need CMOS?

   _____

   _____

8. When troubleshooting a computer, when might you have to enter CMOS setup? List at least three reasons.

   _____

   _____

   _____

4

LAB 4.2 USE A MOTHERBOARD DIAGNOSTIC UTILITY

Objectives

The goal of this lab is to help you learn how to use a motherboard diagnostic utility. After completing this lab, you will be able to:

➤ Download and install the AMIDiag utility

➤ Use the AMIDiag utility to examine your motherboard

Materials Required

This lab will require the following:

➤ Windows 9x operating system

➤ Internet access

Activity Background

AMIDiag, distributed by American Megatrends, Inc., is a well-known diagnostic utility that you can use to solve a variety of computer problems. The utility is DOS-based and works under both DOS and Windows 9x. In this activity, you will download a demonstration version of AMIDiag from the Internet and then learn how to use it.

| Estimated completion time: **30 minutes** |

ACTIVITY

1. Use your favorite search engine, such as *www.google.com*, to search for Diagdemo.zip, which is an archive (a collection of compressed files) containing the files necessary to install the demo version of AMIDiag 4.5, a shareware version of AMIDiag for PC diagnostics. Look for this version, rather than later versions that don't have as much functionality, by searching for "AMIDiag 4.5".

2. Download Diagdemo.zip to your PC. Your instructor might ask you to save the file to a specific folder on your hard drive. If so, what is the name of the folder?

3. Close your browser, open Explorer, and then expand the file **Diagdemo.zip** by double-clicking it.

4. Open a command-prompt window, and then switch to the directory where the demo software files are stored.

5. At the command prompt, type **amidiag**, and then press **Enter**. The screen shown in Figure 4-1 appears.

Figure 4-1   AMIDiag opening menu

Many times a support technician is not given step-by-step directions when using utility software, but must discover how to use the software by exploring menus and using the software's help functions. The following exercise gives you practice in doing that. Use the AMIDiag software to answer these questions:

1. Perform the test of processor speed. What is the detected speed?

2. On the Memory menu, perform all the tests that this demonstration version of the software allows. Record any errors detected.

3. On the Misc. menu, perform the serial port test. Write down any error messages that appear. If you get an unexpected error, perform the test more than once. Do you get the same results each time?

4. On the Option menu, select **System Information**. If you received errors in Step 3, this program might lock up, and you might need to reboot. If you completed the information check successfully, record the results:

5. On the System board menu, select **DMA Controller Test**. Why does this test not work?

6. Exit the program, and then close the command prompt window.

Challenge Activity (additional 15 minutes)

Copy the AMIDiag software to a Windows 9x startup disk and execute the software from the startup disk on a Windows 2000/XP computer.

    1. Describe how the software works using this method.

_____

    2. When might this method be useful?

_____

Review Questions

    1. Does the AMIDiag utility run with a GUI interface?

_____

    2. What menu in AMIDiag contains the serial port test?

_____

    3. What are some tests included in the shareware version of AMIDiag?

_____

    4. What menu in AMIDiag contains the System Information program?

_____

    5. At what points in the test process did you receive error messages? What do these error messages tell you about your computer?

_____

In the following table, list at least three situations where you think it would be appropriate to use AMIDiag for troubleshooting. Describe the problem as the user would describe it to you. For example, "My serial mouse does not work." Then write the suspected source of the problem and the appropriate AMIDiag test. The table includes one example to help you get started.

Description of problem as the user sees it	Suspected source of the problem	AMIDiag test
"My serial mouse does not work."	Serial port does not work	Serial port test

LAB 4.3 IDENTIFY A MOTHERBOARD AND FIND DOCUMENTATION ON THE INTERNET

Objectives

The goal of this lab is to learn to identify a motherboard and find online documentation for it. After completing this lab, you will be able to:

➤ Physically examine a motherboard

➤ Determine a motherboard's manufacturer and model

➤ Search the Internet for motherboard documentation

Materials Required

This lab will require the following:

➤ PC designated for disassembly

➤ Internet access

➤ Adobe Acrobat

➤ PC toolkit with ground strap

Activity Background

You may often be asked to repair a PC for which the documentation is lost or not available. Fortunately, you can almost always find documentation for a device online as long as you have the device's manufacturer name and model number. In this lab, you will learn to find the manufacturer's name and model number on a motherboard. Then you will locate documentation for that device on the Internet.

Estimated completion time: **30 minutes**

ACTIVITY

1. Boot the PC and use SANDRA, which you installed in Chapter 1, Lab 1.3, to learn the type of CPU installed on your computer. Record that information:

2. Following safety precautions, including using a ground strap, remove the PC's case cover and then remove any components obscuring your view of the motherboard. In some cases you may have to remove the motherboard itself, but this is usually unnecessary.

3. Look for a stenciled or silkscreened label printed on the circuit board itself that indicates the manufacturer and model. Note that other components sometimes have labels printed on a sticker affixed to the component. On a motherboard, the label is generally printed directly on the circuit board itself. Common motherboard manufacturers include Abit, Asus, and Intel.

Also, note that the manufacturer name is often printed in much larger type than the model number. Model numbers often include both letters and numbers and many contain a version number as well. Figure 4-2 shows an example of a motherboard label.

Motherboard manufacturer (ASUS)

Model number (P5A)

Figure 4-2   Label printed directly on motherboard

4. Record the information on the motherboard label.

5. Take your information to a PC with Internet access and open a browser.

6. If you know the URL of the manufacturer, go directly to the Web site. (Table 4-2 shows the URLs for some motherboard manufacturers.) If you do not know the URL of the manufacturer's site, search for the manufacturer or model with your favorite search engine, as shown in Figure 4-3. In the search results, click a link that is associated with the manufacturer. If this link does not take you directly to the documentation, it will usually get you within two or three links away. Continue until you find the manufacturer's Web site.

Table 4-2   URLs for major motherboard manufacturers

Manufacturer	URL
motherboards.com	www.motherboards.com
American Megatrends, Inc.	www.megatrends.com
ASUS	www.asus.com
Dell	www.dell.com
Diamond Multimedia	www.diamondmm.com
First International Computer, Inc.	www.fica.com
Gateway	www.gateway.com
Giga-Byte Technology Co., Ltd.	www.giga-byte.com
IBM	www.ibm.com
Intel Corporation	www.intel.com
Supermicro Computer, Inc.	www.supermicro.com
Tyan Computer Corporation	www.tyan.com

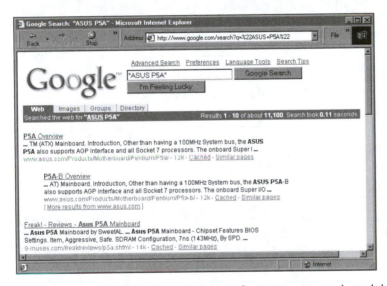

Figure 4-3   Search results using manufacturer name and model number

7. When you have found the site of your motherboard's manufacturer, look for a link for service or support. Click this link, and, if necessary, select the appropriate product category and model number. Sometimes knowing the type of CPU the board supports can be useful in finding the right board.

8. Continue working your way through the site until you find the motherboard documentation. The documentation may include a variety of documents covering technical specification and installation instructions. The documentation will probably also include a basic manual, which is usually a combination of technical and installation specifications.

9. When you find the documentation, you might also find a link to updated drivers. If you see such a link, click it and note the release date of these drivers. If they are newer than the current drivers, it is often advisable to update these as well. If possible, record the release dates for the updated drivers:

   _____

10. Return to the main documentation page, and, if it is available, select the manual. If it is not available, select the installation instructions.

11. The manual is probably in PDF format, so you will need to have a copy of Adobe Acrobat Reader installed. If you have the browser plug-in, you can open the document from the source location, or you can download the manual to your computer and then open it. Using your preferred method, open the document and print the motherboard documentation. Save this documentation for use in Lab 4.4.

Review Questions

1. How is the label usually applied to a motherboard? How is it most often applied to other components?

   _____

2. On the label of a motherboard or other component, how can the manufacturer often be differentiated from the model number?

   _____

3. What type of link on a manufacturer's Web site will usually lead you to manuals and other documentation?

   _____

4. What other information about your motherboard might you want to examine on the manufacturer's Web site?

   _____

5. In what format is documentation most often available for download?

   _____

6. What other information, such as BIOS update and drivers, can be obtained besides motherboard documentation at this site?

   _____

LAB 4.4 REMOVE AND REPLACE THE MOTHERBOARD

Objectives

The goal of this lab is to familiarize you with the process of replacing an old or faulty motherboard. After completing this lab, you will be able to:

➤ Use SANDRA to determine the specifications of your CPU

➤ Remove a motherboard

➤ Configure a new motherboard according to its documentation

➤ Install a replacement motherboard

Materials Required

This lab will require the following:

➤ A computer designated for this lab

➤ SANDRA, Standard version, installed in Lab 1.3

➤ Workgroup of 2-4 students

➤ PC toolkit with ground strap

Activity Background

In this lab you will exchange a motherboard with another workgroup to simulate the process of replacing a faulty motherboard. When you install the new motherboard, you must configure it for your system by adjusting jumper and CMOS settings according to the documentation printed in Lab 4.3. Then you will install the replacement motherboard.

Estimated completion time: **45 minutes**

ACTIVITY

In this activity, follow safety precautions as you work to remove the motherboard. Be sure to use a ground strap.

1. Launch SANDRA (which you installed in Lab 1.3) and use the CPU & BIOS information utility to examine the CPU in your system. Record the information listed in the Processor section.

_____

_____

_____

2. Power the system down, unplug everything, and remove the case cover. Then remove the cabling and expansion cards from the motherboard. Take all necessary precautions (including using a ground strap), and make a sketch of cabling and component placement.

3. Six screws usually attach the motherboard to the case via spacers. The spacers prevent the printed circuitry from shorting out on the metal case and provide space for air circulation. Remove the screws attaching the motherboard, and set them aside in a cup, bag, or bowl so that you don't lose them.

4. Carefully lift the motherboard out of the case. You may have to tilt the board to clear the drive bays and power supply. In some cases you may have to remove the drives to get the motherboard out.

5. Exchange the motherboard and the motherboard documentation with that of another team. You might also exchange the CPU and memory, depending on whether your current CPU and memory modules are compatible with the new motherboard. Follow directions given by your instructor as to what to exchange. Be sure you have the new motherboard's documentation, which should have been found on the Internet in Lab 4.3.

Critical Thinking

Your instructor might ask you to remove jumpers and reset DIP switches on your motherboard before passing it to the other team. These modifications will make the other team's configuration more challenging. As an alternative, your instructor might have a display motherboard somewhere in the lab that uses jumpers and DIP switches for part of its configuration.

1. With the new motherboard in front of you, consult the new board's documentation and find any jumpers that must be configured to match your system. Older boards use jumpers to adjust clock multipliers and memory speeds, as well as to clear the CMOS settings. Unless otherwise instructed, *do not* remove the jumper to clear CMOS settings. Note that newer boards are often "jumperless," with all configuration settings done within CMOS setup. The only jumper these boards will have is the one to clear CMOS settings. Remove and replace the jumpers in the configuration specified to match your processor information.

2. Install the motherboard, cabling, and expansion cards, and any other components you removed.

3. Boot the system and enter the CMOS setup utility. For jumperless motherboards, make any adjustments specified in the motherboard's documentation.

4. Save settings and exit CMOS setup.

5. Reboot the system and verify that the system is functioning correctly. Describe any error messages:

6. What steps do you plan to take to troubleshoot this error?

Critical Thinking (additional 30 minutes)

To learn more about motherboards, do the following:

1. Once the PC is working, ask your instructor to configure a startup password on your computer.

2. Without knowing the password, boot the computer.

3. List the steps required to accomplish this.

Review Questions

1. How many screws usually attach the motherboard to the computer case?

2. What is the purpose of spacers?

3. A jumperless motherboard is likely to have one jumper. Which jumper is it?

4. Where can you access the configuration settings for a jumperless motherboard?

LAB 4.5 IDENTIFY MOTHERBOARD COMPONENTS AND FORM FACTORS

Objectives

The goal of this lab is to help you learn to identify motherboard form factors and components. After completing this lab, you will be able to:

➤ Identify a motherboard's CPU type

➤ Identify connectors

➤ Identify the form factor based on component type and placement

Materials Required

Instructors are encouraged to supply a variety of motherboards, some common and others not so common. At the very least, this lab will require the following:

➤ Three different motherboards

Note: If three motherboards are not available, look on the Web sites of the motherboard manufacturers listed in Lab 4.3 for three boards.

Activity Background

As a PC technician, you should be able to look at a motherboard and determine what type of CPU, RAM, and form factor you are working with. You should also be able to recognize any unusual components the board might have. In this lab, you will examine various motherboards and note some important information about them.

> Estimated completion time: **30 minutes**

ACTIVITY

Fill in the following table for your assigned motherboards. If you have more than three motherboards, use additional paper. When the entry in the Item column includes a question mark (such as "PCI Bus?") write a yes or no answer.

4

Item	Motherboard 1	Motherboard 2	Motherboard 3
Manufacturer/model			
BIOS manufacturer			
CPU type			
Chipset			
RAM type/pins			
PCI bus?			
ISA bus?			
AGP bus?			
SCSI controller?			
IDE controller?			
Embedded audio, video, etc.			
Jumperless?			
Form factor			
Describe any unusual components			

1. How can you determine if a motherboard is an AT board or an ATX board based on the location of the CPU in relation to the expansion slots?

_____

_____

2. Of the motherboards you examined, which do you think is the oldest? Why?

_____

_____

_____

3. Which motherboard best supports old and new technology? Why?

_____

_____

_____

4. Which motherboard appears to provide the best possibility for expansion? Why?

_____

_____

_____

5. Which motherboard is most likely the easiest to configure? Why?

_____

6. Which motherboard do you think is the most expensive? Why?

_____

7. What are some considerations that a motherboard manufacturer has to contend with when designing a motherboard? (For example, consider room for large CPUs and cooling fans, where the power supply is located in relationship to the power connector, new technologies and so forth.)

_____

_____

CHAPTER FIVE

MANAGING MEMORY

Labs included in this chapter

➤ Lab 5.1 Research RAM on the Internet

➤ Lab 5.2 Explore the Kingston Web Site

➤ Lab 5.3 Upgrade RAM

➤ Lab 5.4 Troubleshoot Memory Problems

➤ Lab 5.5 Use Himem.sys

LAB 5.1 RESEARCH RAM ON THE INTERNET

Objectives

The goal of this lab is to help you learn how to find important information about RAM that you will need when upgrading memory. After completing this lab, you will be able to:

➤ Find documentation on your system's motherboard

➤ Read documentation for your system's RAM specifications

➤ Search the Internet for RAM prices and availability

Materials Required

This lab will require the following:

➤ Windows 98 or Windows 2000/XP operating system

➤ Internet access

Activity Background

At one time, RAM was literally worth more than its weight in gold. When building a system back then, most people made do with the minimum amount of RAM required for adequate performance. These days RAM is much cheaper, which means you can probably buy all the RAM you need to make your system perform at top speed. Graphics editing software, in particular, benefits from additional RAM. In this lab, you will research how to optimize RAM on a graphics workstation with a memory upgrade budget of $150.

Estimated completion time: **30 minutes**

ACTIVITY

1. Use My Computer to determine the amount of RAM currently installed. Record the amount of RAM here:

   _____

2. Using skills learned in Lab 4.3, determine the manufacturer and model of your motherboard. (If you don't have the motherboard documentation available, search for it on the Web and print it.)

Use the documentation for your motherboard to answer these questions:

1. What type (or types) of memory does your motherboard support? Be as specific as the motherboard documentation is.

   _____

   _____

2. How many slots for memory modules are included on your motherboard?

   _____

3. How many memory slots on your motherboard are used and how much RAM is installed in each slot?

   _____

   _____

4. What is the maximum amount of memory that your motherboard supports?

   _____

5. What size and how many memory modules will be needed to upgrade your system to the maximum amount of supported memory?

   _____

Now that you have the necessary information about your system's memory, go to a local computer store that sells memory or, using the Internet, go to *Pricewatch.com* or a similar Web site, and complete the following:

1. What is the price of the memory modules required to configure your system for maximum memory?

   _____

2. Will your budget enable you to install the maximum supported amount of RAM?

   _____

3. Can you use the existing memory modules to upgrade to the maximum amount of supported memory?

   _____

4. What is the most additional memory that you could install and still stay within your budget? (Assume you will use the existing memory modules.)

   _____

5

Explore other types of memory on *Pricewatch.com* or a similar Web site and answer the following questions:

1. On average, what is the least expensive type of memory per MB that you can find? What is its price?

_____

_____

2. On average, what is the most expensive type of memory per MB that you can find? What is its price?

_____

3. Is SO-DIMM memory for a notebook computer more or less expensive than the equivalent amount of Rambus memory for a desktop PC? Give specific information to support your answer.

_____

_____

Review Questions

1. Why might you want to upgrade RAM on a system?

_____

_____

2. How many pins are found on a DIMM? How many on a RIMM?

_____

_____

3. Which is more expensive, DIMM or RIMM?

_____

4. What is a disadvantage of using two 64MB modules instead of a single 128MB module in a system with three slots for memory modules?

_____

_____

5. What are two disadvantages of using only one 256MB module rather than two 128MB modules?

_____

_____

_____

_____

5

LAB 5.2 EXPLORE THE KINGSTON WEB SITE

Objectives

The goal of this lab is to use the Kingston Web site to learn about RAM. After completing this lab, you will be able to:

➤ Identify types of RAM

➤ Determine appropriate memory types for a given system

Materials Required

➤ Internet access

Activity Background

RAM comes in a variety of shapes, sizes, and speeds. Not every type of RAM works with every system. In this lab you will use the Web site of Kingston Technology, a major RAM manufacturer, to learn about RAM and to learn how to make sure you have the right memory module to upgrade your system.

Estimated completion time: **30 minutes**

ACTIVITY

Do the following to begin learning about system memory:

1. Open your browser and go to the Web site *www.kingston.com*.

2. Notice that the Memory Search section of the site allows you to search for memory based on the type of system you have. What other three ways can you search for memory?

_____

_____

_____

When you search the site based on your system, results of the search include a list of compatible memory types with prices, maximum memory supported by your system, processors supported, and number of expansion slots on your system for memory modules. Do the following to find information about a memory upgrade for a motherboard:

1. Select one of the motherboards from the table in Lab 4.5. Which motherboard did you select?

   _____

2. Perform a Memory Search on the Kingston site for information on this motherboard. Answer the following questions:

   ▪ What are the types of memory module this board can use?

   _____

   _____

   _____

   ▪ What types of processor does the board support?

   _____

   _____

   _____

   ▪ How many memory slots are on the board?

   _____

   ▪ What is the maximum amount of memory the board supports?

   _____

Now continue exploring the Kingston site. Do the following:

1. Return to the Kingston home page.

2. Click the Memory Tools link. A drop-down menu appears displaying several tools, one being the Memory Assessor. Selecting this link begins a process whereby you can specify which OS you are researching and Kingston will give you a recommended amount of physical RAM based on usage criteria.

3. Using these tools, and perhaps other areas of the site, answer the following questions:

   ▪ In general, do the operating systems for desktops and workstations require more or less memory than the operating systems for servers?

   _____

   _____

■ How wide is the data path on a 168-pin DIMM?

_____

■ DDR is an extension of what older memory technology?

_____

_____

■ What does the SO in SO-DIMM represent?

_____

■ What is an advantage of loading applications entirely into RAM rather than loading part of an application into virtual memory (a page file)?

_____

_____

_____

■ What is another term for a page file, and why are page files used?

_____

_____

■ How many bits of information does a single cell of a memory chip on a 256MB PC2700 DDR module hold?

_____

■ Why would you have problems with a system in which you installed three known-good RIMMs?

_____

_____

_____

■ A relatively new memory technology uses only a 16-bit path. What acronym defines this type of memory?

_____

■ What type of material is used to make a memory "chip?"

_____

_____

5

- What function(s) does the aluminum plate on a RIMM serve?

  _____

  _____

- Why might you not mind using slower memory (in MHz) if faster memory is available for a marginal price difference?

  _____

  _____

- What are some possible ramifications of installing modules in a way that does not comply with the system's bank schema?

  _____

  _____

- What is a memory performance measurement in which the lower the number, the better the performance?

  _____

  _____

- What memory technology achieves better performance by using both the rising and falling sides of the clock cycle?

  _____

  _____

- List five things to consider when upgrading memory.

  _____

  _____

  _____

  _____

  _____

- In a situation where a motherboard would support either SDRAM or EDO, which would give better performance?

  _____

  _____

■ What memory technology uses a heat spreader?

_____

■ What types of memory do notebook computers typically use?

_____

■ Name two certain characteristics of a system using RAMBUS licensed memory.

_____

_____

5

Review Questions

1. Is a DIMM or a RIMM more expensive given that they both hold the same amount of memory? Why do you think this is the case?

_____

_____

2. Summarize why adding RAM offers a performance advantage.

_____

_____

3. Which tool on the Kingston Web site could you use to find Kingston modules for your system if you know the model number of your system's motherboard?

_____

4. If you were planning to buy a new system, would you choose a motherboard that uses DIMMs or RIMMs? Why?

_____

_____

LAB 5.3 UPGRADE RAM

Objectives

The goal of this lab is to learn to plan an upgrade of memory and then perform the upgrade. After completing this lab, you will be able to:

➤ Estimate how much free memory your system has available during typical and stressed use

> ➤ Determine how much and what kind of memory is needed for an upgrade
> ➤ Upgrade RAM in your system

Materials Required

This lab will require the following:

> ➤ SANDRA, Standard version, installed in Lab 1.3
> ➤ Internet access
> ➤ PC toolkit and anti-static bracelet
> ➤ Additional memory module compatible with your system

Activity Background

In this lab you will examine your system, gather information on its memory sub-system, and establish a memory usage baseline. Using this information, you will determine through further research whether the system will support a RAM upgrade required to run a CAD application. Finally, you will install an additional memory module, re-examine your system, and compare against the baseline.

Estimated completion time: **45 minutes**

ACTIVITY

Use SANDRA to answer the following questions about your system:

1. What OS are you running?

   _____

2. What type of processor is your system using?

   _____

3. What is the manufacturer/model of your motherboard?

   _____

4. How many MB of RAM are currently installed?

   _____

5. What type of memory modules are installed? Be as specific as you can.

   _____

6. At what speed does the memory bus operate?

_____

To establish a memory usage baseline, follow these steps:

1. Leaving SANDRA open, launch one instance each of Windows Explorer, Paint, and Internet Explorer.

2. Use the Windows Memory Information tool in SANDRA and record the amount of free physical memory. This is your memory baseline. How much memory is free?

_____

3. Launch six additional instances of Internet Explorer, browsing to a different site on each. Try to locate and view or listen to a movie trailer or video, because this activity is memory intensive compared with displaying a static Web page.

4. Refresh the information in the Windows Memory Information tool by clicking the blue arrow. Record the free physical memory. How much memory is now free?

_____

The change is the result of the demands of running and displaying six additional Web pages.

Suppose that the engineering department of your employer is interested in deploying a CAD program that requires 1 GB of RAM over and above the OS's memory requirements. Use your investigating skills to document whether your system is able to support the additional RAM required. Do the following:

1. Will your system currently support the CAD program?

_____

2. If your system will not support it, can you upgrade RAM to meet the requirements? How much memory must be added?

_____

3. In the space provided, record how you arrived at your answers to the last two questions. Include where you found the information.

_____

_____

_____

_____

4. If an upgrade will support the CAD program, what is the retail price of the necessary modules required to meet specifications?

_____

Next you will simulate making the upgrade. Do the following:

1. Shut down your system and remove all exterior cabling.

2. Be sure you are wearing your anti-static bracelet. Open the system case and locate the slots for memory modules.

3. Remove any data cabling and other devices preventing you from getting at the slots. Answer the following questions:

   ■ How many modules are currently installed? Are there any empty slots in which to install an additional module?

_____

   ■ At what point during boot-up might you be able to determine how many modules are in use?

_____

4. Notice that the slots have a retaining mechanism at each end to secure the modules in the slot. These mechanisms are typically plastic levers that you spread outward to unseat and remove modules. These modules are inserted and removed straight up and down. Spread the plastic levers apart before inserting or removing the memory modules.

5. Examine an empty slot and note that there are raised ridges that line up with notches on the pin edge of the memory module. Because modules are designed to be inserted in only one orientation, these ridges prevent them from being inserted incorrectly.

6. With the module correctly oriented, insert the module and gently but firmly push it in.

7. Reassemble your system.

Though it is extremely rare to purchase a bad memory module, it is a good idea to give the system every opportunity to detect faulty memory. BIOS tests your physical memory each time the system is booted. If a module is drastically flawed, the system usually will not boot. Instead, the system will issue a beep code indicating memory problems. Assuming that the module is in relatively good shape and the video has initialized, the system BIOS's POST routine will typically display a memory count in bytes as it tests memory.

Most POST routines will run through the test three times before proceeding. You can skip this redundant testing by enabling a "Quick" POST in CMOS setup. Quick POST is great to cut down boot-up time during normal use, but when installing new RAM, it is best to give the system every opportunity to detect a problem. Therefore, you should disable Quick POST until you are confident that the module has no obvious problem. With this in mind, follow these steps to verify that the system properly recognizes the upgrade:

1. Boot the system and enter CMOS setup.

2. Verify that any Quick POST is disabled, and, if necessary, specify that you have installed additional memory. (Telling CMOS about new memory is not necessary unless you have a very old motherboard.)

3. Save your settings and reboot. Record below whether the additional memory was recognized, and how many times it was tested.

_____

4. Being careful to duplicate the steps, perform the same baseline tests that you did earlier in this lab. Record the results here:

   ■ Amount of free memory with SANDRA, Windows Explorer, Paint, and Internet Explorer open:

   _____

   ■ Amount of free memory with the system heavily used:

   _____

5. When you have finished, remove the additional memory and return the system to its previous configuration.

Review Questions

1. What is the minimum memory requirement for the OS your system is running?

_____

2. What are at least two ways you can determine how much RAM is installed?

_____

_____

3. What SANDRA module(s) can be used to display information about system memory?

_____

_____

4. What feature is employed on memory slots and modules to prevent modules from being inserted incorrectly?

_____

5. In what situation might you wish to disable a Quick POST and why?

_____

_____

LAB 5.4 TROUBLESHOOT MEMORY PROBLEMS

Objectives

The goal of this lab is to provide you with hands-on experience troubleshooting memory problems. After completing this lab, you will be able to:

➤ Identify some symptoms that indicate memory problems

➤ Identify a faulty module

➤ Use DocMemory to test installed RAM

Materials Required

This lab will require the following:

➤ Internet connection

➤ Windows 9x

➤ SANDRA, Standard version, installed in Lab 1.3

➤ Printer

➤ Compression utility such as WinZip

➤ Blank floppy disk

➤ Acrobat Reader

➤ PC toolkit and anti-static bracelet

Activity Background

The symptoms of faulty RAM are many and varied. Faulty memory can cause a complete failure to boot, fatal exception errors while working with an application, or catastrophic data loss. But sometimes faulty memory presents itself only as annoying interruptions as you work. RAM that is outright dead is fairly easy to identify. If the dead module is the only module installed, the system will not boot. If it is one of several modules, you will notice the system reports less memory than you expected.

However, it is not common for a module to fail absolutely. More often a module will develop intermittent problems that cause data corruption, applications to hang at unexpected times, or Windows NT/2000/XP to hang and display the Blue Screen of Death. In this lab, you will learn how to detect and isolate faulty memory modules to prevent these situations.

Estimated completion time: **60 minutes**

ACTIVITY

Reliable memory function is essential to system operation. Therefore, when the system is booted, if memory is not detected or has major problems, the startup BIOS will begin emitting a beep code defining a general or particular memory problem. If memory is found adequate by startup BIOS, during POST startup BIOS does a thorough test of physical memory, which is usually repeated three times before the system summary is displayed and boot continues. Then, while Windows is loading, Windows tests all memory above 1MB.

These tests are well and good at startup, but often modules that are partially corrupted will not show a problem until they are running at certain temperatures. Because these faults show up only at certain times and temperatures, they are referred to as thermal intermittents. Although these problems are extremely difficult to nail down and document absolutely, they are actually fairly easy to remedy if the fault is on the memory module instead of on the motherboard.

DocMemory is a utility that allows either a quick test or a "burn in" test that runs until an error is encountered or there is human intervention. This "burn in" is particularly useful in discovering a thermal intermittent fault.

In the following steps, you will use DocMemory to test installed RAM. Note that you can create a boot disk on a Windows 9x machine and then use that bootable floppy disk to boot a PC and test memory on that PC, even if Windows NT/2000/XP is installed. Do the following:

1. On a Windows 9x computer, search the Web for a file called DocMem1_45a.exe and its accompanying documentation named docguide.pdf. This utility can be found at *www.dewassoc.com/performance/memory/diag_memory_2.htm*. DocMem1_45a.exe is the program that is used to create a boot disk that runs the diagnostic routine.

2. Open and print the file Docguide.pdf (the documentation file) for later use.

3. Download and run DocMem1_45a.exe. A dialog box containing support contact information opens. Click **OK** to continue.

4. DocMemory then opens in a command-prompt window. Use the arrow keys and the Enter key or use the mouse to select **Make Boot Disk**. A license agreement appears.

5. Scroll down and accept the license agreement. The license agreement disappears, revealing a prompt to insert a blank disk. Insert the disk and press **Enter**.

6. The formating process begins and ends automatically, transferring system files. Then the utility and Autoexec.bat are added to the disk. When the files have been copied, a message is displayed, indicating that the process is complete. Press any key and the command-prompt window closes. Close the installation window as well.

7. The disk is now ready to be used on any Windows system. For the purpose of this lab, leave the disk in the system and reboot.

8. The system boots into the DocMemory utility. Purchase information is displayed and then disappears, revealing a Select Type of Test dialog box with options to run the Burn-in Test, Quick Test, or Cancel. To test for a thermal intermittent, the Burn-in Test is the best choice. However, in the interest of time, for this lab select the **Quick test**.

9. The test begins and the status is displayed in the upper-left side of the screen. Your processor and RAM are identified in the upper-right side. The bottom of the screen displays pass/fail results. This portion of the lab varies in time due to differences in the amount of RAM and the processor speeds of various systems.

10. While waiting for the test to finish, consult the documentation and answer the following questions.

   ■ What two things happen when a fault is detected?

   _____

   _____

   ■ What two areas can DocMemory test?

   _____

   _____

   ■ What type of fault is the Walk Data "0" & "1" test designed to uncover?

   _____

   _____

11. When the test ends or errors are found, record the results below.

   _____

   _____

   _____

Follow these steps to observe the effects of a faulty memory module and interpret beep codes:

1. Use SANDRA to determine the BIOS manufacturer for your system and record it here.

   _____

2. Search documentation or the Internet for a list of beep codes for that manufacturer.

3. Shut down the system and remove all external cabling.

4. Put on your anti-static bracelet, open the case, remove all memory modules, and set them aside in an anti-static bag.

5. Reassemble the system, leaving out memory.

6. Power up the system and describe the outcome, including any beep codes, below.

   _____

   _____

   _____

7. If you heard beep codes, using the documentation obtained in Step 2, interpret their meaning below.

   _____

   _____

8. Shut down the system, disassemble it, install the RAM, and reassemble.

9. Boot the system to verify that the system is functional.

Using the documentation for DocMemory, summarize the process of using a known-good memory module to provide strong evidence that a particular memory module is faulty.

   _____

   _____

   _____

   _____

Review Questions

1. What are some common symptoms of a thermal intermittent?

   _____

   _____

2. How many times does POST usually test memory?

   _____

3. Why can't a Windows NT–based machine be used to create a DocMemory disk?

   _____

   _____

4. Describe the symptoms created by a dead memory module.

   _____

   _____

   _____

5. Which DocMemory test would be ideal for diagnosing a thermal intermittent?

   _____

Lab 5.5 Use Himem.sys

Objectives

The goal of this lab is to help you investigate ways memory can be used by observing the effects of Himem.sys. After completing this lab, you will be able to:

➤ Configure Himem.sys

➤ Configure Msdos.sys to stay in text mode throughout the boot

➤ Observe the effects Himem.sys has on the system

Materials Required

This lab will require the following:

➤ Windows 98

➤ Two blank floppy disks

➤ Windows 98 setup CD or setup files located in a place provided by your instructor

Activity Background

If you have the need frequently to run programs in MS-DOS mode, setting up Config.sys and Autoexec.bat is important because they help set environmental variables in MS-DOS mode. Himem.sys is necessary to use many DOS utilities. Another key function of Himem.sys is that it independently tests RAM during boot. By observing the effects of changing how the system employs Himem.sys, you can get an idea of its various functions. In this lab, you will configure and observe Himem.sys.

Estimated completion time: **30 minutes**

ACTIVITY

To configure your system to remain in text mode throughout boot-up, complete the following steps:

1. Using Windows Explorer, right-click **Msdos.sys** in the root directory of the system partition. Select **Properties** from the shortcut menu. The Msdos.sys Properties dialog box opens.

2. In the Attributes section, clear the box indicating that the file is read-only. Click **OK** to apply your change and close the dialog box.

3. Again, right-click **Msdos.sys**, this time selecting **Open with...** from the shortcut menu. The Open with dialog box opens.

4. In the field Choose the program you want to use:, select **NOTEPAD**. If necessary, clear the **Always use this program to open this type of file** check box and click **OK**. Notepad opens displaying the entries in Msdos.sys.

5. Under the [Options] heading add the line **Logo=0**. (Be sure to type a zero and not a capital "O".) Using the File menu, save the changes and close Notepad.

6. Reboot the computer and record any messages you see concerning Himem.sys. Notice that the Windows logo screen never appears during startup. This allows you to observe the entire text-based boot sequence, which can be useful in observing and diagnosing boot problems.

_____

_____

_____

In DOS and Windows 3.x, Himem.sys was always loaded using a Device= command line in Config.sys. Himem.sys is automatically loaded by Windows 9x, even if a Config.sys file is not present. However, you can use Config.sys under Windows 9x to load Himem.sys to configure how Himem.sys loads. To do this, you would create a Config.sys file and add the Himem.sys command line to it with appropriate switches. To configure Himem.sys and watch it load, follow these steps:

1. In the root of the system partition, right-click **Config.sys**. Select **Open with...** from the shortcut menu. The Open with dialog box opens.

2. In the field Choose the program you want to use:, select **NOTEPAD**. If necessary, clear the **Always use this program to open this type of file** check box and click **OK**. Notepad opens, displaying the entries in Config.sys.

3. In Config.sys, add the line **Device=C:\Windows\himem.sys**. Using the File menu, save your changes and close Notepad.

4. Reboot the computer, recording any messages you see concerning Himem.sys.

_____

_____

_____

5. Following Steps 1–4, add the switch **/V** (be sure to type a capital V) to the Device= line. The resulting line should appear as Device=C:\Windows\ Himem.sys /V, with a space before the switch. "V" stands for verbose or descriptive. This means that text will be displayed to keep you informed of its progress. Reboot the system, if necessary more than once, and answer the following questions:

   ■ How much high memory did Himem.sys report available?

   _____

   ■ What version of Himem.sys is loaded?

   _____

6. Following the previous process to edit Config.sys, add the switch /TestMem:ON. Reboot and record any changes.

_____

_____

_____

Now you will create a Windows 98 startup disk using the Add/Remove Programs applet in the Control Panel. Then you will use Scandisk on the startup disk to scan your hard drive for errors, which will be a first step in demonstrating why loading Himem.sys from Config.sys is important. Do the following:

1. From Control Panel, launch the **Add/Remove Programs** dialog box.

2. When the dialog box opens, select the **Startup disk** tab.

3. Click the **Create Disk** button and, if prompted, provide the location of the Windows setup files.

4. Insert the floppy disk when prompted, and click **OK** to continue and create a startup disk.

5. When the startup disk is complete, examine its contents in Windows Explorer. Does the startup disk contain both Config.sys and Himem.sys? Open the Config.sys file and write the command line that loads Himem.sys.

_____

6. With the startup disk in the drive, reboot the computer.

7. When prompted, select the option to start the computer without CD-ROM support.

8. When you arrive at the command prompt, type **Scandisk C:** and press **Enter** to scan the hard drive for errors.

9. Observe as Scandisk performs a data scan on drive C. When prompted, do not perform a surface scan. Press **X** to return to the command prompt.

10. Remove the startup disk and reboot the system.

Now you will create a bootable disk and copy the Scandisk utility to it. Then you will attempt to use Scandisk without having Himem.sys loaded. Do the following:

1. In Windows Explorer, insert the second blank floppy disk and right-click drive **A**.

2. Select **Format** from the shortcut menu. The Format dialog box appears.

3. In the Format dialog box, select both **Quick (erase)** and **Copy system files** and click the **Start** button.

4. When the summary appears, click **Close** and then click **Close** again to exit. You have created a bootable disk. Using Windows Explorer, examine the disk and list the files on the disk:

_____

_____

_____

5. Now copy Scandisk.exe from the C:\Windows\Command folder to the bootable disk.

6. Reboot the system with the bootable disk in the drive. When you arrive at the command prompt, type **Scandisk C:** to again attempt to scan the hard drive for errors. Describe what happens.

7. What two files must be put on the bootable disk for Scandisk to work?

Review Questions

1. Other than providing access to memory, what other valuable function does Himem.sys provide?

2. What system file is modified to make text messages during startup easier to view?

3. In a command line, when more than one switch is being used, what should come before each switch?

4. Based on the knowledge you have gained in this lab, name three configuration files that can be used to alter the way an OS loads.

5. Name one MS-DOS utility that requires Himem.sys to be loaded for the utility to run. What does Himem.sys do for this utility?

FLOPPY DRIVES

6

Labs included in this chapter

➤ Lab 6.1 Install and Troubleshoot a Floppy Drive

➤ Lab 6.2 Use TestDrive to Test a Floppy Drive

➤ Lab 6.3 Format a Floppy Disk

➤ Lab 6.4 Use the Diskcopy and Xcopy Commands

LAB 6.1 INSTALL AND TROUBLESHOOT A FLOPPY DRIVE

Objectives

The goal of this lab is to give you practice installing a second floppy drive. After completing this lab, you will be able to:

➤ Install a floppy drive

➤ Verify that a floppy drive is working correctly

➤ Troubleshoot problems related to installing a floppy drive

Materials Required

This lab will require the following:

➤ Windows 98 or Windows 2000/XP operating system

➤ System with one floppy drive installed and an empty 3.5-inch drive bay or empty 5-inch drive bay with mounting adapter for a second floppy drive

➤ PC toolkit

➤ A second floppy drive ready for installation

➤ Bootable disk

Activity Background

If you are in a position where you need to duplicate several floppy disks, having a second floppy drive will speed the process significantly. In this lab you will install and test a second floppy drive. But first, you will experiment with an installed floppy drive to become familiar with the correct orientation of the data cable. This activity will also give you an opportunity to verify that the installed floppy drive is working correctly, something that you should always do before installing a new drive so that you know your starting point. After the installation, if the first drive does not work, you will know that the problem did not previously exist and was introduced during the installation process. When making changes to a system, always know your starting point.

> Estimated completion time: **45 minutes**

ACTIVITY

To experiment with the cable orientation on an installed floppy drive:

1. Verify that you can boot from drive A with a bootable disk.

2. Turn off the computer, open the case and examine the data cable to drive A. Look for the twist in the cable. Verify that the cable is connected to the drive so that the twist is between the drive and the motherboard.

3. Adjust the cable to remove the twist between the drive and the controller. Turn on the PC and try to boot from drive A again. Describe what happens.

_____

_____

4. Turn off the computer, and restore the cable to its original position.

5. Verify that you can again boot from drive A with a bootable disk.

6. Reverse the orientation of the connection between the floppy drive cable and the floppy drive controller so that the edge connector is not aligned with pin 1.

7. Boot the PC. What problem occurs? Describe the problem as a user would describe it.

_____

_____

8. Turn off the computer, and restore the cable to its correct orientation.

9. Verify that you can boot from drive A again with a bootable disk.

In the following steps you will install and test a second floppy drive:

1. Turn off the computer.

2. Install a second floppy drive in your PC. Install the cable so that the connector without the twist is attached to the new drive. (Your instructor might tell you to remove a floppy drive from another PC to install as a second drive in this PC.)

3. Boot the system and enter the CMOS setup utility. What keys do you press at startup to enter CMOS setup?

_____

4. Use the Standard CMOS Setup option (or a similar option) to find the fields on the CMOS setup screen that are used to configure floppy drives. Find the field to enable the B drive. This is the default drive letter assigned to a second floppy drive, the drive that does not require a twist in the floppy drive cable.

5. According to your setup utility, does the ROM BIOS for your computer support an extra-high density 3.5-inch floppy disk drive? List the drive types it does support.

_____

_____

_____

6. Select the option for 1.44MB (or extra-high density 3.5-inch drive) as the drive type for the new drive B just installed.

7. Save CMOS settings and exit the CMOS setup utility. List the steps required to save your settings and exit the utility.

   _____

   _____

8. Allow the system to reboot from the floppy disk in drive A. Watch the new drive to see if the activity LED comes on. This will be the first indication that the drive has been installed properly.

9. When the system has reached the command prompt, remove the floppy disk from drive A and insert it in drive B.

10. Type **DIR B:** and press **Enter**. Did the drive read the floppy disk as expected?

    _____

11. Verify that you can change the default drive to drive B by typing **B:** and pressing **Enter**. What is the new command prompt?

    _____

12. Shut down the system.

13. Reverse the drive cabling so that drive A is B and drive B is the new A. Then test by booting from the new drive A.

14. Return the drives to their original assignments, and verify that both function as expected.

15. Change the floppy drive type in CMOS setup to an incorrect setting. (Make sure you don't change the hard drive type accidentally.)

16. Reboot. What error did you see?

    _____

17. Now correct the setting and reboot to make sure all components work again.

18. Remove the second floppy drive from your system, and change the CMOS setup to disable drive B so that the BIOS expects to see only a single drive A.

19. Verify that the original drive is functioning correctly. How did you go about verifying that the drive is working properly?

    _____

    _____

Review Questions

1. Why is it important to verify that original drives already installed in a system are functioning correctly before installing a new drive?

_____

_____

2. Which drive should be attached to the connector that has a twist in the cable?

_____

3. What letter is assigned to any second floppy drive that does not have the twist?

_____

4. What is the capacity of an extra-high density floppy disk?

_____

5. What is one advantage of having two floppy drives on a system?

_____

6

LAB 6.2 USE TESTDRIVE TO TEST A FLOPPY DRIVE

Objectives

The goal of this lab is to familiarize you with floppy drive diagnostic software. After completing this lab, you will be able to:

➤ Use TestDrive to examine and diagnose problems with floppy drives and floppy disks

➤ Describe errors reported by TestDrive

Materials Required

This lab will require the following:

➤ Windows 98 operating system

➤ Internet access

➤ A floppy disk

Activity Background

MicroSystems Development provides a diagnostic program called TestDrive for examining and diagnosing problems with floppy drives and floppy disks. You will learn to use some functions of this utility in this lab. You will begin by downloading a demo version from the company's Web site. Note that most of the options on the TestDrive menu require that you have a DDD (digital diagnostic disk) for testing the drive, but you can perform a few tests without one.

Estimated completion time: **30 minutes**

ACTIVITY

To download and install a demo copy of TestDrive:

1. Open your browser and go to *www.msd.com/diags/*.

2. Download the TestDrive software.

3. Insert a disk containing no important data into the floppy drive. Open a command prompt window and switch to the directory containing the Testdriv.exe program. Type **testdriv.exe** and press **Enter** to launch the program. When the program launches, press any key to continue.

Now that you have installed the TestDrive software, you can begin using it. Note that the main window, shown in Figure 6-1, tells you which function key to press to perform various tasks. Follow these steps:

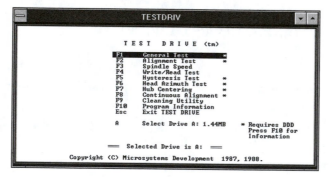

Figure 6-1   TestDrive main menu

1. Press the **F4** key to perform the Write/Read test. The warning box shown in Figure 6-2 appears.

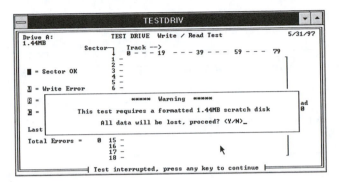

Figure 6-2   TestDrive Write/Read test

2. Press **Y** to continue. While the test is running, answer these questions:

■ In what order are these components of the floppy disk tested: heads, tracks, and sectors.

_____

_____

■ Did you get any errors? If so, describe each error.

_____

_____

3. If you got a significant number of errors, try another disk. Do you see any consistency in errors when switching from one disk to another? If you get a pattern of errors when using several disks, the problem is most likely with the drive. If the errors are isolated to only one disk, the problem is most likely with the disk and not the drive.

_____

4. Press any key to return to the Main Menu.

5. Select the Spindle speed test, and record the spindle speed below. What is the acceptable range for spindle speed?

_____

6. Press any key to return to the Main Menu.

7. Select Program Information and answer the following questions:

■ What type of disk do most of the TestDrive tests require?

_____

- What is one function of the software that is not a test?

  _____

- What type of disk is required for this function?

  _____

- What five measurements of floppy disks can be diagnosed by TestDrive?

  _____

  _____

Review Questions

1. What type of drive is TestDrive designed to test?

   _____

2. What are the only two tests that can be run without a special disk?

   _____

3. What is the symbol that TestDrive uses to indicate a write error?

   _____

4. Suppose you run the Write/Read test with several floppy disks and receive the same errors with each of the disks. What might you conclude?

   _____

   _____

5. Why do you think TestDrive allows you to try some free tests before you must purchase the software?

   _____

   _____

LAB 6.3 FORMAT A FLOPPY DISK

Objectives

The goal of this lab is to help you use various formatting options available from the command prompt and in Windows Explorer. After completing this lab, you will be able to:

➤ Use switches for different formatting options

➤ Format a floppy disk using Windows Explorer

Materials Required

This lab will require the following:

➤ Windows 98 or Windows 2000/XP operating system

➤ Blank, unformatted floppy disk

Activity Background

Floppy disks must be formatted before you can use them. These days, floppy disks usually come preformatted from the factory. But you may often be required to reformat a used disk. The formatting process defines track and sector spacing so that data can be written to a known location. Formatting also creates the File Allocation Table, or FAT, which lists the locations of files on the disk. You can format a disk from within Windows Explorer or from the command line. When formatting disks from the command line, you can use switches to make decisions about exactly how the disk will be formatted. These switches allow you to cut some corners to speed the formatting process or to streamline the process of making a bootable disk. In this lab, you will format a floppy disk in several different ways.

Estimated completion time: **45 minutes**

ACTIVITY

To practice formatting a floppy disk from the command prompt, follow these steps:

For Windows 98:

1. Insert a blank, unformatted floppy disk into drive A.

2. Open a command-prompt window. Use the **Dir** command to examine drive A. Describe what you see on the screen.

_____

_____

3. The system cannot provide information about the contents of the disk because the disk has not yet been formatted. Type **Format /?**, and press **Enter**. This command displays a list of 11 switches that you can use to modify the Format command. What is the correct syntax for a Format command to test clusters on the disk in drive A that are currently marked as bad?

_____

4. To format the disk, type **Format A:**, then press **Enter**.

5. When prompted, press **Enter**. The formatting process begins. Throughout the process, you see a message indicating the percent completed.

6. When the formatting reaches 100%, the system gives you the opportunity to name the volume. Name the volume **FTEST**, then press **Enter**.

7. Next the system displays the formatting summary and prompts you to format another.

8. Type **n**, and press **Enter**.

9. Use the **Dir** command to examine drive A. Now the system is able to give you information about the floppy disk because it has been formatted.

10. A quick format does not write track and sector markings on the disk and is a quick way to reformat a previously formatted disk. To do a quick format, type **Format A: /q** and press **Enter**. Compare the time it took to do a quick format to the time it took to do a full format.

_____

11. Again, use the **Dir** command to examine drive A. Is there a difference between the outcome of the quick format and that of the full format?

_____

For Windows 2000:

1. Insert a blank, unformatted floppy disk into drive A.

2. Open a command-prompt window. Use the **Dir** command to examine drive A. Describe what you see on the screen.

_____

_____

3. The system cannot provide information about the contents of the disk because the disk has not yet been formatted. Type **Format /?** and press **Enter**. This command displays a list of 12 switches that you can use to modify the Format command. What is the correct syntax for a Format command to format only one side of a disk?

_____

_____

4. To format the disk, type **Format A:**, then press **Enter**.

5. When prompted, press **Enter**. The formatting process begins. Throughout the process, you see a message indicating the percent completed.

6. When the formatting reaches 100%, the system gives you the opportunity to name the volume. Name the volume **FTEST**, then press **Enter**.

7. Next the system displays the formatting summary and prompts you to format another.

8. Type **n**, and press **Enter**.

9. Use the **Dir** command to examine drive A. Now the system is able to give you information about the floppy disk because it has been formatted.

10. A quick format does not write track and sector markings on the disk and is a quick way to reformat a previously formatted disk. To do a quick format, type **Format A: /q**, and press **Enter**. Continue through the formatting procedure. Compare the time it took to do a quick format to the time it took to do a full format.

_____

_____

11. Again, use the **Dir** command to examine drive A. Is there a difference between the outcome of the quick format and that of the full format?

_____

_____

For Windows XP:

1. Insert a blank, unformatted floppy disk into drive A.

2. Open a command-prompt window. Use the **Dir** command to examine drive A. Describe what you see on the screen.

_____

_____

3. The system cannot provide information about the contents of the disk because the disk has not yet been formatted. Type **Format /?** and press **Enter**. This command displays a list of nine switches that you can use to modify the Format command. What is the correct syntax for a Format command to format a 1.2-MB floppy disk?

_____

_____

4. To format the disk, type **Format A:**, and then press **Enter**.

5. When prompted, press **Enter**. The formatting process begins. Throughout the process, you see a message indicating the percent completed.

6. When the formatting reaches 100%, the system gives you the opportunity to name the volume. Name the volume **FTEST**, then press **Enter**.

7. Next, the system displays the formatting summary and prompts you to format another.

8. Type **n**, and press **Enter**.

9. Use the **Dir** command to examine drive A. Now the system is able to give you information about the floppy disk because it has been formatted.

10. A quick format does not write track and sector markings on the disk and is a quick way to reformat a previously formatted disk. To do a quick format, type **Format A: /q**, and press **Enter**. Continue through the formatting procedure. Compare the time it took to do a quick format to the time it took to do a full format.

11. Again, use the **Dir** command to examine drive A. Is there a difference between the outcome of the quick format and that of the full format?

Suppose that you wished to make a bootable floppy disks so that you could add utilities and use it for troubleshooting. You can use more than one switch at a time with most commands. To demonstrate this fact with the Format command, complete the following steps:

For Windows 98:

1. Type **Format a: /q /s**, then press **Enter**. This command instructs the system to do a quick format and then to copy the system files required to make the disk bootable.

2. Describe the format process.

   _____

   _____

   _____

   _____

3. How many bytes of free space are now included on the disk? What command did you use to get your answer?

   _____

   _____

4. Close the command-prompt window.

For Windows 2000:

1. Type **Format a: /q /s**, then press **Enter**. This command instructs the system to do a quick format and then to copy the system files required to make the disk bootable.

2. What message did you receive? Suppose that you have a copy of a bootable floppy disk. What command might you use to create another bootable floppy disk using the one that you already have?

_____

_____

3. Now type **Format a: /q/A:512**, and press **Enter**.

4. Describe the format process.

_____

_____

5. How many bytes of free space are now included on the disk? What command did you use to get your answer?

_____

_____

6. Close the command-prompt window.

For Windows XP:

1. Type **Format a: /q /s**, then press **Enter**. This command instructs the system to do a quick format and then to copy the system files required to make the disk bootable.

2. What message did you receive about creating a Windows XP bootable floppy disk?

_____

_____

3. Now type **Format a: /q/A:512,** and press **Enter**.

4. Describe the formatting process.

_____

_____

5. How many bytes of free space are now included on the disk? What command did you use to get your answer?

_____

_____

6. Close the command-prompt window.

To practice formatting a floppy disk from within Windows Explorer, follow these steps:

1. Open Windows Explorer.

2. With the floppy disk inserted in drive A, right-click drive A, then click **Format** in the shortcut menu. The Format window opens.

3. Observe the layout of the Format window, and describe the options provided by the Format window.

Review Questions

1. Suppose you formatted a floppy disk on a Windows 98 system. Would you then be able to reformat the same disk using the /q switch on another Windows 98 system? Why or why not?

2. Suppose you want to format a disk in drive B, making it a bootable disk. What command would you use in Windows 98?

3. In general, what difference did you see in a disk's directory listing after formatting the disk with the /s switch?

4. Why might it be less important for Windows 2000 and Windows XP to provide a switch for creating a bootable floppy disk?

5. What is the difference between a Windows 98 startup disk and a boot disk created using the Format A: /S command?

Lab 6.4 Use the Diskcopy and Xcopy Commands

Objectives

The goal of this lab is to help you observe differences in the Diskcopy and Xcopy commands. After completing this lab, you will be able to:

➤ Copy files and folders using the Xcopy command

➤ Duplicate a disk using the Diskcopy command

➤ Explain when to use Xcopy and when to use Diskcopy when copying files and folders

Materials Required

This lab will require the following:

➤ Windows 98 operating system

➤ Two blank floppy disks

➤ Safety pin

➤ Windows 2000/XP operating system (optional)

Activity Background

The Copy command allows you to copy files from one folder to another folder. Using a single Xcopy command, you can copy files from multiple folders, duplicating an entire file structure in another location. The Diskcopy command allows you to make an exact copy of a floppy disk. You will learn to appreciate the differences between these commands in this lab.

> Estimated completion time: **45 minutes**

Activity

Before you begin using the Xcopy and Diskcopy commands, you need to create a test directory to use when copying files. Follow these steps:

1. Open a command-prompt window, and make the root of drive C the current directory. Note that the quickest way to change to the root of a drive is to type **X:** (where **X** is the drive letter), then press **Enter**.

2. Make a directory in the drive C root called **copytest**.

Now you can begin experimenting with the Xcopy command. Follow these steps:

1. Type **Xcopy /?** and press **Enter**. Xcopy Help information appears. Notice all the switches that you can use to modify the Xcopy command. In particular, you can use the /e switch to instruct Xcopy to copy all files and all subdirectories in a directory, including the empty subdirectories, to a new location.

2. Type **Xcopy C:\"program files"\"internet explorer" C:\copytest /e** and then press **Enter**. You will see a list of files scroll by as they are copied from the C:\program files\internet explorer folder to the C:\copytest folder. Notice that in the command line, you had to use quotation marks to surround a folder name that contains spaces.

3. When the copy operation is complete, check the copytest directory to see that the files have been copied and the subdirectories created.

4. Insert a blank floppy disk into drive A, type **md A:\copytest**, then press **Enter**. This creates a directory named copytest on drive A.

5. To copy all the files in the Copytest directory on the hard drive to the Copytest directory on drive A, type the command **Xcopy C:\"program files"\ "internet explorer" A:\copytest**, then press **Enter**.

6. The system begins copying files, but the floppy disk lacks the capacity needed to hold the entire \Internet Explorer directory. As a result, the system displays a message indicating that the disk is out of space and asking you to insert another disk. What is the exact error message?

_____

_____

7. In this case, you do not really want to copy the entire directory to the floppy disk, so you need to stop the copying process. To do that, hold down the **Ctrl** key, then press the **Pause/Break** key. You return to the command prompt.

You have used the Xcopy command to copy some files to a floppy disk. Next, you will use the Diskcopy command to make an exact copy of that floppy disk, which is referred to as the source disk. (The disk you copy files to is known as the target disk.) You'll begin by writing down a list of the files and directories on the source disk. Later, you will compare this list to the list of files actually copied to the target disk. Follow these steps:

1. Display a directory listing for the A:\copytest directory.

2. Write the complete summary of files, directories, and space on the A drive:

_____

_____

_____

_____

3. Verify that the floppy disk you used in the preceding set of steps is inserted in drive A, then type **Diskcopy A: A:** and press **Enter**. This instructs the system to copy files from one floppy disk to another using a single floppy disk drive. (If your system contained a drive B, you could copy files from a disk in drive A to a disk in drive B or vice versa.)

4. Press **Enter** to begin copying.

5. Because you are copying from drive A to drive A, the system prompts you to remove the source disk and to insert the target disk. When prompted, insert a blank floppy disk and press **Enter**.

6. When the copy operation finishes, a message appears asking if you want to copy another disk. Type **n** and press **Enter** to indicate that you do not wish to copy another disk. (When using Windows 98, you must also indicate that you do not wish to make another duplicate.)

7. With the target disk still in drive A, use the **Dir** command to compare the newly copied files with the file list from the source disk, which you recorded in step 2. The disks should be identical.

CRITICAL THINKING (additional 30 minutes)

1. Format one floppy disk. Use any method from Lab 6.3 to format the disk.

2. Use a safety pin to damage one of the floppy disks created in this lab by sliding back the disk's protective guard and punching a small hole about ½ inch from the edge of the disk.

3. Attempt to copy the files on the damaged disk to the newly formatted disk using Xcopy by first copying them to a folder on the hard drive. List the steps you used to do this and describe the outcome.

_____

_____

_____

4. Attempt to recover from the damaged disk the files that the system could not copy. Explain how you were able to do this.

_____

_____

5. Run TestDrive on the damaged disk and describe the outcome.

_____

_____

CRITICAL THINKING (additional 15 minutes)

Do the following to create and use a Windows 2000/XP bootable floppy disk:

➤ Using Explorer on a Windows 2000/XP computer, format a floppy disk.

➤ Copy Ntldr, Ntdetect.com, and Boot.ini from the root of drive C to the root of the floppy disk.

➤ Use the bootable floppy disk to boot the system. What appears on your screen after the boot?

➤ How might this bootable floppy disk be useful to you in troubleshooting?

Review Questions

1. Can a single Copy command copy files from more than one directory?

   _____

2. What switch can you use with Xcopy to copy subdirectories?

   _____

3. What is the complete Diskcopy command required to copy files on a disk in drive A to a disk in drive B?

   _____

4. What is one disadvantage of using the Diskcopy command with only one floppy disk drive?

   _____

5. Which Xcopy switch suppresses overwrite confirmation?

   _____

UNDERSTANDING AND INSTALLING HARD DRIVES

Labs included in this chapter

➤ Lab 7.1 Install and Partition a Hard Drive

➤ Lab 7.2 Format a Drive and Test It with ScanDisk

➤ Lab 7.3 Test Hard Drive Performance Using SANDRA

➤ Lab 7.4 Use Hard Drive Utilities

➤ Lab 7.5 Troubleshoot Hard Drives

➤ Lab 7.6 Critical Thinking: Sabotage and Repair a Hard Drive Subsystem

LAB 7.1 INSTALL AND PARTITION A HARD DRIVE

Objectives

The goal of this lab is to help you master the process of installing a hard drive in a computer. After completing this lab, you will be able to:

➤ Physically install a drive

➤ Set CMOS to recognize the drive

➤ Partition the drive

Materials Required

This lab will require the following:

➤ Windows 9x startup disk

➤ Hard drive with unpartitioned drive space

Activity Background

As a technician, you definitely need to know how to install a hard drive in a computer. You might have to replace a failed drive with a new one, or, if you have a hard drive that is running out of storage space, you might need to install an additional drive. In either case, you need to know the steps involved in installing a new hard drive.

In this lab you will install and partition a new hard drive. Ideally, you would install a second hard drive in a system that already has a working drive. However, this lab also gives you the option of removing the hard drive from your system, trading your hard drive for another student's hard drive, and then installing the traded hard drive in your computer. Ask your instructor which procedure you should perform. Because the steps in this lab allow for both possibilities, you need to read the steps carefully to make sure you are performing the right steps for your particular situation.

In any case, after you install the hard drive, you will have to partition it. If you are installing a hard drive that has been used as a boot device, the drive will already have a primary DOS partition. In that case, you need to verify that the drive contains at least some unpartitioned space. If it does contain unpartitioned space, you can add an extended partition to the drive. Again, ask your instructor for specific directions.

Estimated completion time: **45 minutes**

ACTIVITY

Do the following to physically install the drive in the computer case:

1. Remove the case cover. Remove the hard drive and exchange it for another student's hard drive. (If your instructor has provided you with a second hard drive to install in your system, simply open the case cover.)

2. Examine the case and decide where to place the drive. Consider whether to place the drive on the primary or secondary IDE channel and if you will need a bay kit to fit a 3.5-inch drive into a 5-inch drive bay. In most cases, you should use the primary channel for your hard drive and, if possible, it should be the only drive on that channel.

3. Place the drive in or near the bay to test its position. Make sure that all cables will reach in that position. If the cables won't reach, try a different bay or obtain longer cables.

4. When you are satisfied everything will fit, remove the drive and set the jumpers to their proper setting. If the drive is to be the only drive on an IDE channel, set it to single. If it is sharing the IDE cable with another drive, set it to master and set the other drive to slave. If the jumpers are not marked on the drive, consult the drive documentation for jumper configuration. You might have to search the Web site of the drive manufacturer for information on the drive.

5. Install the drive in the bay, and secure it with screws on each side of the drive.

6. Attach the power cord and data cable and close the case.

Now that you have physically installed your hard drive, you need to configure CMOS to recognize the new hard drive. Follow these steps:

1. Attach the keyboard, monitor, and mouse.

2. Boot your computer and enter the CMOS setup utility.

3. If IDE hard drive autodetect is not enabled, enable it now. In CMOS, what is the name of this entry? If you have just enabled autodetect, reboot the system so the drive can now be detected.

4. Check the drive parameters that were set by autodetect, and change them if they were not detected correctly. If your system does not have autodetect, set the drive parameters now. When in doubt use Logical Block Addressing (LBA) or consult the drive documentation. What are the drive parameters in CMOS?

5. Save and exit CMOS setup. The system reboots.

6. While the system boots, watch for the drive to appear during POST.

Now that the drive has been recognized, use the Fdisk utility to create or delete partitions. The following sections show you how to create and delete the primary partition, an extended partition, and a logical DOS drive.

Enter Fdisk by following these steps:

1. Insert a Windows 98 startup disk in drive A, and reboot the computer.

2. When you get a command prompt, type **Fdisk** and then press **Enter**.

3. Select **Y** and then press **Enter** to enable Large Disk Support. Large Disk Support uses FAT32 to enable partition sizes above 2GB. The Fdisk Options menu appears as shown in Figure 7-1.

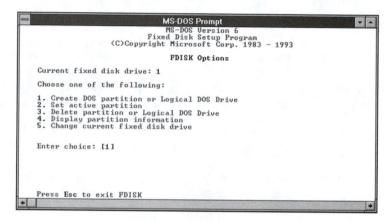

Figure 7-1 Fixed Disk Setup Program (FDISK) menu

On the Fdisk screen, the current fixed disk drive is drive 1. If you are installing a second hard drive, you must first change to drive 2 using the following steps. (If you are installing the only drive in the system, skip these steps and go to the next section, where you will determine what types of partition currently exist on your newly installed drive.)

1. Select option **5** on the menu, then press **Enter**. A list of drives appears.

2. Select drive **2**, then press **Enter**. You return to the Fdisk Options menu shown earlier in Figure 7-1.

Now that you have the correct drive selected, you need to find out what kinds of partition currently exist on the drive. Whether you are installing the only drive on the system or a second drive, follow these steps:

1. To display partition information, select option **4** on the menu, then press **Enter**. Answer these questions about your drive:

   ■ What is the total disk space reported?

   _____

   ■ What is the available disk space reported?

   _____

- Do any partitions currently exist?

- If partitions exist, what kind of partitions are they?

---

2. Press **Escape** to return to the Fdisk Options menu.

If the drive does not already have a primary DOS partition, the next step is to create one. If you are installing a second hard drive on your system, you need to create a primary DOS partition on the second hard drive by using the following steps. (If you have only one hard drive installed or if your second hard drive has a primary partition containing an operating system, skip these steps and move on to the next section, where you will create an extended partition.)

1. To select the second hard drive, from the Fdisk options menu, select option **5** on the menu, then press **Enter**.

2. To select the second hard drive, select option **2** on the menu, then press **Enter**. You return to the Fdisk Options menu.

3. To create a DOS partition, select option **1** on the menu from the Fdisk Options menu, then press **Enter**. The Create DOS Partition or Logical DOS Drive menu appears.

4. To create a primary DOS partition, select option **1** from the Fdisk Options menu, then press **Enter**.

5. The system verifies disk space and displays a progress update. When space on the drive has been verified, Fdisk prompts you to use the maximum available space for the primary DOS partition. Type **N**, then press **Enter**.

6. Fdisk again verifies disk space and prompts for the amount of disk space that you want to use for the primary partition. Type a numerical value that is half of the total available space, then press **Enter**.

7. Fdisk tells you that the primary DOS partition has been created. It displays a summary of the new partition and assigns the partition a drive letter. Record the summary.

Note that Fdisk may slightly increase the partition size to accommodate the disk's geometry. You might also see an error message saying that you do not yet have an active partition.

8. Press **Escape** to return to the Fdisk Options menu.

With a primary partition in place, you are ready to install an extended partition on the last part of the drive. Follow these steps to create an extended partition and one logical DOS drive within that extended partition:

1. In the Fdisk Options Menu, select option **1**, then press **Enter**.

2. To create an extended DOS partition, select option **2**, then press **Enter**.

3. Fdisk verifies disk space and prompts you to enter the amount of disk space to use for the extended partition. Press **Enter** to use the remaining disk space to create the extended partition. Fdisk displays a summary of the extended partition. Note that the extended partition has no drive letter assigned.

4. Press **Escape**. A message appears indicating that no logical drives are defined, and Fdisk again verifies disk space.

5. Fdisk prompts you to enter the amount of space to use for a logical drive. Press **Enter** to use the maximum amount of disk space to create a logical drive.

6. Fdisk assigns a drive letter and displays a summary. Press **Escape** to return to the Fdisk Options menu.

7. Select option **4**, then press **Enter** to display the disk summary. Note that the system column displays Unknown because the drive has not been formatted.

8. Press **Escape** to return to the Fdisk Options menu.

You will now practice deleting partitions. Fdisk is particular about the order in which you create and delete partitions. To delete a primary partition, you must delete an extended partition, and to delete an extended partition, you must delete all the logical DOS drives in the extended partition. A word of warning: If you have an operating system installed on the drive and you have only a single hard drive, *do not delete the primary partition*. Doing so will destroy the operating system installed on the drive.

To delete the extended partition you just created, you must first delete the logical DOS drive in that partition. Follow these steps:

1. From the Fdisk Options menu, select option **3**, then press **Enter**.

2. On the next screen, select option **3**, then press **Enter** to indicate that you are about to delete a logical DOS drive.

3. Type the drive letter assigned to the logical DOS drive, then press **Enter** to confirm that you wish to delete that drive.

4. Enter the volume label (or leave it blank), then press **Enter**. Select **Y** and then press **Enter** to confirm that you wish to delete the drive. Fdisk confirms that the drive has been deleted.

5. Press **Escape** once. The No Logical Drive Defined message appears.

6. Press **Escape** to return to the Fdisk Options menu.

Now that you have deleted the logical DOS drive, you can delete the extended partition. Follow these steps:

1. From the Fdisk Options menu select option **3**, then press **Enter**.

2. On the next screen, select option **2**, then press **Enter** to delete an extended partition.

3. Type **Y**, then press **Enter** to confirm that you want to delete an extended partition. Fdisk confirms that the partition has been deleted.

4. Press **Escape** to return to the Fdisk Options Menu.

If you are working with a second hard drive, you can now delete the primary partition. (Remember, do not delete the primary partition if you are working with a single hard drive.) Follow these steps:

1. From the Fdisk Options menu, select option **3**, then press **Enter**.

2. On the next screen, for the first partition select option **1**, then press **Enter**.

3. Enter the volume label (or leave it blank if there is no volume label), then press **Enter**.

4. Select **Y**, then press **Enter** to confirm that you wish to delete the partition. Fdisk confirms that the drive or partition has been deleted.

5. Press **Escape** to return to the Fdisk Options menu.

   Based on what you have learned, re-create a partition using half of the total disk space. If you have only a single hard drive, create an extended partition. If you have a second hard drive, create only a primary partition, thus leaving half of the drive space unused. Answer these questions:

   - What kind of partition did you create (primary or extended)?

   _____

   - How much space did you use for your partition?

   _____

   - What drive letter was assigned to the logical drive on the new partition?

   _____

To exit the Fdisk utility, follow these steps:

1. With the Fdisk Options menu displayed, press **Escape**.

2. A message is displayed indicating that the system must be rebooted for the changes to take effect. Reboot the system while pressing the **Ctrl** key.

3. Select **Command Prompt Only**.

4. To confirm that the drive is set up correctly, type the drive letter followed by a colon, then press **Enter**. The command prompt now includes the drive's letter.

Review Questions

1. When physically installing a hard drive, what steps should you take before you permanently fix the drive in place with screws?

_____

_____

2. What CMOS setup tool can you use to recognize your hard drive?

_____

_____

3. What are two types of partition?

_____

_____

4. What must you do before you can delete an extended partition?

_____

_____

5. What must you do before you can delete a primary partition?

_____

_____

6. What would prevent your partitions from being recognized after you exit Fdisk?

_____

_____

LAB 7.2 FORMAT A DRIVE AND TEST IT WITH SCANDISK

Objectives

The goal of this lab is to help you prepare a partitioned drive for use. After completing this lab, you will be able to:

➤ Format a drive

➤ Use ScanDisk to test the drive's condition

Materials Required

This lab will require the following:

➤ Windows 98 operating system

➤ Floppy disk containing no essential data

Activity Background

Before your computer can read from and write to a drive, you must format the drive. It is also a good idea to test a drive to ensure that it is in working order before you put it to use. In this lab, you will format and test your newly partitioned drive. You will begin by creating a bootable floppy disk and adding some important utility files to it. Then you will use the disk to boot your computer and then format and test your drive. The utility files you will include are:

➤ Scandisk.exe, which is used to detect and repair hard drive errors

➤ Himem.sys, which is used to manage memory above 1 MB

➤ Format.com, which is used to format a drive

You will also include the system file, Config.sys, which contains configuration settings.

Estimated completion time: **30 minutes**

ACTIVITY

Follow these steps to create a bootable disk, then copy the necessary files to it:

1. Create a bootable floppy disk. If you need help, see Lab 2.2.

2. Copy the file named **Scandisk.exe** from **C:\Windows\Command** to the bootable floppy disk.

3. Copy the file named **Himem.sys** from **C:\Windows** to the bootable floppy disk. Himem.sys is necessary to run Scandisk on a hard drive.

4. Copy the file named **Format.com** from **C:\Windows\Command** to the bootable floppy disk.

5. Edit or create the **Config.sys** file on your floppy disk. Add the line **Device=A:\himem.sys**. (Note that if you fail to edit the config.sys file on your boot disk, when you attempt to start ScanDisk you will receive a message indicating it is necessary to do so.)

Now that you have prepared a bootable disk, follow these steps to format your new drive:

1. Boot your system from the floppy disk.

2. At the command prompt, type **Format *x*:** (where *x* is the drive letter assigned to the partition you created in Lab 7.1), then press **Enter**.

3. The system warns you that all data will be lost and prompts you to continue. Type **Y**, then press **Enter** to confirm that you want to format this drive.

4. The system begins formatting the drive. When the formatting process is complete, you are prompted to enter a volume label. You will name the volume New. Type **New** and then press **Enter**.

5. At the command prompt, type the drive letter followed by a colon, then press **Enter**. The newly formatted drive is now the current directory.

6. Use the DIR command to view the drive summary. Record the summary information:

_____

_____

_____

_____

_____

Now that the drive has been formatted, you can use ScanDisk to check the condition of the drive. Follow these steps:

1. Type **A:\Scandisk *x*:** (where *x* is the drive letter of the volume named New).

2. ScanDisk begins checking the following:
   - Media descriptor
   - File Allocation table
   - Directory structure
   - File system
   - Free space

3. If ScanDisk finds any file fragments or errors, it prompts you to correct the problem. If no errors are found (or after all errors are corrected), ScanDisk displays a summary and prompts you to run a surface scan.

4. A surface scan is a lengthy process in which the disk is scanned block by block until the surface condition of each platter has been checked. Type **Y** to begin a surface scan.

5. ScanDisk begins the surface scan and displays an illustration of the process. While the surface scan continues examining the disk, answer the following questions. ScanDisk can take a long time to complete. For the purposes of this lab, you can cancel the surface scan after you have answered the following questions.

- How many total clusters does the disk contain?

_____

- How many clusters does each block represent?

_____

- What symbol indicates a bad cluster?

_____

Review Questions

1. Write the command you would use to format drive D.

_____

2. When is Himem.sys required to run ScanDisk?

_____

3. By default, does ScanDisk run a surface scan automatically?

_____

4. Why should you run a surface scan?

_____

5. What happens when ScanDisk finds errors during its automatic check?

_____

LAB 7.3 TEST HARD DRIVE PERFORMANCE USING SANDRA

Objectives

The goal of this lab is to help you use SANDRA to compare the performance of your system's drives against similar drives. After completing this lab, you will be able to:

➤ Use SANDRA to test your drive's performance

➤ Use SANDRA to compare your system's drives with similar drives

Materials Required

This lab will require the following:

➤ Windows 9x operating system

➤ SiSoft SANDRA, Standard version, installed in Lab 1.3

Activity Background

You can use SANDRA to run a routine of several tests on your drive, report the results, and compare your drive to a selection of comparable drives. This activity will give you an indication of how your drive is performing and whether another product is available that better meets your performance needs. Some tasks, such as video editing, are very demanding on the drive where the files are stored; a faster drive can increase productivity. When making an upgrade decision, it's helpful to compare results reported by SANDRA to information on other hard drives. In this lab you will use SANDRA to test your drive.

Estimated completion time: **30 minutes**

ACTIVITY

Follow these directions to test your drive:

1. Start SANDRA.

2. Double-click the **Drives Benchmark** icon. The Drives Benchmark window opens. (If you don't see the Drives Benchmark icon, you installed the wrong version of SANDRA. You should be using the Standard version.)

3. Click the **Select Drive** list arrow, then select the letter of the drive you are testing from the drop-down menu. What message appeared after you selected drive C?

_____

_____

4. Wait until SANDRA has finished testing your drive before moving your mouse or doing anything else with the system. After the test is finished, a summary appears. Use the summary to answer the following questions:

- In the Current Drive field, what drive index is reported?

_____

- What drives were compared to the Current Drive?

_____

_____

5. Click the drop-down menu of one of the compared drives to view it. Note that you can compare your drive against several drives.

6. One by one, select each of the drives, and note their performance ratings. List those drives with a lower performance rating than the current drive:

_____

_____

7. List the size and rpm of the two drives with the lowest performance.

_____

_____

8. Use the bottom field of the Drives Benchmark window to complete the following table. (Scroll down as necessary to display the information you need.)

Category	Value
Drive Class	
Total Space	
Sequential Read	
Random Read	
Buffered Write	
Sequential Write	
Random Write	
Average Access Time	

Review Questions

1. Why might you want to test your drive with SANDRA?

   _____

   _____

2. Based on the drive ratings information you got from SANDRA, do you think a drive performs better if it spins faster or slower?

   _____

3. Based on the drive ratings information you got from SANDRA, do you think a drive performs better if it reads data randomly or sequentially?

   _____

4. Why shouldn't you use the system when SANDRA is testing a drive?

   _____

   _____

LAB 7.4 USE HARD DRIVE UTILITIES

Objectives

The goal of this lab is to let you work with utilities from hard drive manufacturers that examine and diagnose hard drive problems. After completing this lab, you will be able to:

➤ Identify your hard drive manufacturer

➤ Evaluate utilities provided by hard drive manufacturers for their drives

➤ Test for hard drive problems

Materials Required

➤ Windows 9x is preferred, but other versions of Windows can be used

➤ Internet access

➤ File compression software such as WinZip

➤ Acrobat Reader

➤ Printer access

➤ Blank floppy disk

Activity Background

Hard drive problems can manifest themselves in different ways. The drive may experience immediate and total failure so that it does not operate at all. If failure is due to a problem with the platters, you might not be able to boot at all if the area where system files are stored is affected. If system files are not affected, you may be able to boot and work normally but experience file loss or file corruption. Then again, your may never realize you have a hard drive problem if your hard drive has bad sectors because data might not be saved to that particular physical area of the disk. More often, though, once a disk begins to fail, you notice errors. One tool you can use to diagnose hard drive problems is diagnostic software provided by your hard drive manufacturer. In this lab you will identify your drive manufacturer and use its software to examine your drive. You will also use a generic hard drive utility, Hard Drive Mechanic, which will work as diagnostic software for any manufacturer's hard drive.

7

| Estimated completion time: | **60 minutes** |

ACTIVITY

The utilities that you will use in this lab require that you boot from a floppy disk. You cannot use a Windows 9x startup disk for this purpose because there is not enough room on the disk for the hard drive utilities. Use the following steps to create a bootable floppy disk:

1. Insert a blank floppy disk into the drive.

2. From Windows Explorer or My Computer, right-click **drive A:** and select **Format** from the shortcut menu. A Format dialog box appears.

3. In the Format type section of the dialog box, select the **Quick (erase)** option. In the Other options section of the dialog box select the **Display summary when finished** and the **Copy system files** options.

4. Click **Start** in the upper-right corner of the dialog box to format and copy files to make the disk bootable. A summary is displayed after the operation is complete. How much space is available?

_____

5. Click **Close** to close the summary, and click **Close** to exit the Format dialog box.

The next thing to do is to identify your hard drive's manufacturer. To do that, you will use a utility for that purpose from Seagate. Follow these steps to identify your drive:

1. Using your Web browser, navigate to *www.seagate.com/support/seatools/index.html*.

2. Look for the section under the heading SeaTools Online, and follow the links to **Online Drive Self Test**. This will open a new window displaying the SeaTools Online testing options.

3. In the new window, follow the **Online Drive Self Test** link to do a quick test of your drive. You might receive a warning about trusting content from Seagate or Ontrack. If you receive this prompt, click **Yes** to receive their content. By following this link, you are allowing a short program to be downloaded onto your PC and executed to identify your drive.

4. A window now displays your drive information. Record the drive information, as it is presented. If you have more than one hard drive, all the drives in your system are listed. Included in the list is the hard drive manufacturer. You will use the drive manufacturer information later in the lab.

_____

_____

5. To select the drive to test, check the box to the left of your drive information, then click the **Next** button at the bottom of the window. A list of tests appears in the next window.

6. Select the **Run short Drive Self Test**, and click **Next** at the bottom of the window. This will begin the test in the same window. The test might take a few minutes. When it is done, record the results of the test.

_____

_____

_____

_____

7. When you have recorded your results, close this last window by clicking the **X** in the Title bar. A message appears informing you that you might not want to navigate away from the site. Click **OK** to close the window and continue the lab.

Now you will download generic hard drive diagnostic software that should work on any type of hard drive. To download Hard Drive Mechanic, do the following:

1. In your Web browser, navigate to *www.highergroundsoftware.com*.

2. Search the Higher Ground Software site for information on Hard Drive Mechanic (HDM). Answer the following questions:

- What version of Hard Drive Mechanic is available for download in demo form?

_____

- Which operating systems does this version of HDM support?

  _____

- Will HDM run inside or outside of Windows?

  _____

- What files must *not* be present on the boot disk?

  _____

3. Find and follow the link to download HDM. The File Download dialog box appears.

4. Click **Save** and download the file **hdmdemo.zip** to its own folder. You can create a folder from the Save As dialog box. What is the path to the down-loaded file?

  _____

7

Now you will test your hard drive with Hard Drive Mechanic (HDM). Follow these instructions to test any manufacturer's drive:

1. In Windows Explorer or My Computer, browse to the location where you downloaded **hdmdemo.zip** and double-click to extract it.

2. When all the files are extracted, copy them, except for the manual, to your bootable floppy disk. You can do this via the drag-and-drop method.

3. Double-click the **Manual.pdf** file to open it in Acrobat Reader, and then print the manual. This manual will be used to give guidance in how to answer the many questions that might be prompted by HDM.

4. Close all programs and restart your computer with the floppy disk in the drive.

5. The computer will boot and settle at the command prompt. At the prompt type **hdmdemo.exe** and press **Enter**. The HDM splash screen appears, and a graphical menu appears horizontally in the upper-left area of the screen. This menu indicates which key to select to choose an option, which is indicated by a blue letter.

6. To begin diagnosing your drive, press the **D** key to open the diagnostics sec-tion. A second menu, this time vertically arranged below the first, appears.

7. On the new menu you will see four diagnostic options and an Okay option to exit. These options should be performed from in order top to bottom to test your drive. Consult the manual that you printed as to how to answer the questions. Your instructor may provide you with the correct answers if they are not evident.

8. Did HDM discover any problems with your drive? If so, describe them below:

_____

_____

_____

Now you will find out about hard drive utilities that are supplied by several hard drive manufacturers.

Maxtor offers Maxdiag to support its hard drives. Do the following to find out about this software:

1. In your Web browser, navigate to **www.maxtor.co.jp/technology/technotes/20007.html**, and locate the link to download the MAXDIAG utility with the filename hddutil.exe.

2. Examine the information on the page and answer these questions:

   ■ With what types of drive will this utility work?

   _____

   _____

   ■ What types of problem will the software identify?

   _____

   _____

   _____

3. If you have a Maxtor drive, click the link to download hddutil.exe and save it in its own folder. What is the path to the file?

   _____

IBM provides Drive Fitness Test for its hard drives. Do the following to find out about this software:

1. In your Web browser, navigate to **www.storage.ibm.com/hdd/support/download.htm**, and find the link to download the Windows version of the software.

2. Search the information provided about the product, and answer the following questions:

- What types of drive are supported and what two types are expressly not supported?

_____

_____

- What types of analysis are performed by the software?

_____

_____

- What other OS version (besides Windows) is available to download?

_____

3. If you have an IBM drive, click the link to download the Drive Fitness Test utility and save it in its own folder. What is the path to the file?

_____

Western Digital provides Data Lifeguard. Do the following to find out about this software:

1. In your Web browser, navigate to *support.wdc.com/download*, and locate the link to download Data Lifeguard 2.8 under the Data Lifeguard Tools (Archived) section.

2. Examine the information provided and answer these questions:

- What size limitation is placed on this software?

_____

- What would you *not* be able to do if you were using Windows NT, Windows 2000, or Windows XP instead of Windows 98?

_____

3. If you have a Western Digital drive, click the link and save it to its own folder. What is the path to the file?

_____

Seagate offers Data Lifeguard. Do the following to find out about this software:

1. In your Web browser, navigate to ***www.seagate.com/support/seatools/index.html***, and locate the link to download SeaTools Desktop.

2. Examine the information provided and answer these questions:

- In what languages is SeaTools available?

   _____

- What type of OS is required?

   _____

3. If you have a Seagate drive, click the link and save the file to its own folder. What is the path to the file?

   _____

Now you will use a manufacturer's utility to test your drive. Do the following:

1. If your drive is from one of the previous manufacturers, follow the instructions provided on your drive manufacturer's Web site and perform the test for your hard drive.

2. Summarize the process and results.

   _____

   _____

   _____

   _____

If your hard drive is not made by one of the previous manufacturers, go to the Web site of your manufacturer and search for diagnostic software.

- What software did you find?

   _____

Review Questions

1. What are some symptoms of hard drive problems listed on the hard drive manufacturers' Web sites? List three in order of seriousness.

   _____

   _____

   _____

2. Which hard drive manufacturer's Web site was the most informative and easiest to use? Why?

_____

_____

_____

3. Which utility from a hard drive manufacturer seemed to be the most powerful? Why?

_____

_____

_____

4. What was the most common method used to run the utilities?

_____

LAB 7.5 TROUBLESHOOT HARD DRIVES

Objectives

The goal of this lab is to help you troubleshoot common hard drive problems. After completing this lab, you will be able to:

➤ Simulate common hard drive problems

➤ Diagnose and repair common hard drive problems

➤ Document the process

Materials Required

This lab will require the following:

➤ A computer with a hard drive subsystem that you can sabotage

➤ Bootable disk

➤ PC toolkit with ground strap

➤ Workgroup of 2–4 students

Activity Background

This lab will give you practice diagnosing and remedying common hard drive problems.

Estimated completion time: **60 minutes**

ACTIVITY

1. Verify that your hard drive is working by using a command prompt or Windows Explorer to display files on the drive.

2. Switch computers with another team.

3. Sabotage the other team's computer by doing one of the following:

   ■ Remove or incorrectly configure the drive jumpers

   ■ Remove the power connector from the drive

   ■ Switch data cables to place devices on incorrect IDE channels

   ■ Disable IDE controllers in CMOS setup

   ■ If allowed by your instructor, delete partitions on the hard drive

4. Return to your computer and examine it for any symptoms of a problem.

5. On a separate piece of paper, answer the following questions relating to the problem's symptoms:

   ■ What symptoms would a user notice? (Describe the symptoms as the user might describe them.)

   ■ Does the system boot from the hard drive?

   ■ Does POST display the hard drive?

   ■ Can you boot from a floppy disk and change to the drive in question?

   ■ Does the CMOS HDD Autodetect option detect the hard drive?

6. On a separate piece of paper, before you actually begin your investigation, state your initial diagnosis.

7. Diagnose and repair the problem.

8. On a separate piece of paper, list the steps required to confirm your diagnosis and solve the problem.

9. Answer the following questions relating to your final conclusions:

   ■ What was the problem?

■ What did you do to correct the problem?

_____

_____

_____

■ Was your preliminary diagnosis correct?

_____

10. Repeat steps 1–9, choosing actions at random from the list in step 3, until your team has performed all the items listed in step 3. Be sure to write down the relevant information (as instructed in the steps) for each problem.

7

Review Questions

1. What was the first indication that the power was disconnected from your drive?

_____

_____

2. In what incorrect drive configuration would you be able to access files on the hard drive by booting from the floppy drive?

_____

_____

3. What incorrect configurations have similar symptoms?

_____

_____

4. What problem resulted in no drives being detected except for the floppy drive?

_____

_____

5. List the steps required to use a drive whose partitions have been deleted.

_____

_____

_____

_____

_____

LAB 7.6 CRITICAL THINKING: SABOTAGE AND REPAIR A HARD DRIVE SUBSYSTEM

Objectives

The goal of this lab is to learn to troubleshoot a hard drive by repairing a sabotaged system.

Materials Required

This lab will require the following:

➤ A PC designated for a sabotage (containing no important data)

➤ Workgroup of 2–4 students

Activity Background

You have learned about several tools and methods for troubleshooting and recovering from a hard drive failure. This lab gives you the opportunity to use these skills in a troubleshooting situation. Your group will work with another group to sabotage a system first and then recover your own sabotaged system.

Estimated completion time: **45 minutes**

ACTIVITY

1. If your system's hard drive contains important data, back up that data to another media. Is there anything else you would like to back up before the system is sabotaged by another group?

_____

2. Trade systems with another group and sabotage the other group's system while they sabotage your system. Do one thing that will cause the hard drive to fail to work or give errors after the boot. Use any of the problems suggested in Lab 7.5, or you can introduce a new problem. (Do *not* alter the operating system files.) What did you do to sabotage the other team's system?

_____

_____

3. Return to your system and troubleshoot it.

4. Describe the problem as a user would describe it to you if you were working at a help desk.

_____

_____

5. What is your first guess as to the source of the problem?

_____

6. List the steps you took in the troubleshooting process.

_____

_____

_____

_____

_____

7. What did you do that finally solved the problem and returned the system to good working order?

_____

_____

7

Review Questions

1. Now that you have been through the previous troubleshooting experience, what would you do differently the next time the same symptoms present themselves?

   _____

2. What software utilities did you use or could have used to solve the problem?

   _____

3. What third-party software utility might have been useful in solving this problem?

   _____

4. In a real-life situation, what might happen that would cause this problem to occur? List three things.

   _____

   _____

   _____

CHAPTER EIGHT

SUPPORTING I/O DEVICES

Labs included in this chapter

➤ Lab 8.1 Gather Information on Your System

➤ Lab 8.2 Identify Hardware Conflicts Using Device Manager

➤ Lab 8.3 Diagnose Simple Hardware Problems

➤ Lab 8.4 Plan and Design a Null Modem Cable

➤ Lab 8.5 Use a Multimeter to Inspect Cables

➤ Lab 8.6 Critical Thinking: Sabotage and Repair a System

LAB 8.1 GATHER INFORMATION ON YOUR SYSTEM

Objectives

The goal of this lab is to teach you how to use SANDRA, the Control Panel, and other sources to compile information on your system specifications. After completing this lab, you will be able to:

➤ Use various SANDRA modules to get information about your system

➤ Use Control Panel applets to get information about your system

➤ Compile a documentation notebook

Materials Required

This lab will require the following:

➤ Windows 98 or Windows 2000/XP operating system

➤ Documentation that you collected about your computer in Lab 3.2

➤ SANDRA, Standard version, installed in Lab 1.3

Activity Background

As you continue to work with different kinds of computers, you will find it extremely useful to maintain a report listing the components installed on each computer. This is especially important if you are responsible for a large number of computers. In this lab, you will create such a document. (Note that you will need to refer to this document in future labs.) You will use SANDRA in this lab, which you installed earlier.

Estimated completion time: **45 minutes**

ACTIVITY

Fill in the following charts, which will become part of the total documentation that you will keep about your PC. When necessary, refer to the documentation about your computer that you collected in Lab 3.2 or use the SANDRA software. After you have finished the charts, make copies of them and place them in your computer's documentation notebook. If you are not sure which menus and applets to use in SANDRA, experiment to find the necessary information. Some information can be found in more than one place.

Table 8-1   Computer Fact Sheet

Location of computer	
Owner	
Date purchased	
Date warranty expires	
Size and speed of CPU	
Type of motherboard	
Amount of RAM	
Type of monitor	
Type of video card	
Hard drive type and size	
Size of disk drive A	
Size of disk drive B (if present)	

8

Table 8-2   Software Installed

Software install name	Version	Installed by	Date

Table 8-3   Other Devices

Name of device	IRQ	I/O address	DMA channel device	Driver filename
Serial port 1				
Serial port 2				
Parallel port				
Mouse				
Modem				
CD-ROM drive				
Display adapter				
Network card				

Create a documentation notebook or binder for your computer that includes copies of these charts, as well as any other documentation that you have collected about your computer. Save space for troubleshooting steps that you will learn in future labs. You will need this notebook in future labs.

Review Questions

1. How did you determine the CPU type?

_____

_____

2. How did you determine the driver used by your display adapter?

_____

_____

3. List two ways to determine the amount of RAM installed on a system.

_____

_____

4. Why would it be important for a PC technician to keep documentation on the computers for which he or she is responsible?

_____

_____

LAB 8.2 IDENTIFY HARDWARE CONFLICTS USING DEVICE MANAGER

Objectives

The goal of this lab is to help you learn to use Device Manager to identify hardware conflicts. After completing this lab, you will be able to:

➤ Use Device Manager to investigate your system specifications

➤ Detect hardware conflicts using Device Manager

➤ Use Device Properties to determine which resources are causing a conflict

Materials Required

This lab will require the following:

➤ Windows 98 or Windows 2000/XP operating system

➤ Workstation with no hardware resource conflicts

➤ Hardware device that you can install to create a hardware resource conflict

➤ Access to the Windows installation CD or the setup files stored at another location

Activity Background

Device Manager is an excellent tool for finding information about your hardware specifications. You can also use it to diagnose problems with hardware devices, including those caused by two or more devices attempting to use the same system resources (a situation called a hardware resource conflict). Among other things, Device Manager can identify faulty or disabled devices, conflicting devices, and resources currently in use. This lab will teach you how to use Device Manager to discover this information. You will start by examining your system and verifying that no hardware resource conflicts currently exist on your system. Then you will install a device that creates a resource conflict and observe the effects.

Estimated completion time: **30 minutes**

8

ACTIVITY

You can use Device Manager to print a report about your system. It is a good idea to print such a report when your system is working correctly. You can then use that report later as a baseline comparison when troubleshooting conflicts or other problems.

1. Open Device Manager and print a report that provides information on all devices and also provides a system summary. If you are using a lab PC that does not have access to a printer, you can save the report to a floppy disk and go to another computer to print it.

2. Answer the following:

   - What were the steps you used to print the report?

     _____

     _____

   - How many pages are included in the report?

     _____

   - In one or two sentences, describe the type of information included on the report.

     _____

     _____

     _____

   - List two items in the report that are not displayed in the Device Manager windows.

     _____

3. Put the Device Manager report in your documentation notebook (which you created in Lab 8.1).

Now you will use Device Manager to verify that there are no hardware conflicts.

1. Using Device Manager, check for conflicts among devices. If any conflicts exist, they will be identified by a yellow triangle with an exclamation point. (Note that if a device has been disabled and is not working at all, a red circle with a slash through it will appear over the yellow triangle and exclamation point.)

2. Shut down the system and install the component and its drivers provided by your instructor, which should conflict with another component already installed on the system. If you don't have a device that will cause a conflict, remove a nonessential device such as a modem card or sound card, which will at least cause Device Manager to report an error.

3. Reboot and install drivers if prompted. You might be asked to provide access to the Windows setup files. Did you see a message indicating a conflict or other error? If so, record the message here:

_____

_____

4. Open Device Manager. Does Device Manager report any conflicting devices? Describe the problem as Device Manager reports it, listing all problematic devices:

_____

_____

5. For each device reporting a conflict, access the device's Properties window by right-clicking the device and selecting **Properties** from the shortcut menu. What messages do you see in the Device Status field?

_____

_____

6. Still using the device's Properties window in Device Manager, click the **Resource** tab. What message do you see in the Conflicting Device field?

_____

7. Examine the Resource Type and Settings field. What resources is the device using?

_____

_____

_____

8. Does it appear that you may be able to change the settings for this device?

_____

9. Close the device Properties window.

CRITICAL THINKING (additional 15 minutes)

While the two devices are in conflict, use Device Manager to print a report on your system. Remember that, if your PC is not connected to a printer, you can save the report to a floppy disk and print it from another computer. Compare the report created when the system was working properly to the report created when conflicts existed. Note the differences in the two reports.

Now that you have observed two devices in conflict, you'll remove one of the conflicting devices. When you remove a device, you should first uninstall it in Device Manager. If you don't first uninstall the device before removing it from your system, later, when you want to install a similar or the same device, you will end up with two of them installed under Device Manager, which can cause the new device to not work.

Follow these steps to uninstall the device under Windows and then remove it:

1. For Windows 98, highlight the problem device in Device Manager and click **Remove**. For Windows 2000/XP, right-click the device and then click **Uninstall** in the shortcut menu. If prompted to restart the computer, click **No**.

2. Close Device Manager and shut down the system.

3. Remove the device you installed earlier.

4. Restart the computer, open Device Manager and verify that no conflicts exist.

Review Questions

1. What symbol in Device Manager indicates a component is not working properly?

_____

2. What two devices in your system were in conflict?

_____

3. What resource(s) was causing a conflict?

_____

_____

4. Before physically removing a device from a system, what should you do first?

_____

5. What would happen if you did not uninstall the device before removing it from your system?

LAB 8.3 DIAGNOSE SIMPLE HARDWARE PROBLEMS

Objectives

The goal of this lab is to give you practice diagnosing and repairing simple hardware problems. After completing this lab, you will be able to:

➤ Start with a functioning PC, introduce a problem, and remedy the problem

➤ Diagnose a problem caused by someone else

➤ Record the troubleshooting process

Materials Required

This lab will require the following:

➤ Windows 98, Windows 2000, or Windows XP operating system

➤ PC toolkit including screwdrivers and ground strap

➤ Pen and paper

➤ Documentation notebook that you began creating in Lab 8.1

➤ Workgroup of 2-4 students

Activity Background

If you ever work in a shop dealing with the general public, about half of the problems you see will be the result of an inexperienced person making a slight mistake when configuring a system and lacking the knowledge to diagnose and remedy the problem. Unless you are very good and very lucky, you yourself will make many of the same mistakes from time to time. Your advantage is that you will have the experience to narrow down and identify the problem and then to fix it. This lab provides experience troubleshooting and repairing simple problems. Before you begin this lab, team up with another workgroup in your class. Your team will work with this other group throughout the lab.

Estimated completion time: **60 minutes**

ACTIVITY

1. Verify that your team's system is working correctly. Also, verify that you have the completed charts for your system from Lab 8.1.

2. Make one of the following changes to your team's system:

   - Remove the power cable from the hard drive on the primary interface or highest SCSI ID
   - Reverse the data cable for the floppy drive
   - Remove the RAM and place it safely inside the case so the other team cannot see it
   - Disable IDE, SCSI, or Serial ATA controllers in CMOS
   - Remove the power-on wire from the motherboard connection
   - Partially remove the data cable from the hard drive
   - For IDE drives, swap master/slave jumper assignments or set both drives to the same setting

3. Switch places with the other team, and then diagnose and remedy the problem on your team's PC. Record the troubleshooting process on a separate sheet of paper.

   - Describe the problem as a user would describe it to you if you were working at a Help desk.

     _____

   - What is your first guess as to the source of the problem?

     _____

   - What did you do that solved the problem and returned the system to good working order?

     _____

4. Repeat Steps 1 through 3, choosing items at random from the list in step 2. Continue until your team has made all the changes listed in step 2.

CRITICAL THINKING (additional 30 minutes)

If time permits, try introducing two changes at a time. This can prove to be a much more difficult situation.

Review Questions

1. What problems resulted in a "non-system disk" error?

   _____

   _____

2. What was typically the first indication that RAM had been removed?

   _____

   _____

3. What was the first indication of a problem with drive assignments?

_____

_____

4. Name three problems resulting in symptoms similar to those related to a problem with the primary slave drive.

_____

_____

_____

5. What was the first indication of a floppy drive problem?

_____

_____

LAB 8.4 PLAN AND DESIGN A NULL MODEM CABLE

Objectives

The goal of this lab is to help you practice visualizing cable and pin-out arrangements by planning a null modem cable. After completing this lab, you will be able to:

➤ Plan a 25-pin null modem cable

➤ Use the Internet to find information on a 9-pin null modem cable

➤ Plan a 9-pin null modem cable

Materials Required

This lab will require the following:

➤ Internet access

Activity Background

A null modem cable can be used for file transfers between PCs. Such a cable is slow compared to the cables used on a modern network, but it will do in a pinch. This lab explains how to plan the pin-outs for a null modem cable.

Estimated completion time: **30 minutes**

ACTIVITY

1. Complete the drawing in Figure 8-1 to illustrate how pins on a 25-pin null modem cable connect. Draw lines between a pin on the left and its corresponding pin on the right. Use the information in Table 8-4 to complete the drawing.

Table 8-4   Connections on a 25-pin null modem cable

Pin number on the left connector	Pin number on the right connector	How the wire connecting the two pins is used
2	3	Data sent by one computer is received by the other.
3	2	Data received by one computer is sent by the other.
6	20	One end says to the other end, "I'm able to talk."
20	6	One end hears the other end say, "I'm able to talk."
4	5	One end says to the other, "I'm ready to talk."
5	4	One end hears the other say, "I'm ready to talk."
7	7	Both ends are grounded.

Figure 8-1   Complete the drawing by connecting each pin on the left to a pin on the right that is used by a 25-pin null modem cable

2. Search the Internet for the pin-out specification for a 9-pin null modem cable and complete Table 8-5.

8

Table 8-5 Connections on a 9-pin null modem cable

Pin number on one connector	Pin number of the other connector	How the wire connecting the two pins is used

3. Use the information entered in Table 8-5 to complete Figure 8-2, which shows how pins on a 9-pin null modem cable connect.

Female Connector

```
   1          5
 ○ ○ ○ ○ ○
   ○ ○ ○ ○
   6          9
```

Female Connector

```
   1          5
 ○ ○ ○ ○ ○
   ○ ○ ○ ○
   6          9
```

Figure 8-2 Complete the drawing by connecting each pin on the left to a pin on the right that is used by a 9-pin null modem cable

CRITICAL THINKING (additional 30 minutes)

If you have access to a null modem cable, use it to network two PCs and pass files between them in both directions. On a separate piece of paper, list the steps you used to do this. If necessary, open Windows Help and search on Direct Cable Connection.

Review Questions

1. Should a null modem cable be used in place of a modern network connection, if a network connection is available? Why or why not?

_____

_____

_____

2. How many pins are normally found on a serial connector on the PC itself? Is it male or female?

_____

_____

3. With what industry standard should serial cables comply?

_____

_____

4. Describe a situation in which it is appropriate to use a null modem cable that has a 9-pin connector on one end and a 25-pin connector on the other.

_____

_____

8

CRITICAL THINKING (additional 15 minutes)

Draw a diagram showing the pin-outs for a 9-pin to 25-pin null modem cable.

LAB 8.5 USE A MULTIMETER TO INSPECT CABLES

Objectives

The goal of this lab is to teach you how to use a multimeter to test cables. After completing this lab, you will be able to:

➤ Set up a multimeter to measure resistance

➤ Test cables for resistance to determine pin arrangements

➤ Test cables for broken connections

➤ Measure resistance in a resistor

Materials Required

This lab will require the following:

➤ A multimeter

➤ Three assorted cables

➤ Assorted resistors

➤ Pin-out specifications for cables from Lab 8.4

> ➤ Internet access (optional)
>
> ➤ Workgroup of 2-4 students

Activity Background

One of the multimeter's many uses is to determine if a cable is good or bad. You can also use a multimeter to determine the cable's pin arrangement. All of this is done by measuring resistance in the cable. Resistance is measured in Ohms, with infinite resistance indicating that no electricity can flow. A measure of zero Ohms or zero resistance means that electricity can flow (a state referred to as continuity). A resistor is a device that resists or controls the flow of electricity in a circuit, and a multimeter can be used to measure a resistor. You will begin the lab by setting up and testing your multimeter. Then you will measure resistance in cables and resistors.

> Estimated completion time: **45 minutes**

ACTIVITY

To set up and test your multimeter:

1. Set the multimeter to measure resistance.

2. With the probes not in contact with anything, observe the reading on the meter. The reading should be infinity, or 99999.99999, or similar.

3. With the probes touching each other, observe the reading on the meter. The reading should be 0 or similar.

Now that you have verified that your multimeter is working properly, you can use it to measure the resistance or continuity in a cable. Examine cables provided by your instructor. In the following steps you will use your multimeter to discover the pin-outs for each cable:

1. On a separate piece of paper, create a table (similar to Table 8-4) for each cable indicating the cable's pin-outs. Can you identify the cable from your table and your knowledge of cables?

2. For Cable 1, complete the following:
   - Description of cable connectors: _____
   - Number of pins on each end of the cable: _____
   - Number of pins on each end of the cable that are used: _____
   - Type of cable: _____

3. For Cable 2, complete the following:
   - Description of cable connectors: _____
   - Number of pins on each end of the cable: _____

- Number of pins on each end of the cable that are used: _____
- Type of cable: _____
4. For Cable 3, complete the following:
   - Description of cable connectors: _____
   - Number of pins on each end of the cable: _____
   - Number of pins on each end of the cable that are used: _____
   - Type of cable: _____

Suppose a user comes to you with a problem. He has a cable that connects his computer's serial port to a serial printer. He needs to order more of the same cables, but he does not know if this cable is a regular serial cable or a specialized cable made specifically for this printer. One connector on the cable is 9-pin and the other connector is 25-pin. Using this information, answer the following:

1. Describe how to determine what kind of cable he needs to order.

_____

_____

_____

_____

2. Suppose the cable is not a regular serial cable but a specialized cable. How might you give the user the pin-outs necessary to order new custom-made cables?

_____

_____

_____

_____

_____

So far you have used a multimeter to discover cable specifications. Next, you will use the multimeter to measure the resistances of several resistors.

1. Measure each resistor and record the results in Table 8-6. Note that resistors have colored bands indicating their intended resistance.

Table 8-6   Resistor measurements

Resistor	Resistance Reading

CRITICAL THINKING (additional 45 minutes)

An Ethernet network uses a patch cable to connect a PC to a hub or other network device but uses a crossover cable to connect a PC to another PC or to connect a hub to another hub. Answer the following questions:

1. How many pins does an RJ-11 patch cable or crossover cable have?

   _____

2. Research the Internet for the pin-outs of a crossover cable and a patch cable. Draw a diagram of the pin-outs of each cable.

3. Have your instructor give you one patch cable and one crossover cable. Can you tell which cable is which by physically examining them?

   _____

4. Use your multimeter to confirm which cable is the patch cable and which is the crossover cable. Which pins did you examine?

   _____

Review Questions

1. When a multimeter is set to measure resistance, what reading would you expect when the probes are touching?

   _____

2. When a multimeter is set to measure resistance, what reading would you expect when the probes are not touching anything?

   _____

3. Suppose all pins match pin-outs except one at each end. Suppose these non-matching pins have no continuity with any other pin. What is the likely condition of the cable?

_____

_____

_____

4. What do the colors on resistors indicate?

_____

5. When you are measuring resistance, is there enough electricity in the wire to cause you harm?

_____

6. In the last lab, you learned you could connect two computers using a null modem cable. What is a faster way to connect two computers when each computer has a NIC installed? What type of cable would you use?

_____

LAB 8.6 CRITICAL THINKING: SABOTAGE AND REPAIR A SYSTEM

Objectives

The goal of this lab is to learn to troubleshoot a system by recovering from a sabotaged system.

Materials Required

This lab will require the following:

> ➤ A PC (containing no important data) that has been designated for sabotage
> ➤ Workgroup of 2-4 students

Activity Background

You have learned about several tools and methods that you can use to troubleshoot and repair a failed system or failed hardware devices. This lab gives you the opportunity to use these skills in a simulated troubleshooting situation. Your group will work with another group to first sabotage a system and then repair another failed system.

Estimated completion time: **45 minutes**

ACTIVITY

1. If the hard drive contains important data, back up that data to another media. Back up anything else you would like to save before the system is sabotaged by another group and note it below.

   _____

2. Trade systems with another group and sabotage the other group's system while they sabotage your system. Do one thing that will cause the system to fail to work or give errors after booting. Use any of the problems introduced in Lab 8.3 or introduce a new problem. (Do *not* alter the operating system files.) What did you do to sabotage the other team's system?

   _____

   _____

3. Return to your system and troubleshoot it.

4. Describe the problem as a user would describe it to you if you were working at a Help desk.

   _____

   _____

5. What is your first guess as to the source of the problem?

   _____

6. List the steps you took in the troubleshooting process.

   _____

   _____

   _____

   _____

   _____

   _____

7. What did you do that finally solved the problem and returned the system to good working order?

_____

_____

Review Questions

1. Thinking back on this troubleshooting experience, what would you do differently the next time the same symptoms present themselves?

_____

2. What software utilities did you use or could you have used to solve the problem?

_____

3. What third-party software utility or hardware device might have been useful in solving this problem?

_____

4. In a real-life situation, what might cause this problem to occur? List three possible causes.

_____

_____

_____

8

MULTIMEDIA DEVICES AND MASS STORAGE

Labs included in this chapter

➤ Lab 9.1 Install a Sound Card

➤ Lab 9.2 Install a PC Video Camera

➤ Lab 9.3 Compare CD and DVD Technologies

➤ Lab 9.4 Install Dual Monitors in Windows XP

➤ Lab 9.5 Research Digital Cameras

➤ Lab 9.6 Explore Windows XP Audio Features

LAB 9.1 INSTALL A SOUND CARD

Objectives

The goal of this lab is to help you install a sound card. After completing this lab, you will be able to:

➤ Physically install a sound card

➤ Install device drivers

➤ Test the card and adjust the volume

Materials Required

This lab will require the following:

➤ Windows 2000 operating system

➤ Windows 2000 installation CD or installation files stored in another location as specified by your instructor

➤ Empty expansion slot

➤ Compatible sound card with speakers or headphones

➤ Sound card device drivers (on an installation floppy disk or CD, or stored in another location as specified by your instructor)

➤ Motherboard documentation if your system uses embedded audio

➤ PC toolkit with ground strap

➤ Internet access (optional)

Activity Background

Two of the most popular multimedia devices are the sound card and the embedded audio device. A sound card enables a computer to receive sound input and to output sound such as when playing a music CD. Alternatively, many newer systems have audio embedded on the motherboard. As an A+ computer technician you will need to know how to install a sound card, either when you are putting together a computer from scratch, repairing a failed device, or upgrading components on an existing system. In this lab, you will install, configure, and test a sound card.

Estimated completion time: **45 minutes**

ACTIVITY

First you must discover whether your system has a sound card, embedded audio device, or perhaps both or neither. Use the skills you have learned to discover and describe what audio configuration your system currently has. Describe the configuration below, and then work through the necessary steps to complete the lab in the following general order:

- Disable any existing audio devices in Windows.

- Remove or disable the hardware device(s).

- Verify that the audio is disabled.

- Physically install the sound card.

- Install the drivers in Windows.

- Verify the function of audio features.

- Return the system to its original state (optional, per instructor's directions).

_____

_____

_____

Follow these steps to uninstall a sound card or embedded audio device in Windows:

1. After you have logged on as an administrator, open the Control Panel.

2. From the Control Panel, double-click the **Add/Remove Hardware** icon to launch the Add/Remove Hardware Wizard. The wizard opens.

3. In the Add/Remove Hardware Wizard dialog box, select the radio button next to **Uninstall/Unplug a device**. Click **Next** to continue.

4. In the Add/Remove Hardware Wizard dialog box, select the radio button next to **Uninstall a device**, as shown in Figure 9-1. Click **Next** to continue.

9

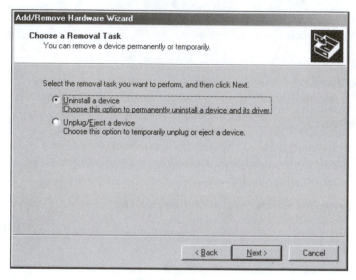

Figure 9-1 Select Uninstall a device to uninstall the sound card or embedded audio device

5. In the Devices list of the Add/Remove Hardware Wizard dialog box, scroll down until you locate your audio device. Click your device to select and highlight it, then click **Next** to continue.

6. In the Add/Remove Hardware Wizard dialog box, select the radio button next to **Yes, I want to uninstall this device**. Figure 9-2 shows this dialog box. Click **Next** to continue.

Figure 9-2 Confirm that this device is to be uninstalled

7. When the Add/Remove Hardware Wizard reports that you have successfully uninstalled your audio device, click **Finish** to close the dialog box.

8. Shut down your computer.

Follow these steps to physically remove the sound card:

1. Disconnect all external cables from the case.

2. Remove the case cover and locate the sound card. List any cables connected to the sound card.

_____

_____

3. Disconnect any cables from the sound card and secure them. Remove the sound card and place it in a safe place.

4. Reassemble the system and boot to Windows to verify that audio does not function.

Follow these steps to disable the embedded audio device:

1. Consult the motherboard documentation and learn the means to disable the embedded audio device. Also, take note of any internal audio cables. The means to disable the device is often a jumper setting, but in other cases you may have to disable the device in the CMOS setup utility. If you must disable the device in CMOS, describe the steps that you took in the space provided, then complete steps 2 and 3.

_____

_____

_____

2. Disconnect all external cables. Remove the case cover and locate the means to disable the embedded audio (if applicable). List the steps, then remove and secure any internal audio cables.

_____

_____

3. Reassemble the system and boot to Windows to verify that audio does not function.

Follow these steps to physically install a sound card:

1. Shut down the computer and disconnect all external cables from the case.

2. Remove the case cover.

3. Locate an empty expansion slot that you can use for the sound card. On some systems, expansion cards are attached to a riser card, which you might have to remove at this time. If necessary, remove the expansion slot faceplate on the case so that the sound card will fit into the expansion slot.

4. Insert the sound card into the expansion slot on the motherboard (or insert the sound card into the riser card and the riser card into the motherboard). Line up the sound card on the slot and press it straight down, making sure that the tab on the backplate (the metal plate on the rear of the card where sound ports are located) fits into the slot on the case. It normally requires a little effort to seat the card, but do not force it. If the card does not insert with just a little effort, something is preventing the card from seating. Check for obstructions and try again, removing components that are in the way, if necessary.

5. Once the card is installed, secure it with a screw. The screw goes through a hole in the card's backplate, securing the backplate to the case.

6. Attach any cable required to carry an audio signal from other multimedia devices, such as a CD-ROM drive.

7. Replace any components that you removed while installing the sound card, and replace and secure the cover on the case.

8. Reattach all cables from external devices to the appropriate ports. Attach speakers or headphones. (Some speakers receive power from the computer, and others have to be plugged into an external power source such as a wall outlet.)

Next, you will configure the drivers and other software for your sound card. If you have the documentation for your sound card, follow the exact instructions given in the documentation. Otherwise, follow these general steps to install software for most sound cards, keeping in mind that your sound card might require a slightly different procedure.

1. Start the computer, and log on as an administrator. Windows displays a Found New Hardware dialog box, attempts to determine what type of new hardware is present, and displays the result.

2. The Add New Hardware Wizard launches, informing you that it will help you install a driver. Click **Next** to continue.

3. The Add New Hardware Wizard displays a message asking how you want to install the software. Click the **Search for a suitable driver for my device (Recommended)** option button, and click **Next** to continue.

4. The Add New Hardware Wizard displays a message asking where the drivers for the new device are located. See Figure 9-3. Insert the floppy disk or CD containing the drivers and select the appropriate check box to indicate the location of the drivers. (If the CD Autorun program launches when you insert the CD, close the application.) Click **Next** to continue. If your files are not located on removable media, choose **Specify a location**. A dialog box opens prompting

you to type the path or browse to the file location. Use either method you prefer, and when you finish, click **OK** to continue.

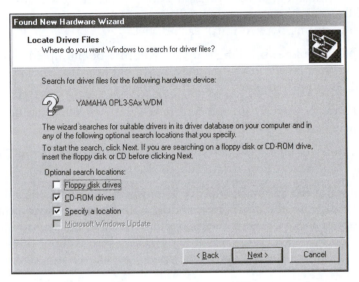

Figure 9-3   Use the appropriate method to direct the New Hardware Wizard to the correct location of the drivers

5. If the Add New Hardware Wizard is able to locate the correct driver, it displays a message identifying the sound card model name, driver location, and driver file name. Click **Next** to continue and then skip to step 7. If the wizard reports that it is unable to find the drivers, proceed to step 6.

6. If the Add New Hardware Wizard reports that it was unable to locate the drivers, click **Back** and repeat step 4, but this time select the **Specify Location** option and then click **Browse**. This opens the Browse for a Folder window. Browse to the location of the setup files, expanding folders as necessary, and look for a folder named Win2000, Win2k, or similar. (If you are not sure which .inf file to choose, consult the readme.txt file. This file should include instructions and last-minute information. Do not be surprised if you are instructed to use Windows NT 4 drivers for some devices!) After you select the correct folder, click the **OK** button to close the Browse for Folder window, and then click **Next** in the Add New Hardware Wizard. If the wizard finds the driver, continue to step 7; otherwise, consult the documentation further for the correct installation procedure.

7. After locating and installing the drivers, the Add New Hardware Wizard displays a message notifying you that the installation of the device is complete. Click **Finish** to close the Add New Hardware Wizard. At some point during the process, you may be required to supply the location of the i386 directory holding Windows installation files.

8. After the sound card is completely installed, Windows may detect additional devices. Sound cards sometimes include embedded features such as MIDI Wave Audio, SB16 Emulation, Game Port, and so on. The Add New Hardware Wizard will launch as necessary to install each of these devices separately. Follow the preceding steps to install each device.

9. When Windows finishes installing software, you may be prompted to reboot. If you are prompted, go ahead and reboot. You should hear the Microsoft sound (the default sound played on startup) after you log on.

Follow these steps to test the sound card and customize Windows sound settings. You will start by adjusting the volume.

1. In Control Panel, double-click the **Sounds and Multimedia** icon. The Sounds and Multimedia Properties dialog box appears.

2. At the bottom of the Sounds tab of the Sounds and Multimedia Properties dialog box, make sure the box corresponding with **Show volume control on the taskbar** is checked, then move the volume slider all the way to high, as shown in Figure 9-4. Click **OK** to close the dialog box. Reboot the system.

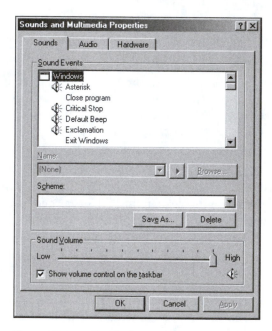

Figure 9-4   Check the settings on the Sounds tab of the Sounds and Multimedia Properties dialog box

3. On the right side of the taskbar on the desktop, you should see the speaker volume setting represented by a speaker icon. Click the speaker icon. A pop-up window opens where you can adjust speaker volume.

4. Drag the volume slider all the way to the top, and then click on the desktop. The pop-up window closes.

5. Double-click the speaker icon. The Play Control dialog box opens. Note that this dialog box gives you more control than the pop-up window you used in step 4. Among other things, it allows you to adjust the volume of various inputs including the master volume, which controls the actual volume of the signal fed to the speakers. List here the various volume controls from left to right and identify two settings (other than volume) that can be changed.

_____

_____

_____

9

6. Set the master volume slider (the one on the far left) to half volume and close the Volume Control window.

Follow these steps to control which sounds play for certain Windows events:

1. Open the Control Panel, and double-click the **Sounds and Multimedia** icon. The Sounds and Multimedia Properties dialog box opens. Scroll down the Sound Events list box on the Sounds tab, and note that a speaker icon next to an event indicates that a specific sound will play when that event occurs. Complete Table 9-1 by clicking each event listed in the table and noting the sound associated with that event. (The name of the sound file associated with the selected event appears in the Name list box.) Also note that not all Windows events are assigned a sound.

Table 9-1 Associated sounds with events

Event	Sound name
Start Windows	
Empty Recycle Bin	
Critical Stop	

2. In the Sound Events list box, click **Empty Recycle Bin** and then click the **Play** button to the right of the Name list box. The recycle sound plays.

3. Use the Name list arrow to select and play several different sounds until you find one that you like better than the recycle sound. In the Scheme list box, select **Windows Default**. Click **Save As** in the Schemes section. In the **Save Scheme As** dialog box that appears, type **Custom** to change the name of the

scheme from Windows Default to Custom, and then click **OK** to close the Save Scheme As dialog box. What sound did you choose?

_____

4. Click **OK** to apply and save the revised Sounds and Multimedia Properties. Next, you will test the new sound by emptying the Recycle Bin.

5. Right-click the **Recycle Bin** on the desktop, and then click **Empty Recycle Bin** in the shortcut menu. Click **Yes** to confirm. Note that if there are no files in the Recycle Bin, this option is unavailable.

6. Using the Sounds applet in Control Panel, change the sound that plays when Windows starts. What sound did you use?

_____

7. Restart Windows and listen to the new sound.

8. After you have verified that the new sound plays, repeat the process and return the sound to the original settings.

9. If you have Internet access, use a search engine and locate a Lion.wav file and play it to hear a lion's roar. What was the Web site where you found the file?

_____

Review Questions

1. What Windows feature walks you through the process of installing drivers for a new device?

_____

2. Other than driver files included with the sound card, what other software might be requested by Windows 2000 when configuring a new sound card?

_____

3. What other devices embedded on the sound card might Windows detect after the sound card installation is finished?

_____

_____

4. How does Windows handle the installation of these additional devices?

_____

_____

5. What Control Panel applet, and which specific tab in its properties dialog box, allows you to test the sound card by playing sounds for Windows events?

_____

6. Besides the output to the speakers on the sound card or embedded audio device interface, what other outputs/inputs are available on the card? What are their uses?

_____

_____

_____

LAB 9.2 INSTALL A PC VIDEO CAMERA

Objectives

The goal of this lab is to help you complete the process of installing and testing a PC camera. After completing this lab, you will be able to:

➤ Install a PC video camera

➤ Use Windows XP Movie Maker to test your PC camera

➤ Use Windows 98 NetMeeting to test your PC camera

Materials Required

This lab will require the following:

➤ Windows XP or Windows 98 operating system

➤ Windows installation CD or installation files stored in another location as specified by your instructor

➤ USB connective PC camera compatible with your system

➤ Spare USB port on the system

➤ Device drivers for the camera

➤ Sound card, speakers, and microphone (optional)

➤ Internet access (optional)

Activity Background

PC cameras are becoming increasingly popular. Using these cameras, you can set up a video conference, record or send video images to your family and friends, and monitor your house over the Internet. You can even detach some PC cameras and use them to take still pictures while away from your system, uploading them to the computer when you return. Most PC cameras install via the USB port, making physical installation a relatively simple process. In this lab, you will install, configure, and test a basic PC camera.

Estimated completion time: **45 minutes**

ACTIVITY

For Windows XP, follow these steps to install a PC camera:

1. Start the computer and, if necessary, log on as an administrator.

2. Locate an unused USB port. Insert the PC camera's cable into the USB port. (Do not force it. If the cable does not insert easily, flip the connector over, and try again; it should insert easily.)

3. Windows detects the new USB device and the Found New Hardware icon appears in the Taskbar Notification area (think System Tray). A balloon tip above the icon informs you that new hardware has been found. Next the balloon tip will identify the hardware as a camera, and then it will notify you that it has identified the particular model of camera. Finally, the balloon tip will notify you that the camera has been successfully installed. Windows XP likely will not give you the opportunity to use the camera manufacturer's device drivers. However, if it is requested, insert the camera installation CD or floppy disk. (If the Autorun program launches, close it.)

Now you will use Windows XP My Computer to collect information about your camera. Complete the following steps and list the information indicated:

1. Open My Computer. List the section title that the camera appears under in the right pane of My Computer.

   _____

2. Right-click the icon for your camera and choose **Properties** from the shortcut menu. The *Cameraname* **Properties** dialog box opens. List the five types of information available in the **Camera Status** section of the **General** tab.

   _____

   _____

   _____

3. Click the **Test Camera** button in the Diagnostics section of the dialog box. A new dialog box appears. Describe below the results reported, then click **OK** to close the dialog box. Click **OK** again to close the *Cameraname* Properties dialog box.

_____

_____

4. Now double-click the camera icon in My Computer. Record what happens and what tasks are available in the Camera Tasks section.

_____

_____

_____

5. Use what you know about Windows and list two ways, other than My Computer or Windows Explorer but within Windows XP, where you can find information about the camera. Briefly describe any differences from My Computer on the amount of information available or the way it is presented for each source.

_____

_____

_____

_____

Now you will use a feature new to Windows in Windows XP called **Windows Movie Maker** to put your camera to use. Complete the following steps:

1. From the Start Menu select **All Programs**, then **Accessories**, then click **Windows Movie Maker**. Windows Movie Maker launches. See Figure 9-5.

Figure 9-5   Windows Movie Maker

2. On the Windows Movie Maker toolbar, click **Record**. The Record dialog box opens.

3. On the Record dialog box, click the arrow for the **Record:** field drop-down menu and list the choices you have for recording.

_____

_____

4. On the Record dialog box, click the **Change Device** button. The Change Device dialog box opens. What devices are currently selected?

_____

5. In the Change Device dialog box, click the arrow for the **Line:** field drop-down menu and select the microphone on the camera. If your camera does not have a microphone, leave the default setting. Click **OK** to close the dialog box.

6. To record a video clip, click the **Record** button on the Record dialog box. See Figure 9-6. The Record button changes to **Stop** and the **Elapsed** time counter starts ticking. Take several seconds of footage, then click **Stop**. What is

the title of the dialog box that appears? What is the default path in the new dialog box?

_____

_____

_____

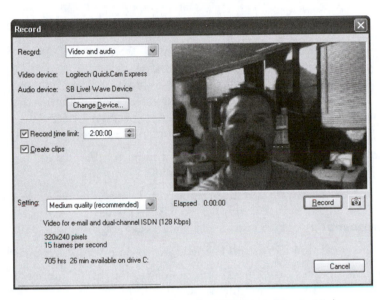

Figure 9-6   Record dialog box for Windows Movie Maker

7. Save your file as a test with the default extension. The Record dialog box closes and a **Creating Clips** dialog box appears showing the Save progress, then closes automatically when the clip is saved. Where does your clip appear in the Windows Movie Maker screen?

_____

_____

8. When you click a clip and highlight it, you can play that clip in the interface on the right side of your screen. In addition, you can drag and drop a clip to the Timeline/Storyboard interface at the bottom of Windows Movie Maker to edit it. Take a few minutes to explore and experiment with Windows Movie Maker, then record and save a clip describing what features you find interesting about the capability to record and edit video on your system.

For Windows 98, follow these steps to install a PC camera:

1. Start the computer and log on, if necessary.

2. Insert the PC camera's installation CD or floppy disk. (If the CD Autorun program launches, close it.)

3. Locate an unused USB port. Insert the PC camera's cable into the USB port. (Do not force it. If the cable does not insert easily, flip the connector over and try again; it should insert easily.)

4. Windows detects the new USB device and the Found New Hardware window opens, informing you that a USB device has been detected. A second window opens, informing you that Windows is forming a New Driver Database; when the new database is finished, the second window closes. The Found New Hardware window closes as well. (If Windows does not detect the camera, check the Device Manager or BIOS settings to discover whether the USB controller has problems or has been disabled. If necessary, enable the USB controller in Device Manager and CMOS setup and begin again with step 1.)

5. The Add New Hardware Wizard opens and indicates that it will begin searching for drivers for a USB device. Click **Next** to continue.

6. The Add New Hardware Wizard prompts you to specify a driver or search for the best driver. Click the **Search for the Best Driver for Your Device (Recommended)** option button and click **Next** to continue.

7. Locate the installation files as you learned how to do in Lab 9.1 and click **Next**.

8. The wizard indicates that it has found the driver for the PC camera and displays the driver's location and file name. Click **Next** to continue.

9. The wizard copies all necessary files and displays a message indicating that the installation is complete. Click **Finish** to close the wizard. Many PC cameras have built-in microphones as well as other devices. If this is the case, the wizard may launch again for each device. It is also possible that during any installation, the wizard will prompt you to provide the location of Windows 98 installation files.

Now you will use Windows 98 NetMeeting to test your camera. NetMeeting is video conferencing software included with Windows 98. To perform a full video conference with two or more people, you can use a directory service, an online database that NetMeeting uses to locate participants in a NetMeeting conference. One such directory service is Microsoft Internet Directory. When you install NetMeeting, you are prompted to enter information about yourself and are then given the opportunity to be added to the Microsoft Internet Directory. The following steps tell you to use the Microsoft Internet Directory, although your instructor might ask you to use a different directory service. Follow these steps to install NetMeeting if it is not already installed:

1. Open the Control Panel, open the **Add/Remove Programs** applet, and then click the **Windows Setup** tab. Windows searches for Windows Components.

2. Double-click the **Communications** group in the Components list box. The Communications dialog box opens.

3. Scroll down the Components list box, select the **Microsoft NetMeeting** check box, and then click **OK**. The Communications dialog box closes.

4. Click **OK** to close the Add/Remove Properties dialog box. The Copying Files dialog box appears, indicating that the copying process has begun. If prompted, supply the location of Windows 98 installation files. When the files are copied, the Copying Files dialog box closes. Reboot your PC if prompted to do so.

Now you will launch Windows 98 NetMeeting and configure it. Follow these steps:

1. Click **Start** on the taskbar, point to **Programs**, and then look for Microsoft NetMeeting on one of the submenus. You might find it located under Internet Explorer or under Accessories\Communications.

2. Click **Microsoft NetMeeting**.

3. Microsoft NetMeeting begins configuring your connection. Click **Next** to continue.

4. In the NetMeeting dialog box shown in Figure 9-7, accept **Microsoft Internet Directory** as the server name (unless your instructor gives you different directions) and then click **Next**.

Figure 9-7   By default, installing NetMeeting adds you to the Microsoft Internet Directory

5. Supply the requested identification information, including your name and e-mail address, and then click **Next** to continue. (Keep in mind that your identification information will be available to other NetMeeting users on the directory server.)

6. What you see on the next screen depends on the version of NetMeeting installed. You might see a screen asking you what category to use for your personal info (personal use for all ages, business use for all ages, or adults–only use). Select a category and click **Next**. For some versions of NetMeeting, the screen will give you the option of selecting a directory server. In this case, the default is Microsoft Internet Directory. Leave the default selected and click **Next**.

7. On the next screen, you are asked to specify your connection speed. Select **Local Area Network** (or other speed as specified by your instructor) and then click **Next** to continue.

8. You are asked to specify your video capturing device. Select your camera from the drop-down menu, if it is not already selected, and then click **Next** to continue.

9. NetMeeting informs you that it will help tune your audio settings. Click **Next** to continue.

10. Set and test your audio settings. When they are satisfactory, click **Next** to continue.

11. When the installation is complete, click **Finish**. NetMeeting launches.

12. Click **Current Call** and then click the **Play** button in the My Video frame. You should be able to see video supplied by your PC camera in the My Video screen. This demonstrates that your video camera was installed correctly.

CRITICAL THINKING (additional 20 minutes)

If others in the lab are connected to NetMeeting and you have access to a sound card, speakers, and microphone, join someone else in a video conference. To make the connection, you can use an IP address of another computer on the LAN, instead of using a directory server. To use Windows 98 to determine the IP address of a workstation, enter **winipcfg** in the Run dialog box and then select the network adapter from the drop-down list. Figure 9-8 shows a full NetMeeting video conference complete with shared whiteboard, chat window, and video.

Figure 9-8   NetMeeting provides three windows during a session

Review Questions

1. Typically, via what type of port do PC cameras attach to a system?

   _____

2. What type of audio device may be embedded in a PC camera?

   _____

   _____

3. Do you have to power down the system before connecting a USB camera? Why or why not?

   _____

   _____

4. What feature of Windows XP is designed to create video content?

   _____

   _____

   _____

5. What application can you use to test the video supplied by your PC camera?

   _____

   _____

6. When would using a PC camera be beneficial to you?

   _____

   _____

9

LAB 9.3 COMPARE CD AND DVD TECHNOLOGIES

Objectives

The goal of this lab is to help you use the Internet to research CD and DVD standards. After completing this lab, you will be able to:

➤ Recognize CD and DVD specifications

Materials Required

This lab will require the following:

➤ Internet access

Activity Background

Many multimedia PCs include CD or DVD drives (and sometimes both). These drives may be of three types: read-only (ROM), write/record (R), or write/record and re-write (RW or RAM). (The last two types can only write and record to specialized disks.) You will research the features and limitations of CD and DVD standards in this lab.

Estimated completion time: **60 minutes**

ACTIVITY

Use the Internet and your favorite search sites such as Google (*www.google.com*) or Yahoo! (*www.yahoo.com*) to answer the following questions on CD standards. Print the source page or pages supporting your answers.

1. What is the maximum storage capacity of a CD?

   _____

2. Briefly, how is information recorded on a CD-ROM disk?

   _____

   _____

3. Are CDs capable of storing data on both sides of the disk?

   _____

4. What type or color of laser is used in a CD drive?

   _____

5. What is a limitation of a CD-R drive that is not an issue with a CD-RW drive?

   _____

   _____

6. What kind of problems might occur if you tried to use an older CD–ROM drive or a CD player to play a CD–R or a CD–RW disk?

_____

_____

7. Define "constant angular velocity" and explain how it applies to CD standards.

_____

_____

8. Define "constant linear velocity" and explain how it applies to CD standards.

_____

_____

9. What term is used to refer to the process of writing data to a disk?

_____

10. Can any CD hold video data? Explain.

_____

11. On a CD disk, is data written in concentric circles or in a continuous spiral track?

_____

12. What are three common standards CD drives use to interface with a system?

_____

13. What does the X factor of a drive indicate? What is the specification of one X?

_____

_____

9

14. Briefly describe how a CD-RW writes data to a disk and how it is able to rewrite data.

_____

_____

_____

_____

_____

15. How much would you pay for a package of CD-R disks? How much for a package of CD-RW disks? How many disks are in a package of each type?

_____

Use the Internet and your favorite search sites to answer the following questions on DVD standards. Print the source page or pages supporting your answers.

1. What is the maximum storage capacity of a DVD disk?

_____

2. What two characteristics give a DVD disk more storage capacity than a CD disk?

_____

_____

_____

3. Describe the difference between DVD-R and DVD-RAM.

_____

_____

_____

_____

4. Besides DVD-R, what other standards are available for burning DVDs?

_____

5. Explain how DVD audio and CD audio differ.

_____

_____

_____

6. How many CDs worth of data can a single DVD hold?

_____

7. How many layers of data can be stored on one side of a DVD?

_____

8. How many data areas are on a single side of a DVD-R?

_____

9. List the versions and maximum capacities of DVD-RAM.

_____

_____

10. Can DVDs be used in CD devices? Explain.

_____

11. Explain the use of the UDF file system and how it applies to a DVD.

_____

_____

_____

_____

_____

Review Questions

1. What factors, other than storage capacity, would you consider when choosing between a DVD drive and a CD drive?

_____

_____

2. What characteristics do DVD and CD drives share?

_____

_____

3. If you wanted to create a disk that would never need to be altered and could be used on the maximum number of systems, what type of disk would you use and why?

_____

_____

_____

4. Why do you think motion pictures are released on DVDs instead of CDs?

_____

_____

_____

LAB 9.4 INSTALL DUAL MONITORS IN WINDOWS XP

Objectives

The goal of this lab is to help you set up a second monitor on a system. After completing this lab, you will be able to:

➤ Install a display adapter and its drivers

➤ Attach a second monitor

➤ Configure the system to use both monitors at the same time

Materials Required

This lab will require the following:

➤ Windows XP operating system

➤ PC toolkit with ground strap

➤ Second display adapter with drivers

➤ Second monitor

Activity Background

It is often quite handy to have two monitors on a system. For instance, if you have a second monitor, you can have a Web browser maximized on one and a video editing application maximized on the other. This has the effect of making your desktop larger and making it easier to work with multiple applications simultaneously, which is often very useful when developing multimedia presentations. In this lab, you will install and configure a second monitor on a computer.

> Estimated completion time: **45 minutes**

ACTIVITY

It is important to verify that the original hardware is working properly before you try to add a second display adapter and monitor. That way, if a problem arises after you install new hardware, you can be pretty sure that something is amiss with the newly added components rather than with the original equipment. It is also important to make sure that the hardware is either on the Windows XP HCL (recommended) or, at the very least, that the device manufacturer offers drivers and specific instructions for use with Windows XP.

Follow these steps to physically install the second display adapter:

1. Check to make sure that the original display adapter uses the PCI or AGP standard, and decide whether it will be the primary or secondary monitor.

2. Install the second adapter card in the PCI slot nearest to the AGP slot (if the original is an AGP adapter) or in the PCI slot immediately next to the original PCI adapter (if the original is a PCI adapter). If you need additional guidance on installing a card, refer to Lab 9.1.

3. Attach the second monitor to the port on the back of the display adapter.

4. Boot your PC and enter CMOS setup. If your setup has the display settings for dual monitors, adjust them so that the primary display adapter is initialized first. If you don't see this setting, then your BIOS does not support, it so you can exit CMOS setup and wait for your system to reboot.

5. In CMOS setup, if you see the settings for dual monitors, for a system with an AGP slot, make sure the AGP adapter is selected as your primary adapter and the PCI adapter as the secondary adapter. For a system that uses two PCI adapters, it does not matter which adapter is the primary one; you can leave the setting as is. For additional guidance on adjusting BIOS settings refer to Lab 4.1. Exit CMOS setup and wait for your system to reboot.

Follow these steps to install device drivers and adjust Windows display settings:

1. When the system reboots, log on as an administrator. Windows XP recognizes the new adapter and displays a Found New Hardware icon in the Notification area of the taskbar (next to the clock). Above the Found New Hardware icon, a balloon tip appears with the notification.

2. At this point, Windows may automatically install the drivers for you (if the drivers were available when XP was published) or launch the Found New Hardware Wizard if the adapter is new enough that XP is not aware of the correct drivers. Complete the steps in the wizard to install the adapter. When installation is complete, reboot. Refer to Lab 9.1 if you need additional information on using the wizard.

Before you use a second monitor, you must activate it. You will activate your second monitor in the following steps:

1. Log on as an administrator, open the Control Panel, and click the **Appearance and Themes** icon. Then click the **Display** icon. The Display Properties dialog box appears.

2. Select the Settings tab on the Display Properties dialog box, as shown in Figure 9-9. The field at the top of the settings tab now displays two monitors. Click the image of the monitor with the number 2 in it, or in the Display list box select the video adapter that you just installed.

Figure 9-9   You must choose to activate a second monitor before it can be used by Windows

3. Adjust the resolution and color settings to your preference, and then select the **Extend My Windows Desktop Onto This Monitor** check box.

4. Click **Apply** to apply the settings. The second monitor displays the desktop.

Follow these steps to test your dual-monitor configuration:

1. Open Paint, and then drag and drop it to the second monitor. Does your desktop extend to the second monitor as expected?

_____

2. Open Windows Explorer and maximize it on the original monitor. Can you see your mouse move as expected from one monitor to the next? Does the mouse interact with applications on each monitor?

_____

3. Close Paint and Windows Explorer and open Device Manager.

Follow these steps to remove the second adapter and return to a single monitor configuration:

1. Open Device Manager, find the second display adapter, and highlight it. (Make sure you are looking at the second adapter and not the first.)

2. Click **Uninstall**. If prompted, verify that you do wish to remove the device, and when asked if you want to restart the computer, click **No**.

3. Shut down the computer. Do not restart the computer at this time.

4. Remove the secondary monitor and adapter card. If necessary, reverse any BIOS changes you made that affect the display initialization sequence, and reboot the system to verify that the adapter card is no longer recognized by the system.

Review Questions

1. Before installing a second monitor, why is it important to know if your existing configuration is working properly?

_____

2. Why might it be necessary to change the sequence in which the system initializes display adapters?

_____

_____

3. In Display Properties, what is one way to select the monitor you wish to adjust?

_____

4. What would probably happen if the new adapter was on the Windows XP HCL and was in production prior to the release of Windows XP?

_____

5. Does adjusting the settings of one monitor affect the settings of the other?

_____

6. Why would a user want to install multiple monitors on a system?

_____

_____

7. Which would be cheaper, adding a second 17" monitor to an existing system or buying a 21" monitor in single-monitor mode?

_____

_____

_____

8. How did you arrive at your answer to Question 7?

_____

_____

LAB 9.5 RESEARCH DIGITAL CAMERAS

Objectives

The goal of this lab is to help you research digital cameras and learn how you might integrate them with a multimedia PC. In this lab, you will research:

➤ Camera picture quality and compatibility

➤ Camera storage technology

➤ Methods of transferring images to a PC

Materials Required

This lab will require the following:

➤ Internet access

Activity Background

As digital cameras have become more common and popular, they have also become more refined. Their special features, image quality, methods of file storage, and methods of transferring image data to the PC have improved over earlier models. Also, the prices of digital cameras have decreased significantly. In this lab, you will research digital cameras and learn how they are used with multimedia PCs.

Estimated completion time: **60 minutes**

ACTIVITY

Research digital photography on the Internet. Try searching for "digital camera" or "digital photography" on your favorite search engine. Web sites that might be useful include:

➤ *www.cnet.com* by CNET Networks, Inc.

➤ *www.dpreview.com* by Digital Photography Review

➤ *www.shutterline.com* by Shutterline

➤ *www.keyworlds.com/d/digital_photography.htm* by KeyWorlds.com

Answer these questions about general camera topics. Print the Web page or pages supporting your answer.

1. How is image quality measured? Will all digital cameras produce the same image quality?

   _____

   _____

2. What are three storage technologies that digital cameras might use to store images in a camera?

   _____

   _____

   _____

3. Name four technologies a camera might use to transfer images to a PC. What requirements must a PC meet for each?

   _____

   _____

   _____

   _____

9

4. Name and print information about at least two digital cameras that offer features such as changeable lenses, manual focus, aperture settings (f-stops), and shutter-speed settings (exposure).

_____

_____

Answer these questions regarding basic image characteristics.

1. What three file types might a digital camera use to store images?

_____

2. Name three factors that affect the number of images that a camera can store on a single storage device.

_____

_____

_____

3. Do most digital cameras offer the ability to control image quality? Explain.

_____

4. Can you remove an image that you do not like from a camera without transferring the image to a PC? Explain.

_____

5. What are three means of obtaining an actual printed photo of an image taken by a digital camera?

_____

_____

_____

6. Will any digital cameras record images other than still shots?

_____

Answer these questions about how cameras transfer images to a PC.

1. Which means of transfer offers the highest transfer speed and what is that speed?

_____

_____

2. Which means of transfer requires the least specialized hardware on the PC?

_____

3. Which storage technologies allow the direct transfers of images by removing the storage device from the camera and inserting it in the PC?

_____

_____

4. What devices can be added to a PC to allow it to directly read flash memory cards?

_____

_____

_____

_____

5. What means of image transfer does not require you to remove a device from the camera or use cabling to the PC?

_____

6. Does image resolution have any effect on transfer speed? Explain.

_____

_____

_____

_____

Answer these questions about photo-quality printers:

1. What resolution would you recommend for a printer capable of reproducing digital pictures?

_____

9

2. Do you need special paper to get the best quality in photo printing? Explain.

_____

3. Describe one way you could get your pictures from your digital camera to the printer.

_____

_____

_____

Review Questions

1. What are three advantages of a digital camera over a 35mm camera?

_____

_____

_____

2. What are some disadvantages of a digital camera compared to a 35mm camera?

_____

_____

3. What are some features that you would like on a digital camera if you were to buy one? Explain your choices.

_____

_____

_____

4. What could be done to maximize the number of images stored on the camera without modifying the storage device capacity?

_____

_____

_____

5. Typically, would a 3.1 megapixel camera have a superior or inferior picture quality compared to a 4.9 megapixel camera?

_____

6. When purchasing a photo printer, would you consider the cost of purchasing ink refills? Why or why not?

_____

_____

LAB 9.6 EXPLORE WINDOWS XP AUDIO FEATURES

Objectives

The goal of this lab is to let you experiment with different audio features and capabilities of Windows XP. After completing this lab, you will be able to:

➤ Identify audio media types

➤ Download and install Nullsoft Winamp, a third-party sound software application

➤ Control audio CD playback with Windows Media Player and Nullsoft's Winamp

➤ Customize sounds that Windows plays for events

Materials Required

This lab will require the following:

➤ Windows XP operating system

➤ Windows XP CD or installation files

➤ Internet access

➤ CD-ROM drive and an audio CD

Activity Background

Windows XP provides various features that let the user experience and use audio files in different ways. Various Windows events may be configured to play a certain sound when the event occurs. These features can be used simply to make using Windows more enjoyable to the average user, but to a sight-impaired user they can be vital tools.

Windows XP provides Windows Media Player as a means to experience audio CDs as well as other multimedia types. In this lab you will experiment with Windows audio capabilities and use Nullsoft's Winamp, a third-party sound software application.

Estimated completion time: **40 minutes**

ACTIVITY

Follow these steps to adjust the Windows volume level:

1. On the right side of the taskbar, you should see the Windows volume represented by a speaker symbol. Click once on the speaker symbol. This opens the Volume Control pop-up window.

2. Drag the volume slider all the way to the top, and click on the desktop. The Volume Control dialog box closes.

3. Double-click the speaker symbol. This opens the Play Control window. Note that this window lets you adjust the volume of various inputs independent of and including the master volume. The number of volume controls offered here depend on the capabilities of your sound card. List here the various volume controls from left to right, and identify two settings (other than volume sliders) that can be made.

_____

_____

_____

_____

_____

4. Set the "master" volume slider (the one on the far left) to half volume and close the Volume Control window.

Follow these steps to customize Windows sound settings:

1. From the Control Panel, double-click the **Sounds, Speech and Audio Devices** icon, then click the **Sounds and Audio Devices Control Panel** icon to open the Sounds and Audio Devices Properties dialog box.

2. On the Sounds tab of the Sounds and Audio Devices Properties dialog box, scroll down the Program Events field, and note that each event with a speaker symbol has a sound assigned that plays when the event occurs, as shown in Figure 9–10. Click **Start Windows** in the Program event-field, and then click the **Play** button between the Sounds field and the Browse button. The Windows XP Startup sound plays. If you do not hear the sound, check your volume levels and make sure that the volume is not muted.

Figure 9-10   A speaker symbol indicates which events will initiate a sound when activated

3. From the drop-down menu of the Sounds field, select and play several different sounds until you find one that you like better than the Microsoft sound. Click **Save As** in the Sound scheme section, type **Custom** in the dialog box that appears, and click **OK** to save the new settings. (You could also apply the Windows Default scheme by selecting it from the Schemes drop-down menu.)

4. Click **OK** to apply and save Sound Properties. Restart Windows and log on to the same account to hear the new sound.

Follow these steps to play an audio CD with Windows Media Player:

1. Insert the audio disk in the CD-ROM drive. An Audio CD dialog box will appear. In the Audio CD dialog box, select **Play Audio CD using Windows Media Player**, then click **OK** to close the dialog box.

2. Windows Media Player should launch and automatically begin playing the CD. Adjust the volume so it is not distracting to others.

3. The right pane of Windows Media Player displays the tracks on the CD. The center section displays different images to accompany the audio output. Experiment with customizing this image by right-clicking this section and selecting something from the shortcut menu. List below three of your favorite selections.

_____

_____

4. Windows Media Player, has the standard set of control features that you would expect with a CD player. On the left of Windows Media Player are a number of other features. Experiment with Windows Media Player and answer the following questions:

- Which feature would change the appearance of the entire Windows Media Player interface?

  _____

  _____

- What are some of the featured stations in Radio Tuner?

  _____

  _____

- What types of information are available via Media Guide?

  _____

  _____

Follow the steps below to install Winamp and use it to play the audio CD. Bear in mind that new versions of software are released often, so these directions might differ slightly, depending on the latest release:

1. In your Web browser, go to the Nullsoft Winamp Web site at *www.winamp.com*. Follow the Download Now! link and download the default version of Winamp. (This file will be named Winamp3_0-full.exe or something similar.) What is the name of the file you found to download?

   _____

2. In Windows Explorer find your download location and double-click **winamp3_0-full.exe** to launch Winamp Setup and begin the installation process. The Winamp Setup process is very similar to other installation wizards you have previously completed. Work through the installation using default settings for everything. If you do not wish to receive e-mail from Nullsoft, select the **Stop Bugging Me** check box if it appears on the information screen for Winamp Setup. When prompted, click **Run Winamp** to launch Winamp, which will download additional information in the Winamp browser.

3. Close Winamp and the Winamp browser. Remove the audio CD and then insert the audio CD again. This time, when the Audio CD dialog box opens, select **Play Audio CD using Winamp3**. Winamp will launch again and begin playing your audio CD.

4. Experiment with Winamp to answer these questions:

■ Does Winamp have the same basic features as Windows Media Player?

_____

■ What feature does Winamp provide that allows you to customize the sound tone?

_____

■ Name three popular music file types that Winamp supports.

_____

■ Could you set up a playlist that would play all the files on your CD in an order that you chose, instead of first to last? Explain your answer.

_____

_____

_____

Review Questions

1. What icon do you single-click to access the Windows volume control?

_____

2. What feature of Windows Media Player would allow you to listen to streaming audio content?

_____

3. What is the default sound played during Windows XP startup?

_____

_____

4. Which player provided more features, and which was easier to use? Explain your answers.

_____

_____

_____

_____

5. How can you lower the volume of CD playback while keeping the Windows event sounds volume the same?

_____

_____

CHAPTER TEN

SUPPORTING MODEMS

Labs included in this chapter

➤ Lab 10.1 Simulate Serial Port Communication

➤ Lab 10.2 Install and Test a Modem

➤ Lab 10.3 Use AT Commands to Control a Modem

➤ Lab 10.4 Simulate Modem Problems

 ➤ Lab 10.5 Critical Thinking: Use Two Modems to Create a Multilink Connection

LAB 10.1 SIMULATE SERIAL PORT COMMUNICATION

Objectives

The goal of this lab is to illustrate serial communication using a game. After completing this lab, you will be able to:

➤ Identify pin arrangements

➤ Explain which pins are used for handshake and data transfer

Materials Required

This lab will require the following:

➤ Eight pieces of string, each approximately four feet long

➤ Workgroup of eight students

Activity Background

RS-232 standards specify cabling and communication methods for the PC. Among other things, they specify the sequence of signals that must travel across a serial cable in order to complete a handshake and transmit data between devices. In this lab, to keep things simple, you will simulate a handshake and data transfer on a null modem cable. You and your fellow students will play the part of the serial ports, using pieces of string for the cable.

Estimated completion time: **30 minutes**

ACTIVITY

Follow these steps to simulate a cable connection between two devices:

1. Position eight students in two rows facing each other, with four on each side. Designate the students on one side as Students A through D. Designate the students on the other side as Students E through H. Students E and A should be facing each other, as should Students B and F, and so on down the line. The two groups of students make up Computer ABCD and Computer EFGH.

2. Stretch seven strings between the eight students as shown in Figure 10-1. Student A's left hand and Student E's right hand are Pin 1 on their respective serial ports. The numbers should proceed down the line until Pin 8 is Student D's right hand and Student H's left hand. Table 10-1 describes the null modem cable communication you are simulating. Notice that Pins 1 and 9 are not used in a null modem cable communication and are therefore omitted from this simulation.

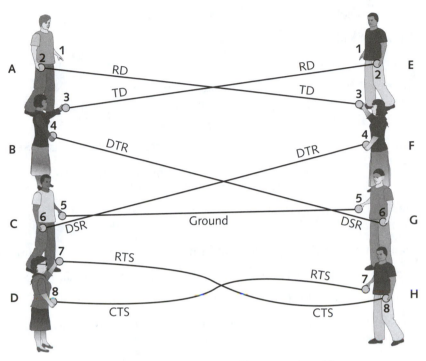

Figure 10-1   Simulating null modem cable communication

Table 10-1   Pin connections for a 9-pin null modem cable

Pin number on one connection	Pin number of the other connector	How the wire connecting the two pins is used
1	1	Not used
2 (RD)	3 (TD)	Data sent by one computer is received by the other
3 (TD)	2 (RD)	Data received by one computer is sent by the other
4 (DTR)	6 (DSR)	One end says to the other end, "I'm able to talk"
5 (Ground)	5 (Ground)	Both ends are grounded
6 (DSR)	4 (DTR)	One end hears the other end say, "I'm able to talk"
7 (RTS)	8 (CTS)	One end says to the other, "I'm ready to talk"
8 (CTS)	7 (RTS)	One end hears the other say, "I'm ready to talk"
9	9	Not used

Here are the meanings of the acronyms in the table:

RD – Receive data

TD – Transmit data

DTR – Data terminal ready

DSR – Data set ready

CTS – Clear to send

RTS – Request to send

Follow these steps to perform the handshake and then to send and receive data. Suppose that Computer EFGH has initiated communication to Computer ABCD, and that Computer ABCD is ready to receive data from Computer EFGH.

1. Student G raises his left hand indicating that he is able to talk (DSR high).

2. Student B raises his hand on the other end of the same string to indicate that he has received Student G's communication.

3. Student C raises his right hand, indicating he understands that Computer EFGH is able to talk (DTR high).

4. Student F raises his left hand indicating he has received the communication.

5. Student H raises his right hand indicating he is ready to talk (RTS high).

6. Student D raises his hand indicating he has received the communication.

7. Student D raises his left hand indicating he is ready to receive data from Computer EFGH.

8. Student H raises his hand indicating he has received the communication.

   Computer ABCD has just indicated that it is able and ready to have a conversation. (As you'll recall, DTR indicates that Computer ABCD is open to having a conversation, and RTS tells Computer EFGH to go ahead and start talking.) Computer EFGH is now ready to start talking to Computer ABCD.

9. Student F repeatedly raises and lowers his hand—which represents the TD (TXD) pin—to indicate that data is being sent. (Each raise of the hand represents one bit transmitted.)

10. Student A sees this signal and repeatedly raises and lowers his right hand—which represents the RD (RXD) pin—to indicate the reception of each bit.

    Now suppose that computer EFGH has been transmitting for a while and Computer ABCD has noticed that its buffer is getting full. (That is, it has to process what Computer EFGH has said.) This ability of the receiving computer to stop transmission so it can catch up is called flow control.

11. Student D lowers his left hand (RTS) to indicate that Computer ABCD is processing and doesn't want to hear any more right now.

12. Student H quits receiving CTS high and lowers his hand to indicate he has received the communication.

13. Other students keep their hands raised, indicating that the conversation is still not yet over.

14. Student F quits sending data and keeps his hand down.

At this point, computer EFGH has quit talking, but has not yet finished sending all the data. After a pause, computer ABCD finishes processing and the buffer is empty. Computer ABCD is now ready to listen again.

15. Student D raises his hand, raising RTS high.

16. Student H raises his hand, indicating CTS high. In response, Student F starts sending data again until all data is sent.

17. Students H and G lower their hands indicating that Computer EFGH has nothing more to say and wants to end the conversation.

18. All students then lower their hands in response to Students H and G. The conversation is ended.

Now that you have seen how Computer EFGH sends data to Computer ABCD, answer the following questions regarding communication from Computer ABCD to Computer EFGH.

- Which hands should be raised to indicate that Computer EFGH is able to communicate with Computer ABCD?

_____

- Which hands should be raised to indicate that Computer EFGH is ready to receive data?

_____

- Which hands should be raised to indicate data flowing from Computer ABCD to Computer EFGH?

_____

- Which hands should be lowered when Computer EFGH's buffers are full?

_____

- Which hands should be lowered when the communication is finished?

_____

19. Now raise and lower your hands to simulate communication from Computer ABCD to Computer EFGH.

Review Questions

1. Pins 1 and 9 are not used for communication via a null modem cable. How are they used by a modem?

   _____

   _____

2. What is indicated by a signal raised on Pin 8?

   _____

3. Pin 4 on one end of the cable is connected to Pin _____ on the other end of the cable.

4. Data passes from Pin _____ on one end of the cable to Pin _____ on the other end of the cable.

5. What is the sole purpose of Pin 5's participation in the network communication?

   _____

LAB 10.2 INSTALL AND TEST A MODEM

Objectives

The goal of this lab is to help you install and test a modem. After completing this lab, you will be able to:

➤ Physically install a modem

➤ Test the modem using Modem Properties

Materials Required

This lab will require the following:

➤ Windows 98 operating system

➤ Windows 98 installation CD or installation files stored in another location

➤ Modem with drivers

➤ PC toolkit with ground strap

➤ Windows 2000/XP operating system and installation files (optional activity)

Activity Background

Most users dial in to their ISP using a modem and Plain Old Telephone Service (POTS). Such dial-up connections can be unreliable, for several reasons. So as an A+ technician, you need to be prepared to install modems and troubleshoot modem connections. In this lab, you will install a modem and then run some simple diagnostics to test the modem.

Estimated completion time: **30 minutes**

ACTIVITY

Follow these steps to install a modem:

1. Remove all cables from the case and remove the case cover.

2. Locate the expansion slot that you will use to install the modem and then remove the slot's cover.

3. Install and secure the modem card.

4. Replace the case cover and reattach all cables, including the telephone cable, to the Line-In port on the back of the modem card.

5. Boot the computer and log on, if necessary. The Found New Hardware Wizard launches and informs you that it is ready to search for drivers. Click **Next** to continue.

6. The wizard asks how you want to locate the drivers. Select the **Search for the Best Driver for Your Device (Recommended)** option button and click **Next** to continue.

7. The wizard asks you to specify a location for the drivers. Insert the floppy disk or CD containing the drivers and select the appropriate check box to indicate the location of the drivers. (If the CD Autorun program launches when you insert the CD, close the application.) Note that you can temporarily disable Autorun by holding down the Shift key while you insert the CD.

8. The wizard reports the device name and location of the driver. Click **Next** to continue.

9. The wizard informs you that the installation was successful. Click **Finish** to close the Found New Hardware Wizard.

10. Additional Found New Hardware Wizards might launch for any devices embedded in the modem, such as voice or fax devices. Complete the wizards for these devices. Be prepared to provide any Windows 98 installation files as necessary.

Follow these steps to verify that your modem is working properly:

1. Check that your modem is displayed in Device Manager. Device Manager should report no problems with the modem. If necessary, review Chapter 2, Lab 2.1 for a reminder of how to use Device Manager.

2. Open the Control Panel, double-click the **Modems** icon to open the Modems Properties dialog box, and then select the **Diagnostics** tab. What type of port information does the Diagnostics tab provide?

_____

3. Select the modem you just installed, and note the port it is associated with. Record that information here.

_____

4. Click the **More Info** button.

5. The More Info dialog box opens. The system uses its modem diagnostic tool to test the modem and then displays the test results. Take and print a screen shot of this dialog box and then click **OK** to close the More Info dialog box. Answer these questions:

  ■ When you open the More Info dialog box, what type of commands are used to test the modem?

  _____

  ■ List two commands and the purpose of each command.

  _____

  _____

6. Click **OK** to close the Modems Properties dialog box.

Leave the modem installed for use in upcoming labs in this chapter.

CRITICAL THINKING (additional 30 minutes)

Install a modem in a Windows 2000 or Windows XP system. When you start up the system, the Found New Hardware Wizard launches to install the modem drivers. Verify that the modem is working using Device Manager. In Device Manager, right-click the modem and select **Properties** from the shortcut menu. The modem's Properties box opens. Click the **Diagnostics** tab and then click the **Query Modem** button. What are the results of this query?

_____

_____

_____

_____

Review Questions

1. Were any devices embedded in your modem? How could you tell?

   _____

   _____

2. What are two system resources that a modem requires?

   _____

3. What is the format of the diagnostic commands shown in your screen shots?

   _____

4. In what situation might you use the modem diagnostic tool?

   _____

LAB 10.3 USE AT COMMANDS TO CONTROL A MODEM

10

Objectives

The goal of this lab is to help you use AT commands to initiate and receive calls. After completing this lab, you will be able to:

➤ Install HyperTerminal

➤ Use several modem commands to control a HyperTerminal session, dial a number, receive a call, and test your modem

Materials Required

This lab will require the following:

➤ Windows 98 or Windows 2000/XP operating system

➤ Windows installation CD or installation files in another location

➤ Access to a phone line that can send and receive calls

➤ The line's telephone number

➤ A lab partner to whom you can make modem calls

Note that you might not have access to a phone line in a classroom lab environment. In this case, this lab might have to be completed at home.

Activity Background

The AT command set is a set of commands that can be used to control a modem. When the modem receives commands, each command line is prefaced with AT for ATtention. A modem stays in command mode any time it is not connected to another modem. When a modem is in command mode and bits and bytes are sent to it from a PC, the modem interprets the bytes as commands to be followed, rather than as data to be sent over a phone line. It leaves command mode when it either receives an incoming call or dials out, and returns to command mode when a call is completed or a special escape sequence is sent to it by its computer. A modem responds to a command with OK or gives the results after performing the command. AT commands allow you to control virtually every aspect of modem behavior and are useful in troubleshooting modem hardware and connections. Table 10-2 lists a few of the core AT commands that most modems understand.

Table 10-2   AT commands for Hayes-compatible modems

Command	Description	Some values and their meanings
AT	Gets the modem's attention	AT (Modem should respond with OK)
*70	Disable call waiting	ATDT*70,4045551212
+++	Escape sequence: tells the modem to return to command mode. You should pause at least 1 second before you sequence. After you end it, wait another second before you send another command. Don't begin this command with AT.	+++ (Follow each + with a short pause; use this when trying to unlock a hung modem; don't begin the command with AT)
O*n*	Go Online: tells the modem to return to online data mode. This is the reverse command for the escape sequence above.	ATO0 Return online ATO1 Return online and retrain (perform training or handshaking again with the remote system)
A/	Repeat last command: repeat last command performed by the modem. Don't begin the command with AT, but do follow it with Enter. Useful when redialing a busy number.	
I*n*	Identification: instructs the modem to return to product identification information	ATI0 Return the product code ATI3 Return the modem ROM version
Z*n*	Reset: instructs the modem to reset and restore the configuration to that defined at power on	ATZ0 Reset and return to user profile 0 ATZ1 Reset and return to user profile 1

Table 10-2   AT commands for Hayes-compatible modems (continued)

Command	Description	Some values and their meanings
&F	Factory default: instructs the modem to reload the factory default profile. In most cases, use this command to reset the modem rather than using the Z command	AT&F (This method is preferred to ATZ when trying to solve a modem problem)
A	Answer the phone: instructs the modem to answer the phone, transmit the answer tone, and wait for a carrier from the remote modem	
Dn	Dial: tells the modem to dial a number. Several parameters can be added to this command. A few are listed on the right.	ATD5551212 Dial the given number ATDD Causes the dialing to pause ATDP Use pulse dialing ATDT Use tone dialing ATDW Wait for dial tone ATD& Wait for the credit card dialing tone before continuing with the remaining dial string
Hn	Hang up: tells the modem to hang up	ATH0 Hang up ATH1 Hang up and enter command mode
Mn	Speaker control: instructs the modem as to how it is to use the speaker	ATM0 Speaker always off ATM1 Speaker on until carrier detect ATM2 Speaker always on
Ln	Loudness: sets the loudness of the modem's speaker	ATL1 Low ATL2 Medium ATL3 High
Xn	Response: tells the modem how it is to respond to a dial tone and busy signal	ATX0 Blind dialing; the modem does not need to hear the dial tone and will not hear a busy signal. ATX4 Modem must first hear the dial tone and responds to a busy signal (This is the default value.)

You can type a command from a communications software window to be executed immediately or enter a command from a dialog box for the modem configuration to be executed later when the modem makes a call. HyperTerminal is an excellent utility you can use to make a quick and easy phone call from a Windows PC. HyperTerminal is installed by default under Windows 2000/XP but is not automatically installed by Windows 98. By using HyperTerminal, you can test a newly installed modem with AT commands. In this lab, you will use AT commands to make and receive calls and to adjust modem settings.

10

Estimated completion time: **45 minutes**

ACTIVITY

For Windows 98, follow these steps to install HyperTerminal:

1. Open the Control Panel, double-click the **Add/Remove Programs** icon, and then click the **Windows Setup** tab.

2. In the Components list box, double-click the **Communications** group. The Communications dialog box opens.

3. Select the **HyperTerminal** check box and then click **OK**. The Communications dialog box closes and you return to the Add/Remove Programs Properties dialog box.

4. Click **OK** to close the Add/Remove Programs dialog box. Supply Windows 98 installation files as necessary.

For Windows 98 andWindow 2000/XP, follow these steps to use AT commands in HyperTerminal:

1. Click **Start** on the taskbar, point to **Programs** (for Windows XP, **All Programs**), point to **Accessories**, point to **Communications**, and then click **HyperTerminal**. This opens the HyperTerminal folder.

2. For Windows 98, double-click **Hypertrm.exe**. HyperTerminal starts, with the Connection Description dialog box displayed.

3. In the Connection Description dialog box, type **Test 1** in the Name field and then click **OK**. The Connect To dialog box opens.

4. Select your modem from the drop-down list and then click **Cancel** to close the Connect To dialog box. The Connect To dialog box closes, and the main HyperTerminal window is active.

5. Click in the blank field in HyperTerminal to position the cursor there.

At this point, if you start typing AT commands, the commands will be executed but you might not actually be able to see the commands as you type them in the HyperTerminal window. To make it possible to see the AT commands as you type them (if displaying commands has not already been enabled), you must begin with the AT echo command, ATE1. To practice using this command, follow these steps:

1. Type **ATE1** and press **Enter**. The modem's response (OK) appears under the cursor. Note that you couldn't see the command, ATE1, as you typed it. But from now on you should be able to see commands as you type.

2. Type **ATE0** and press **Enter**. (Be sure to type a zero and not the letter "o.") The command ATE0 appears on the screen as you type. OK appears below ATE0 after you press Enter.

3. Type **AT** and press **Enter**. The AT command issued by itself should always return an OK response, and, in fact, OK does appear on the screen. But this time the command you typed is not displayed on the screen. Which command caused the text not to appear as you typed (i.e., caused the text not to "echo")?

_____

4. Execute the ATE1 command to again echo the commands as you type.

Now that you know how to make commands appear as you type, you are ready to test your modem using HyperTerminal. Follow these steps:

1. To verify that a working phone line is connected to the modem, type **ATD** followed by your computer's telephone number (for example, ATD5551212) and then press **Enter**. You should hear the modem dial. What message does HyperTerminal return?

_____

2. Type **ATL3**, press **Enter**, and then use the ATD command to dial your computer's number again.

   ■ What difference do you notice from the first time you dialed the number?

   _____

   _____

   ■ What do you think the L in the ATL command stands for?

   _____

3. HyperTerminal can also be controlled using commands on its menu bar. Click **Call** on the HyperTerminal menu bar and then click **Wait for a Call**.

4. Give your lab partner your computer's number and have him or her dial and connect to your computer. What messages does HyperTerminal display on your computer?

   _____

   _____

   _____

5. Click the button that shows the phone handset hanging up on the phone cradle (shown in Figure 10-2 for Windows 98). Your modem disconnects.

10

Disconnect icon

Figure 10-2   HyperTerminal window

6. Type **AT&T1** and press **Enter**. HyperTerminal runs a local analog loop to make sure the modem is working correctly. Record the results below.

_____

_____

_____

_____

7. To end the test, type **AT&T0** and press **Enter**. (Ending the test might take a few moments.)

8. Click the disconnection button on the toolbar.

9. If you begin testing a working modem with AT commands and the modem begins to experience problems, you can use the AT&F command to reset the modem to factory settings. Type **AT&F** and press **Enter**. The modem's default settings are restored.

10. To close HyperTerminal, click **File** and then click **Exit**. When asked if you wish to disconnect, click **Yes**. When asked if you wish to save the session, click **No**.

Review Questions

1. What Windows application is commonly used for working with AT commands?

_____

2. What command turns on the text echo so that you can see what you are typing?

_____

3. What command dials a number?

_____

4. What command returns the modem to its default settings?

_____

5. What method, other than an AT command, can be used to receive an incoming call?

_____

_____

6. Look in Table 10-2 for additional AT commands. What are some other AT commands not used in this lab that you would find useful in debugging a modem?

_____

_____

_____

10

LAB 10.4 SIMULATE MODEM PROBLEMS

Objectives

The goal of this lab is to help you simulate, diagnose, and remedy common modem problems. After completing this lab, you will be able to:

➤ Diagnose problems with a modem

➤ Remedy problems with a modem

Materials Required

This lab will require the following:

➤ Windows 98 or Windows 2000/XP operating system

➤ Modem installed in a PC and connected to a phone line

➤ PC toolkit with ground strap

➤ Modem installation drivers

➤ Windows installation CD or installation files

➤ Standard phone

➤ Lab partner with whom you can swap PCs

Activity Background

Dial-up connections are notoriously unreliable. One of the challenges of troubleshooting such connections is determining whether a dial-up failure is related to a problem with the modem itself or to a problem with the phone line. In this lab, you will diagnose and remedy common modem problems. Mastering these skills will make it easier for you to determine when the modem itself is the source of trouble in a dial-up connection.

Estimated completion time: **90 minutes**

ACTIVITY

1. To verify that your modem is working, start HyperTerminal, dial any reliable phone number, and listen for the sound of the modem dialing and attempting to connect. (The actual connection is not necessary at this point.) Disconnect the call and close HyperTerminal.

2. Sabotage your modem by introducing one of the problems listed below:

   - If your modem has jumpers or DIP switches, record the original settings and then change the settings.
   - In BIOS or Device Manager, disable the modem's COM port.
   - Loosen the modem card in the expansion slot so that it does not make good contact.
   - Unplug the phone cord from the wall.
   - Change the port the phone line connects to on the back of the modem.
   - Uninstall the modem in Device Manager.
   - Change or disable the IRQ for the modem.
   - Using Device Manager, disable the modem in the current hardware configuration.

3. Swap PCs with your partner and then troubleshoot and repair your partner's PC.

4. Answer these questions:

   - What is the initial symptom of a problem as a user would describe it?

   _____

   _____

■ How did you discover the source of the problem?

_____

_____

_____

_____

■ What did you do to resolve the problem?

_____

_____

_____

_____

5. Introduce another problem from the list in step 2 and swap again. Continue this process until you have introduced and remedied all of the problems listed in step 2.

10

Review Questions

1. What was the easiest problem to diagnose and why?

_____

_____

2. Which problems would not be apparent in Device Manager but would result in no dial tone when dialing?

_____

_____

3. Did all of the problems listed in step 2 actually prevent the modem from working? Which (if any) did not prevent the modem from working?

_____

4. Which problem prevented the modem from being displayed in Modems Properties?

_____

_____

_____

5. What was the simplest way to determine if there definitely was a dial tone?

_____

_____

6. Suppose a user says, "I can't dial out using my modem." List the first three things you would check, in the order you would check them.

_____

_____

_____

LAB 10.5 CRITICAL THINKING: USE TWO MODEMS TO CREATE A MULTILINK CONNECTION

Objectives

The goal of this lab is to help you set up a Dial-Up Networking connection involving two modems to increase connection performance. After completing this lab, you will be able to:

➤ Install a second modem

➤ Create a Dial-Up Networking connection

➤ Configure a Dial-Up Networking connection for multilink

➤ Download a file to compare single modem and multilink connection performance

Materials Required

This lab will require the following:

➤ Windows 98 operating system

➤ Two modems and any necessary drivers

> ➤ Two phone lines and phone jacks

> ➤ ISP that allows multilink connections

> ➤ User name and password for your ISP connection, as provided by your instructor

> ➤ Dial-up phone number for your ISP, as provided by your instructor

Note that if you don't have a second modem and phone line and an ISP that supports multilink connections, you can still do most of this lab to create and test a single-link connection.

Activity Background

A broadband connection is the best option when you need to transfer lots of data at high speeds. But if you don't have access to a broadband connection, you can make do by using two phone lines and two modems to create a multilink connection. (Note that not all ISPs support multilink connections, and those that do will charge extra for the service.) Assuming both modems connect at the same speed, a multilink connection can roughly double your usual dial-up connection speed. In this lab, you will configure a multilink connection and compare its performance to a single modem connection. You will start by creating a dial-up connection for the modem you installed in Lab 10.2. You will then install a second modem and combine the two modems in a multilink connection.

10

Estimated completion time: **90 minutes**

ACTIVITY

Follow these steps to create a Dial-Up Networking connection using the modem you installed in Lab 10.2:

1. In Windows Explorer, click the **Dial-Up Networking** icon to view Dial-Up Networking icons in the left pane of Explorer.

2. Double-click the **Make New Connection** icon to open the Make New Connection dialog box.

3. Type in the name for the connection you are about to create, select the modem to use in the drop-down menu if it is not already selected, and then click **Next** to continue.

4. The Make New Connection dialog box opens. Here you need to specify the number your computer will dial to complete the dial-up connection. Enter your ISP's area code and phone number (as provided by your instructor), and select the country code from the drop-down menu. Click **Next** to continue.

5. The Make New Connection dialog box informs you that the connection was created successfully. Click **Finish** to close the Make New Connection dialog box. Your new connection appears in the Dial-Up Networking window.

Follow these steps to configure and test your connection:

1. Double-click your connection in the Dial-Up Networking window.

2. The Connect To dialog box opens, showing the connection name. Enter the User Name and Password supplied by your instructor, and then click **Dial Properties** to open the Dialing Properties dialog box.

3. Select the **I am Dialing From:** text box and replace its contents with **LAB**.

4. Click **Area Code Rules** to open the Area Code Rules dialog box, select the **Always Dial the Area Code (10-digit dialing)** check box, and then click **OK**. The Area Code Rules dialog box closes.

   Note that creating multiple dial-up connections is a useful technique on a portable computer. You can configure a separate connection for each location where you intend to travel, with separate dialing rules for each connection. For example, suppose you live in Kentucky and have a dial-up connection to a local ISP. You could create one dial-up connection for your home office that does not require an area code (because the ISP is local). You could also create a connection for dialing into your ISP from a hotel in Boston. This connection might include dialing 9 for an outside line as well as dialing your ISP's area code. You could create yet another connection for dialing into your ISP from a private home in Orlando where you have the local phone number for your ISP's point of presence (POP) in Orlando.

5. Adjust the appropriate settings in the "When Dialing From Here:" section as necessary to reach an outside line or to disable call waiting. What other options can you adjust in the Dialing Properties dialog box?

   _____

   _____

   _____

6. Click **OK** to close the Dialing Properties dialog box.

7. In the Connect To dialog box, notice that the Dialing From: field has changed to "Lab."

8. Select the **Save Password** check box so that you won't have to enter your password each time you connect.

9. Click **Connect** to dial.

10. The Connecting To dialog box appears and displays messages indicating what task is currently being performed ("Dialing…" and "Verifying User Name and Password…," and so forth). When the connection is completed, a connection symbol appears in the system tray, as shown in Figure 10-3.

Connection icon

Figure 10-3   A connection icon appears in the system tray when the connection is completed

11. Double-click the connection symbol in the system tray. The Connected To dialog box opens. Record your connection speed and any other information provided in this dialog box.

_____

_____

_____

Now that you have established a dial-up connection, you can use it to download the driver required by your second modem (which you will install in this lab).

12. Open your Web browser and navigate to the Web site for the manufacturer of your second modem.

13. Download the latest driver for this modem. As the file is being downloaded, take and print a screen shot of the download progress indicator.

Now that you have created a Dial-Up connection and tested it using a single modem, you will create a multilink connection. Do the following:

1. Install a second modem using the driver you just downloaded.

2. Create a Dial-Up connection for the second modem and test it by dialing up your ISP and completing the connection.

Next, you need to adjust the connection properties of your first Dial-Up connection to allow a multilink connection. Follow these steps:

1. Right-click the connection's icon in the Dial-Up Networking window and then click **Properties** in the shortcut menu. The connection's Properties window opens.

2. Click the **Multilink** tab.

3. Select the **Use Additional Devices** check box, and then click **Add**.

4. Select the second modem from the list of available devices, and then click **OK**.

Now you are ready to use the multilink connection.

1. Following the directions given above, use the multilink connection to dial up your ISP.

10

2. Compare the speed of this connection to that of a single connection by downloading the same driver file as you did in step 13, taking and printing a screen shot of the download progress. What are the differences in the connection speed and process?

_____

_____

_____

_____

3. Uninstall the second modem and reconfigure the original modem connection.

Answer the following questions about using an ISP for a multilink connection:

1. What is one other ISP that allows multilink connections?

_____

2. What are the costs associated with multilink connections using this ISP?

_____

_____

Review Questions

1. What Windows feature allows you to configure and save connection information?

_____

2. List the steps required to adjust the number of digits required to dial a local phone number.

_____

_____

3. How does a multilink connection improve performance?

_____

_____

_____

4. What are the requirements for a multilink connection?

_____

_____

5. What is the advantage of creating several Dial-Up connections for a single modem?

_____

_____

10

CHAPTER ELEVEN

PCs ON A NETWORK

Labs included in this chapter

➤ Lab 11.1 Install and Test an Ethernet NIC

➤ Lab 11.2 Inspect Cables

➤ Lab 11.3 Compare Options for a Home LAN

➤ Lab 11.4 Troubleshoot with TCP/IP Utilities

➤ Lab 11.5 Practice Solving Network Connectivity Problems

Lab 11.1 Install and Test an Ethernet NIC

Objectives

The goal of this lab is to install and configure an Ethernet network interface card (NIC). After completing this lab, you will be able to:

➤ Remove a NIC (and network protocols, if necessary)

➤ Install a NIC (and network protocol, if necessary)

➤ Perform a loopback test

Materials Required

This lab will require the following:

➤ Windows 98 operating system with no modem or dial-up networking installed or Windows 2000/XP operating system

➤ NIC and drivers

➤ Windows installation CD or installation files stored in another location

➤ PC toolkit with ground strap

➤ Crossover cable

➤ Workgroup partner

Activity Background

A computer connects to a wired network through a network interface card (NIC). In this lab, you will install a NIC, configure necessary network settings, and verify that the NIC is functioning properly. Working with a partner, you will create a simple network of two PCs. By default, Windows 98 does not install network protocols needed to support a network, but Windows 2000/XP has these components installed. This fact makes installing a NIC under Windows 2000/XP much simpler than under Windows 98.

Estimated completion time: **30 minutes**

Activity

For Windows 98, if your computer does not already have a NIC installed, skip to the next section. Otherwise, follow these steps on your Windows 98 computer to remove the computer's networking components:

1. Right-click the **Network Neighborhood** icon and select **Properties** in the shortcut menu. The Network dialog box opens.

2. If necessary, click the **Configuration** tab, click **Client for Microsoft Networks**, and then click **Properties**. The Client for Microsoft Networks Properties dialog box opens.

3. In the General section, make sure that the **Log on to Windows NT domain** check box is not selected. Click **OK** to close the Client for Microsoft Networks Properties dialog box. Then close the Network Properties dialog box and reboot when prompted.

4. After the computer has rebooted, open the Network dialog box again by right-clicking the **Network Neighborhood** icon and selecting **Properties**. On the Configuration tab of the Network Properties dialog box, click your NIC (indicated by an adapter symbol) and then click **Remove**. The NIC and any protocol associated with it are uninstalled; Client for Microsoft Networks is also uninstalled.

5. Click **OK** to close the Network dialog box. You might see a message indicating that the network is incomplete.

6. Click **Yes** to continue. You are prompted to restart your computer.

7. Click **No**.

8. Shut down your computer, but do not reboot.

9. Remove your computer's NIC, or, if your instructor directs you to do so, remove the network cable but leave the NIC in place.

For Windows 98, follow these steps to install and configure your NIC:

1. If your NIC is not installed, physically install it as you would other expansion cards. If you need a refresher on the process, review Lab 4.4 or Lab 9.1.

2. Boot the system. The Add New Hardware Wizard detects the NIC and begins the driver installation process. Complete the Add New Hardware Wizard as in previous labs. Reboot when prompted.

3. The Network Neighborhood icon reappears on the desktop. Right-click the **Network Neighborhood** icon and then click **Properties**. The Network dialog box opens.

4. Select the **Configuration** tab and examine the Network Components displayed on the tab. List the installed components.

_____

_____

_____

_____

_____

11

5. Verify that your NIC appears in the list and that TCP/IP is installed and bound to the NIC, as indicated by an item in the list that includes TCP/IP with an arrow that points to the name of your NIC. Select this item and then click **Properties**. The TCP/IP dialog box opens.

6. On the IP Address tab of the TCP/IP dialog box, click the **Specify an IP Address** option button.

7. Next you will configure the network connection. For the configuration, you and your partner will need an IP address, a computer name, and a workgroup name, which are all listed in the following table. Write your name and your partner's name in the table.

Your names:		
IP address:	192.168.1.1	192.168.1.2
Computer name:	Lab 1	Lab 2
Workgroup name:	NIC Lab	NIC Lab

8. In the IP Address field of the TCP/IP Properties dialog box, type **192.168.1.1** or **192.168.1.2**. (Your lab partner should use one and you the other.) In the Subnet Mask field, enter **255.255.255.0**. (Both you and your partner should do this.) Note that it is possible for a server (called a DHCP server) to assign these two necessary values (which enable TCP/IP communication), but in this lab, you'll assume no such server is available.

9. Click **OK** to close the TCP/IP dialog box.

10. To identify each computer on the network, click the **Identification** tab in the Network dialog box. Record the computer name displayed in the Computer Name field. Replace this name with either the name **Lab 1** or the name **Lab 2**. (Again, your partner should use one of these names while you use the other.) In the Workgroup field, type **NIC Lab**. Although it's not necessary, you can type a description for your computer if you want. When you are browsing the network, this description will appear in the computer's Properties dialog box (under the Comment Heading). This description can help users determine what resources might be available on the computer. What description, if any, did you enter?

_____

11. Click **OK** to close the Network window and save your settings. Supply the Windows 98 CD or the location of the installation files if prompted. If you receive a message indicating that a file being copied is older than the current file, click **Yes** to keep the current file. (This is usually the best practice, unless you suspect that the newer file has been the source of any existing problem.)

12. Click **Yes** when prompted to restart the computer.

For Windows 2000/XP, follow these steps to install and configure your NIC:

1. Physically install your NIC as you would other expansion cards. If you need a refresher on the process, review Lab 4.4 or Lab 9.1.

2. Boot the system. The Found New Hardware Wizard detects the NIC and begins the driver installation process. In some cases, Windows XP will not give you the opportunity to use non-Microsoft drivers. If given the opportunity, click **Have Disk** and provide the manufacturer's drivers for the NIC. Reboot if prompted to do so.

> If you want to force Windows XP to use manufacturer's drivers, run the setup program on the CD or floppy disk that comes bundled with the NIC *before* you physically install the NIC. Then, after you boot with the new card installed, Windows will find the already-installed manufacturer drivers and use those drivers.

Now you will give the computer an IP address, a computer name, and a workgroup name as listed in the table in step 7.

First you will assign an IP address to the computer.

1. Right-click **My Network Places** and select **Properties** from the shortcut menu. The Network Connections window appears.

2. Right-click **Local Area Connection** and select **Properties** from the shortcut menu. The Local Area Connection Properties dialog box appears.

3. In the list of connection items, select **Internet Protocol (TCP/IP)** and click **Properties**. The Internet Protocol (TCP/IP) Properties dialog box appears. Select **Use the following IP address** and enter your IP address (192.168.1.1 or 192.168.1.2) and subnet mask (255.255.255.0). Click **OK** twice to close both Properties boxes and then close the Network Connections window.

Now you will assign a computer name and workgroup name to your computer.

1. Right-click **My Computer** and select **Properties** from the shortcut menu. The System Properties window appears.

2. For Windows XP, click the **Computer Name** tab, then click the **Change** button. The Computer Name Changes dialog box appears (see Figure 11-1). For Windows 2000, click the **Network Identification** tab, and then click the **Properties** button. The Identification Changes window appears.

3. Enter the Computer name (**Lab 1** in the example shown in Figure 11-1). Each computer name must be unique within a workgroup or domain.

4. Select **Workgroup** and enter the name of the workgroup (**NIC LAB** in this example).

5. Click **OK** to exit the Windows XP Computer Name Changes dialog box or the Windows 2000 Identification Changes window, and click **OK** to exit the System Properties window. You will be asked to reboot the computer for changes to take effect.

6. Reboot your computer.

11

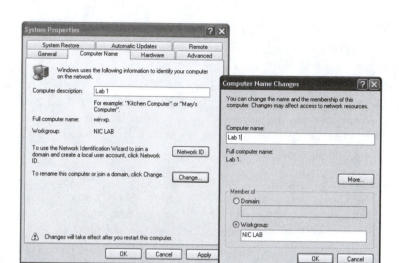

Figure 11-1   Windows XP uses the Computer Name Changes dialog box to assign a host name to a computer on a network

Using Windows 98 or Windows 2000/XP, follow these steps to test your NIC:

1. Open a command-prompt window.

2. Type **ping 127.0.0.1** and press **Enter**. Ping is a TCP/IP utility used to test whether an address is reachable and able to respond. Any 127.x.x.x address is a loopback address. Essentially, a loopback address is a stand-in for your computer's own address. When you use a loopback address in a ping test, the Ping utility sends packets to your local computer's NIC, thereby allowing you to verify that your computer's NIC has a functioning TCP/IP connection. If your computer is connected to a printer, take a screen shot of the results and print the screen shot of the loopback ping command.

3. Examine the results of the loopback test and answer these questions:

   ▪ How many bytes were sent in each packet?

   _____

   ▪ How many packets were sent with one ping command?

   _____

   ▪ How many responses were received from one ping command?

   _____

   ▪ Were any packets lost?

   _____

For Windows 98, use the configuration utility Winipcfg to verify your IP configuration. Do the following to check your NIC's configuration:

1. At the command prompt, type **winipcfg** and press **Enter**.

2. Select your NIC from the drop-down list and examine your IP configuration. Answer the following:

- Is the configuration the same information that you originally configured?

_____

- What is the MAC address of your NIC?

_____

For Windows 2000/XP, use the configuration utility Ipconfig to verify your IP configuration. Do the following to check your NIC's configuration:

1. At the command prompt, type **ipconfig /all |more** and press **Enter**. An IP configuration report is displayed one screen at a time. If necessary, press **Enter** to see each new line. Answer the following:

- Is the configuration the same information that you originally configured?

_____

- What is the physical address (MAC address) of your NIC?

_____

For Windows 98 or Windows 2000/XP, another way to test an NIC is to use its assigned IP address in a ping test.

1. Use the ping command with the IP address you assigned to your computer. The results should be similar or identical to the loopback test results, except for the address listed in the ping results.

2. Now ping your partner's IP address. Describe what happened to the request.

_____

_____

_____

You will now connect the two PCs using the crossover cable. Then you will test your network.

1. Close the command-prompt window and shut down both computers.

2. Connect one end of the crossover cable to the NIC on your partner's computer and the other end to the NIC on your computer.

3. Reboot the computers and open a command-prompt window.

4. Ping your partner's IP address. If your computer is connected to a printer, take and print a screen shot of the results. How do these results differ from your earlier attempt to ping your partner's IP address?

_____

_____

11

Review Questions

1. What window is used to configure network adapters and protocols?

   _____

2. What two name fields are used to identify a computer on a workgroup?

   _____

   _____

3. Other than the IP address, what other information is required for TCP/IP communication?

   _____

   _____

4. What are two ways to use the ping utility to test the local computer's NIC?

   _____

   _____

5. What conclusion should you draw from a loopback test that reports dropped packets or an unreachable host?

   _____

   _____

LAB 11.2 INSPECT CABLES

Objectives

The goal of this lab is to help you visually inspect and use a multimeter to test a set of cables. After completing this lab, you will be able to:

➤ Identify two CAT-5 wiring systems

➤ Test cables with a multimeter

➤ Draw pin-outs for cable connectors

➤ Determine if a cable is a patch cable (also known as a straight-through cable) or a crossover cable

➤ Visually inspect cables and connectors

Materials Required

This lab will require the following:

➤ A variety of cables including a patch cable and a crossover cable

➤ Multimeter

➤ Internet access

Activity Background

Once you narrow down a problem to physical connectivity, you must inspect the connections to verify that they are not loose. If you eliminate that possibility, then you can assume that the cable is the problem. In this lab, you will physically inspect the cables and the connector and then test the cable for continuity and pin-out using the multimeter.

Estimated completion time: **45 minutes**

ACTIVITY

1. Consult the information at *www.atcomservices.com/highlights/cat5notes.htm* or search the Internet for information about a patch cable diagram, a crossover cable diagram, and a CAT-5 wiring diagram. List the two standards of CAT-5 wiring schemes. What Web site did you use?

   _____

   _____

   _____

2. Print a wiring diagram for a patch cable wired to each scheme and for a crossover cable using each scheme.

Follow these steps to visually inspect cables:

1. Examine the length of the cable for obvious damage. The damage could be in the form of a cut or abrasion in the outer sleeve with further damage to the twisted pairs inside. A completely cut strand is an obvious problem, but the proper conductor inside the cable might be broken even if the insulator is intact. Any visible copper is an indication that you need a new cable.

2. Inspect the RJ-45 connectors. Particularly look for exposed twisted pairs between the clear plastic connector and the cable sleeve. This is an indication that the cable was assembled improperly or that excessive force was used when pulling on the cable. The cable sleeve should be crimped inside the RJ-45 connector. It is sometimes possible to identify a nonconforming wiring scheme by noting the color of the insulation through the clear connector, but the cable should be checked with a multimeter to verify the condition.

3. Next, verify that the retaining clip on the connector is present. Often when an assembled cable is pulled, this clip will snag on carpet or other cables and break off. This results in a connector that is likely to become loose or fall out of the jack. Worse still, this connection may be intermittent. Some cables have hooded guards to prevent the clip from snagging when pulled. These guards themselves can cause problems when seating the connector in the jack if the guard has slid too far toward the end of the cable.

4. Test your cables using a multimeter and complete Table 11-1.

11

Table 11-1   Cable Information

	End A			End B			Questions about the cable
	Pin #	Insulator color	Pin tied to pin at End B	Insulator color	Pin tied to pin at End A		Is the cable good or bad?
Cable 1	1						
	2						Wired with what scheme?
	3						
	4						
	5						Is the cable a crossover or a patch cable?
	6						
	7						
	8						
	Pin #	Insulator color	Pin tied to pin at End B	Insulator color	Pin tied to pin at End A		Is the cable good or bad?
Cable 2	1						
	2						Wired with what scheme?
	3						
	4						
	5						Is the cable a crossover or a patch cable?
	6						
	7						
	8						
	Pin #	Insulator color	Pin tied to pin at End B	Insulator color	Pin tied to pin at End A		Is the cable good or bad?
Cable 3	1						
	2						Wired with what scheme?
	3						
	4						
	5						Is the cable a crossover or a patch cable?
	6						
	7						
	8						

Review Questions

1. If you can see a copper conductor in a cable, what should you do with the cable?

_____

_____

2. What type of connector is used with CAT-5 cable?

_____

3. Based on your research, what cabling scheme is more common?

_____

4. On a patch cable, pin 3 on one end connects to pin _____ on the opposite end of the cable.

5. On a crossover cable, pin 2 on one end connects to pin _____ on the other end of the cable.

LAB 11.3 COMPARE OPTIONS FOR A HOME LAN

Objectives

The goal of this lab is to help you research the costs and capabilities of both a wired and a wireless home LAN. After completing this lab, you will be able to:

➤ Research wired and wireless Ethernet

➤ Research 802.11 standards

➤ Identify the strengths and weaknesses of each option

Materials Required

This lab will require the following:

➤ Internet access

Activity Background

As the price of equipment and computers fall, installing a home LAN has become increasingly popular. In this lab, you will research wired and wireless Ethernet and determine which option is best in certain situations.

Estimated completion time: **30 minutes**

ACTIVITY

Use your favorite search site to investigate and answer the following questions regarding wireless LAN standards.

1. List the 802.x standards used to specify wireless networks.

_____

_____

2. What industry name is associated with 802.11b?

   _____

3. What is the simplest form of a wireless network? What devices are needed to create this type of network and what mode does this type of network use?

   _____

   _____

   _____

4. What device connects wireless users to a wired network?

   _____

5. What standard speeds are supported by 802.11x?

   _____

   _____

   _____

6. What kind of encryption is used with 802.11b?

   _____

   _____

7. Give four examples of devices (besides PCs) that will probably eventually run on wireless LANs.

   _____

   _____

   _____

   _____

8. What does the acronym Wi-Fi stand for?

   _____

9. What is the approximate maximum range for 802.11b technology?

   _____

10. What inherent feature of 802.11b, seen as a significant problem by businesses, might affect your decision to not use Wi-Fi at home as well?

_____

_____

11. In the context of how they physically interface with a computer, what are the three basic types of wireless adapter?

_____

_____

_____

12. What mode requires a wireless access point?

_____

13. How many 802.11b devices can be used at one time with a single access point?

_____

14. What radio band and speed does 802.11a use?

_____

_____

15. Which standard offers a faster transfer rate, 802.11a or 802.11b? List their transfer rates.

_____

_____

16. List components and prices required to connect four PCs in ad hoc mode. List the device and extra expense necessary to connect the same four PCs to a cable modem.

_____

_____

_____

_____

_____

11

Use the Internet to research and answer these questions on an Ethernet home LAN:

1. What is the maximum cable length for a 100BaseT Ethernet LAN?

   _____

2. Must you use a hub to connect three PCs? Two PCs? Explain.

   _____

   _____

   _____

3. What type of cabling is typically used for 100BaseT?

   _____

4. Are special tools required when working with CAT-5 cabling to create patch or crossover cables?

   _____

5. What feature included with Windows 98 or Windows XP allows more than one computer to share a connection to the Internet?

   _____

6. What type of cable connector is used for fast Ethernet?

   _____

7. What standard supports a speed of 100 Mbps using two sets of CAT-3 cable?

   _____

8. What is the name for a cable that connects a computer to a hub?

   _____

9. Suppose you have a LAN consisting of a 100BaseT hub, two computers with 10BaseT NICs, and a computer with a 10/100BaseT NIC. At what speed would this LAN operate? Why?

   _____

   _____

10. Given a budget of $200 to connect five computers, would you choose 100BaseT or 10BaseT? Explain your choice.

_____

_____

_____

11. What is the name for a cable that connects a hub to a hub?

_____

12. In theory, if File X is transferred in 4.5 seconds on a fast Ethernet LAN, how long would the same file transfer take on a 10BaseT LAN?

_____

13. Give three examples of ways to physically interface a NIC to a computer.

_____

_____

_____

11

14. What device might you use to connect two or more PCs to a single cable modem?

_____

15. List the components, including cables, required to connect four PCs. Include the price of each component. List the changes and additional devices required to connect all four PCs to a cable modem and provide a hardware firewall.

_____

_____

_____

_____

_____

Review Questions

1. Based on your research, does wireless or 100BaseT offer the best performance for the money?

   _____

   _____

2. Would wireless or 100BaseT be easier to configure in a home? Why?

   _____

   _____

3. What factors dictate the transmission range of 802.11x?

   _____

   _____

   _____

4. What determines the speed of a LAN that consists of both 10Mbps and 100Mbps devices?

   _____

   _____

5. Would a wired or wireless LAN offer better security?

   _____

6. Could you combine a wireless and wired LAN in the same home? Why would you?

   _____

   _____

   _____

LAB 11.4 TROUBLESHOOT WITH TCP/IP UTILITIES

Objectives

The goal of this lab is to help you use Windows 2000/XP TCP/IP utilities to troubleshoot connectivity problems. After completing this lab, you will be able to:

➤ Use IPConfig

➤ Use the Ping utility

➤ Use Tracert

➤ Identify the point at which your packets will no longer travel

Materials Required

This lab will require the following:

➤ Windows 2000/XP operating system

➤ DHCP server

➤ Internet access

Activity Background

Perhaps nothing frustrates users more than a suddenly unavailable network connection. As a PC technician, you might be asked to restore such a connection. In some cases, in fact, you may have to deal with multiple failed connections at one time. When troubleshooting network connections, it helps to know if many users in one area of a network are having the same connection problem. That information can help you narrow down the source of the problem. Once you have an idea of what machine is causing the problem, you can use a few TCP/IP utilities to prove your theory without actually physically checking the system. In this lab, you will learn to use TCP/IP utilities to isolate connection problems.

Estimated completion time: **30 minutes**

ACTIVITY

Follow these steps to display IP settings in Windows 2000/XP:

1. Right-click **My Network Places** and select **Properties** from the shortcut menu. For Windows 2000, the Network and Dialup Connections window opens, and for Windows XP, the Network Connections window opens.

2. In the window, right-click **Local Area Connection** and select **Properties** from the shortcut menu. The Local Area Connection Properties dialog box opens.

3. Click **Internet Protocol (TCP/IP)** and then click **Properties**. The Internet Protocol (TCP/IP) dialog box opens. In the Internet Protocol (TCP/IP) dialog box, notice the different options. What two ways can you set up the IP configuration?

_____

_____

4. Verify that **Obtain an IP address automatically** is selected.

5. Click **OK** to close the Internet Protocol (TCP/IP) dialog box, and then click **Close** to exit the Local Area Connection Properties dialog box. Close the Network and Dialup Connections window (for Windows 2000) or the Network Connections window (for Windows XP).

Follow these steps to adjust the command prompt so that you can view more information at a time:

1. Open a command-prompt window.

2. Right-click the title bar of the command-prompt window and select **Properties** from the shortcut menu. The MS-DOS Prompt Properties dialog box opens.

3. In the Screen Buffer size section of the Layout tab, specify **150** for width and **300** for height. This will allow you to scroll in the command-prompt window and view the last 300 lines of 150 characters. If you wish, you can adjust the Window Size section, but it is generally best to wait to adjust each command-prompt window after it opens. This ensures that you do not make the window too large for your monitor's display settings. Click **OK** to save the settings.

4. The Apply Properties to Shortcut dialog box appears. To specify that you wish to apply the properties every time you open a command-prompt window, select **Modify the shortcut that started this window** and then click **OK**.

Follow these steps to learn how to display IP information from the command line:

1. Open a command-prompt window.

2. Type **IPConfig** and press **Enter**. Displayed are three types of information. List them below.

_____

_____

_____

3. To get more information about your IP settings, type **IPConfig /all** and press **Enter**. Take a screen shot of these results, print the screen shot, and answer these questions.

- What is the purpose of DHCP?

  _____

  _____

- What is the address of the DHCP server?

  _____

4. Because your system is using DHCP to obtain an IP address, type **IPConfig /renew** and press **Enter**. The command-prompt window again displays IP information.

5. Again, type **IPConfig /all** and press **Enter**. Compare the current lease information to the information in the screen shot. What information changed?

  _____

  _____

6. Next, type **IPConfig /release** and press **Enter**. What message is displayed? What implications do you predict this will have on connectivity?

  _____

  _____

7. Using your screen shot as a reference, attempt to ping the DHCP server and the DNS server. What are the results?

  _____

  _____

8. Type **IPConfig** and press **Enter**. Note that your adapter has no IP address and no subnet mask. These two parameters are necessary to communicate using TCP/IP.

9. To re-obtain an IP address lease, type **IPConfig /renew** and press **Enter**. New IP information, which may be the same address as before, is assigned.

10. Find your new lease information. List the command you used to obtain this information. Also list the lease information itself.

  _____

  _____

  _____

11

11. For Windows XP, you can use the Network Connections window to release and renew the IP address. Right-click **My Network Places** and select **Properties** from the shortcut menu. The Network Connections window appears. Select the network connection you want to repair and click **Repair this connection**. Note that you can also right-click the network connection you want to repair and select Repair from the shortcut menu.

If you are connected to the Internet, follow these steps to determine what route your packets take to reach an Internet address:

1. Open a command-prompt window.

2. Type **Tracert** followed by a single space, followed by a domain name on the Internet that you seldom use, and then press **Enter**. (Use a domain name you don't regularly access, because any recently accessed addresses might be cached on your system.)

3. The domain name is resolved by the DNS server and an associated IP address is listed, indicating that you can reach at least one DNS server. This tells you that your packets are traveling at least that far. Next, each hop (or router your packet passed through) is listed with the time in milliseconds the packet took to reach its destination. How many hops will Tracert list? How many hops did the packet take to reach the domain you specified?

_____

4. Now use the Tracert command with an illegal name such as *www.mydomain.c.* What are the results of this command?

_____

When troubleshooting connectivity problems, always consider the number of users experiencing the problem. If many users have similar difficulties, it is unlikely the problem lies with any one user's computer. Thus, you can probably eliminate the need to run extensive local tests on each computer. Instead, you can examine a device that all the computers commonly use.

As a general rule, when troubleshooting, you should start by examining devices close to the computer that is experiencing problems and then move further away. The following steps show you how to apply this principle, by first examining the local computer, and then moving outward to other devices on the network.

1. Verify that the computer is physically connected (that is, that both ends of the cable are connected).

2. Verify that the NIC is installed and that TCP/IP is bound to the NIC.

3. Perform a loopback test to verify that the NIC is functioning properly.

4. Check the IP settings with the following command: **IPCONFIG /ALL**. Verify that an IP address is assigned.

5. Ping other computers on the local network. If you get no response, begin by examining a hub or punch-down panel (a panel where cables convene before connecting to a hub).

6. If you can ping other computers on the local network, then ping the default gateway, which is the first stop for transmissions being sent to addresses that are not on the local network.

7. Continue troubleshooting connections, beginning with nearby devices and working outward until you discover an IP address that returns no response. That will be the source of the trouble.

8. If the device is under your supervision, take the necessary steps to repair it. If the device is out of your control, contact the appropriate administrator.

Review Questions

1. Name four additional pieces of information that the IPCONFIG command with the /ALL switch provides that the IPCONFIG command alone does not.

_____

_____

_____

_____

2. What type of server resolves a domain name to an IP address?

_____

3. Using Windows 2000/XP, what command discards the IP address?

_____

4. What command would you use to determine whether you are able to reach another computer on the local network? Would this command work if the default gateway were down?

_____

_____

11

5. If many users suddenly encountered connection problems, would you suspect problems with their local computers or problems with other devices on the network? Explain.

_____

_____

_____

Lab 11.5 Practice Solving Network Connectivity Problems

Objectives

The goal of this lab is to troubleshoot and remedy common network connectivity problems. After completing this lab, you will be able to:

➤ Diagnose and solve connectivity problems

➤ Document the process

Materials Required

This lab will require the following:

➤ Windows 98 or Windows 2000/XP operating system connected to a network and to the Internet

➤ Windows 98 or Windows 2000/XP installation CD or installation files stored in another location

➤ PC toolkit with ground strap

➤ Workgroup partner

Activity Background

To a casual user, Internet and network connections can be confusing. When users experience a connectivity problem, they usually have no idea how to remedy the situation. In this lab, you will introduce and solve common connectivity problems.

Estimated completion time: **30 minutes**

Activity

1. Verify that your network is working correctly by browsing the network and connecting to a Web site.

2. Do one of the following:
   - Change your PC's IP address
   - Change your PC's subnet mask
   - Remove your PC's network cable
   - Remove TCP/IP from your PC
   - Remove your PC's adapter in the Network dialog box
   - Unseat or remove your PC's NIC, but leave it installed in the Network window
   - Disable your PC's NIC in the Device Manager
   - Release your PC's IP address (if DHCP is enabled)

3. Swap PCs with your partner and troubleshoot your partner's PC.

4. On a separate sheet of paper, answer these questions about the problem you solved:
   - What is the initial symptom of the problem as user might describe it?

   _____

   _____

   - What steps did you take to discover the source of the problem?

   _____

   _____

   _____

   _____

   - What steps did you take to resolve the problem?

   _____

   _____

   _____

   _____

11

5. Repeat steps 1–4 until you and your partner have each used all the options listed in step 2. Be sure to answer the questions in step 4 for each troubleshooting scenario.

Review Questions

1. What problem could you resolve by issuing only one command? What was the command you used?

_____

2. Which problem (or problems) forced you to reboot the computer after repairing it?

_____

_____

_____

_____

3. What two pieces of information are necessary for TCP/IP communication on the local network?

_____

4. When using Windows 98, what problem (or problems) caused the Network Neighborhood icon to disappear?

_____

_____

_____

5. What TCP/IP utility was the most useful, in your opinion, for troubleshooting these problems? Why?

_____

_____

6. What situation would not necessarily cause a communication problem if a network protocol other than TCP/IP (such as NetBEUI) were installed on this and other computers on the network?

_____

CHAPTER TWELVE

NOTEBOOKS, TABLET PCS, AND PDAS

Labs included in this chapter

➤ Lab 12.1 Examine Notebook Documentation

➤ Lab 12.2 Compare Notebooks and Desktops

➤ Lab 12.3 Replace a Notebook Hard Drive

➤ Lab 12.4 Research Software Available for PDAs

➤ Lab 12.5 Battery Calibration and Power Management

LAB 12.1 EXAMINE NOTEBOOK DOCUMENTATION

Objectives

The goal of this lab is to help you acquire documentation for a notebook from a manufacturer's Web site and become familiar with it. After completing this lab, you will be able to:

➤ Locate documentation for specific notebook computer models

➤ Download the documentation

➤ Use a notebook's documentation to find critical information

Materials Required

This lab will require the following:

➤ Internet access

Activity Background

Notebooks are designed for portability, compactness, and energy conservation, and their designs are often highly proprietary. Therefore, establishing general procedures for supporting notebooks is more difficult than for desktop computers. Often it is necessary to consult the documentation for a particular notebook computer to get information on technical specification and support procedures. In this lab, you will locate and download documentation for two different notebook computers and then use that documentation to answer questions about each model.

Estimated completion time: **30 minutes**

ACTIVITY

Follow these steps to locate and download documentation:

1. Choose two notebook manufacturers listed in Table 12-1, go to their Web sites, and select one model from each to research. List your two choices here.

_____

_____

Table 12-1   Notebook manufacturers

Manufacturer	Web site
Acer America	*global.acer.com*
ARM Computer	*www.armcomputer.com*
Compaq Computer	*www.hp.com*
Dell Computer	*www.dell.com*
Gateway	*www.gateway.com*
Hewlett-Packard	*www.hp.com*
IBM	*www.ibm.com*
Micron PC	*www.buympc.com*
PC Notebook	*www.pcnotebook.com*
Sony	*www.sonystyle.com/vaio*
Toshiba America	*www.csd.toshiba.com*
WinBook	*www.winbook.com*

2. On the support section of each Web site, search for documentation on each of the models you chose and follow the directions to download it. Were you able to find documentation for both models? If not, list the models for which you were unable to find documentation. Try other models until you have located documentation for two.

_____

_____

3. Using the documentation you located, answer the following questions for your first model. If you can't answer a question because the information is not included in the documentation, write "information unavailable."

   ■ What type of processor does the notebook use and how much RAM is installed?

   _____

   ■ What operating system does the notebook support?

   _____

   ■ Could you download or save the documentation locally, or did you have to view it on the company's Web site?

   _____

12

- Does the notebook offer quick-launch keys for commonly used applications? If so, can you customize them? How? If they are not customizable, what buttons are offered, and which applications do they launch?

  _____

  _____

  _____

- List the functions assigned to keys F1 through F4.

  _____

  _____

  _____

- Does the notebook have a sleep or hibernation mode? If so, how do you activate it? How does activating this mode differ from shutting down the computer?

  _____

  _____

  _____

- What other types of download are offered besides the manual?

  _____

  _____

- What type of optical storage (CD, CD-RW, DVD, and so forth) does the notebook offer?

  _____

- What type of networking (modem, NIC, infrared port, wireless LAN port, and so forth) comes built-in?

  _____

  _____

4. Using the documentation you located, answer the following questions for your second model. If you can't answer a question because the information is not included in the documentation, write "information unavailable."

- What type of processor does the notebook use and how much RAM is installed?

  _____

- What operating system does the notebook support?

  _____

- Could you download or save the documentation locally, or did you have to view it on the company's Web site?

  _____

- Does the notebook offer quick-launch keys for commonly used applications? If so, can you customize them? How? If they are not customizable, what buttons are offered, and which applications do they launch?

  _____

  _____

  _____

- List the functions assigned to keys F1 through F4.

  _____

  _____

  _____

  _____

- Does the notebook have a sleep or hibernation mode? If so, how do you activate it? How does activating this mode differ from shutting down the computer?

  _____

  _____

  _____

- What other types of download are offered besides the manual?

  _____

  _____

12

- What type of optical storage (CD, CD-RW, DVD, and so forth) does the notebook offer?

  _____

- What type of networking (modem, NIC, infrared port, wireless LAN port, and so forth) comes built-in?

  _____

  _____

Alternate Activity

If you have access to a notebook computer, do the following:

1. Go to the manufacturer's Web site for your notebook computer and download the user manual, if available. List other downloads that are available:

   _____

   _____

   _____

2. From the list of available downloads, choose a device driver or system update for your notebook. Download and install it using instructions on the site. List the driver or update and the steps you took to install it on your notebook.

   _____

   _____

   _____

   _____

Review Questions

1. On a manufacturer's Web site, where do you usually find support and documentation information?

   _____

   _____

2. For which model was it easiest to find documentation? Which manufacturer site did you feel was most user friendly and, in general, offered the best support?

_____

_____

3. Besides the questions you researched in the lab, what other type of information is available in the manuals you reviewed?

_____

_____

4. If you were to purchase one of the notebooks you researched, which one would you choose? Explain your answer.

_____

_____

LAB 12.2 COMPARE NOTEBOOKS AND DESKTOPS

Objectives

The goal of this lab is to help you compare the specifications and costs of notebook and desktop computers. After completing this lab, you will be able to:

➤ Compile a list of specifications for a computer according to its purpose

➤ Locate a desktop computer and a notebook computer with similar specifications

➤ Compare the price of a desktop computer to a similar notebook computer and decide which you would purchase

Materials Required

This lab will require the following:

➤ Internet access

Activity Background

When you shop for and purchase a computer, your decisions are generally driven by questions such as, What will the computer be used for? What features are required to accomplish your goals, and what features would be nice to have but are not essential? What features are you willing to compromise on to gain others?

12

One of the most basic of these decisions is whether to choose a notebook computer or a desktop. Unlike desktops, notebooks are portable; however, to make notebooks portable, manufacturers often choose to sacrifice performance or other features. In addition, you'll usually pay more for a notebook than for a desktop computer with comparable features. In this lab, you will compile a list of requirements for a computer, locate a notebook and desktop computer with those features, and compare the two.

| Estimated completion time: **30 minutes** |

ACTIVITY

1. Determine your requirements by answering the following questions:

   - For what will the computer mainly be used? (Possible uses include office applications, graphics and multimedia, gaming, and software development.)

     _____

   - Based on the purpose listed, what features are required? Include in your list the desired amount of memory and hard drive space. (Some features you might consider include wireless support, display/screen type, software packages supported, PC card support, and external device support.)

     _____

     _____

     _____

     _____

     _____

   - List any additional features that you would like but do not require.

     _____

     _____

     _____

     _____

2. Use computer manufacturer Web sites (such as the ones listed in Table 12-1) or comparison Web sites (such as *www.cnet.com* or *www.pricewatch.com*) to find one notebook and one desktop that fulfill as many of your requirements as possible and that are as similar to each other as possible. Summarize your findings by completing Table 12-2. Print the Web pages supporting this information.

Table 12-2   Desktop and notebook computer specifications

Features	Desktop computer	Notebook computer
Manufacturer and model		
Processor type and frequency		
Memory installed		
Hard drive space		
Operating system		
Drive 1		
Drive 2		
Drive 3		
External ports		
Preinstalled applications		
Cost		

3. Based on your research and the requirements you listed in step 1, would you choose to purchase a desktop computer or a laptop? Explain your answer.

_____

_____

_____

Review Questions

1. Which computer was more expensive, the desktop or the laptop? What was the price difference?

_____

_____

2. About what features, if any, were you unable to find information?

_____

_____

3. What features, if any, were missing from the desktop and from the laptop? How did this influence your purchasing decision?

_____

_____

12

4. Did you find that you changed your requirements or expectations based on the products available? Explain your answer.

_____

_____

_____

5. Was it easier to find a comparable desktop and laptop from the same manufacturer or from a different manufacturer? Why do you think this is the case?

_____

_____

_____

LAB 12.3 REPLACE A NOTEBOOK HARD DRIVE

Objectives

The goal of this lab is to describe the process of replacing a hard drive in a notebook computer. After completing this lab, you will be able to:

➤ Locate the hard drive in a notebook computer

➤ Remove the hard drive from a notebook computer

➤ Replace the hard drive in a notebook computer

Materials Required

This lab will require the following:

➤ Notebook computer or Internet access

➤ PC toolkit with ground strap

➤ Additional, smaller screwdrivers, if necessary

Activity Background

Hard disk drives are by nature delicate devices. Dropping one, even if only a few inches, can cause permanent damage to the read/write heads, the platter surfaces, or both. Notebook systems are, of course, often moved and commonly subjected to forces that most 3.5-inch hard drives will never encounter. Although drives intended for use in notebook systems are designed to be resistant to movement and shock, they are still more likely to fail than any other notebook component. In this lab you will remove a hard drive from a notebook computer and then reinstall the same hard drive. If you do not have access to a notebook, perform the alternate activity at the end of this lab.

Hard drives designed for notebook computers tend to be 75 percent to 100 percent more expensive than the standard 3.5-inch drives of comparable capacity for desktop computers. Also, the majority of newer notebooks support most 2.5-inch drives designed for notebooks, but sometimes a notebook computer requires a proprietary hard drive. For these reasons, it is particularly important to research your replacement options carefully. Read the documentation that came with your notebook to determine what drives the notebook supports. If this information is not available in the documentation, search the manufacturer's Web site. For the purpose of this lab, you will remove the existing drive and then reinstall the same drive. The specific steps required for your notebook might be slightly different from the procedures given, so, again, it's important to study the documentation before you begin.

Estimated completion time: **30 minutes**

ACTIVITY

1. What is the manufacturer and model of your notebook computer?

   _____

2. Based on the notebook's documentation or information on the manufacturer's Web site, what type hard drive can be used to replace the existing hard drive? Be as specific as the documentation or the Web site is.

   _____

   _____

3. Search the Internet for a replacement hard drive that meets the requirements for your notebook. Print the Web page showing the specifications for the drive and its cost. How much space does the hard drive have?

   _____

4. Look for specific directions (in the documentation or on the Web site) for removing and replacing your notebook's hard drive. If you find any, summarize those directions here. (If you are using the Web site as your source of information, print any relevant Web pages.)

   _____

   _____

   _____

   _____

12

Follow these general steps to remove the hard drive from a notebook computer. Note that these directions might not list every single step necessary for your particular model. Refer to specific directions in the documentation or the company's Web site, as necessary.

1. Remove the main battery or batteries and, if necessary, unplug the computer from the AC adapter. Close the screen and turn the computer so that the bottom is facing up.

2. Locate and remove the access panel or component enclosing the drive bay. In many notebooks, the hard drive is located beneath a floppy drive or other removable device. For example, see Figure 12-1.

Bottom of notebook

Floppy drive

Hard drive

Figure 12-1   First remove the floppy drive to reveal the hard drive cavity

3. Once you have gained access to the drive, determine how it is secured within the system. The device is commonly attached to a frame or "cradle" with small screws. The cradle is in turn often attached directly to the system chassis. This cradle helps locate and support the drive inside the drive bay. Remove the screws securing the cradle.

4. In most notebooks, data cables do not connect the hard drive to the motherboard as in desktop computers. Instead, a hard drive connects to the notebook's motherboard by way of an edge connector, similar to those found on expansion cards in desktop computers. This type of direct connection has two advantages. First, it improves reliability because it reduces the total number of connection points; fewer connection points mean fewer connections that could shake loose as the notebook is moved around in daily use. The second advantage of a direct connection is that the lack of data cables reduces the overall size and weight of the notebook. To remove the cradle/drive assembly, slide the cradle away from the connector. Slide the assembly back until all pins are clear of the connector. Once the pins are clear, lift the assembly straight up out of the drive bay.

5. Note the orientation of the drive in the cradle so that, when you reinstall the drive, you will be able to mount the drive in the same direction. Remove the screws securing the drive in the cradle, and then remove the drive.

Follow these general steps to reinstall the hard drive in the notebook computer. Note that these directions might not list every single step necessary for your particular model. Refer to specific directions in the documentation or the company's Web site, as necessary.

1. If necessary, configure the jumper settings to indicate master or slave. Place the drive in the cradle so that the pins are correctly oriented and then secure it with screws.

2. Set the drive-cradle assembly straight down into the drive bay. Gently slide the assembly to the connector and verify that the pins are correctly aligned with the connector. Slide the assembly until the drive is fully seated in the connector. The cradle should now align with the holes in the chassis. If the holes do not align, you should remove the assembly, loosen the drive retaining screws, and adjust the position of the drive in the cradle. You should repeat this process until the drive is fully seated, so that there is no room for the drive to move once the cradle is secured. Once the assembly is seated, secure it with screws.

3. Replace any drives or access covers that you removed to get at the hard drive.

4. Reinstall any batteries and reconnect to AC power, if necessary. As with any other hard drive, a notebook drive must be correctly recognized by BIOS, and then partitioned and formatted before it can be used. This process is not necessary in this lab because you have not installed a new hard drive.

Alternate Activity

If you do not have access to a notebook computer:

1. Using the documentation for one of the notebooks you selected in Lab 12.1 as your source, what are the exact requirements for a replacement hard drive for this notebook? Be as specific as the documentation is.

_____

_____

2. Search the Internet for information on replacement hard drives, and print the Web page showing the correct specifications for a replacement hard drive. What is the cost of the drive? How much space does the drive have?

_____

3. Locate the steps for replacing the hard drive. To find this information, use the manuals that you downloaded in Lab 12.1, the manufacturers' Web sites, and other Internet resources (such as the Web sites of manufacturers of replacement notebook hard drives).

12

4. How do the steps you found differ from the steps provided in this lab? Note the differences here:

_____

_____

_____

_____

_____

_____

_____

_____

Review Questions

1. Why should you thoroughly research hard drives when replacing one in a notebook computer?

_____

_____

2. Why is cabling commonly not included in notebook systems?

_____

3. How was the installation procedure for your computer different from the one listed in this lab?

_____

_____

_____

4. Suppose you need to install a hard drive in a notebook that does not include an access panel for the hard drive. Where should you look for the hard drive inside the notebook?

_____

_____

_____

5. What do you have to do in CMOS setup before a new hard drive can be used?

_____

_____

LAB 12.4 RESEARCH SOFTWARE AVAILABLE FOR PDAS

Objectives

The goal of this lab is to help you research and compare PDAs. After completing this lab, you will be able to:

> Locate and compare information on available PDAs

Materials Required

This lab will require the following:

> Internet access

Activity Background

One common problem with PDAs (personal digital assistants) is finding compatible software (in addition to the software that comes preinstalled on the PDA). There are two basic OS choices for a PDA: Windows Mobile and Palm OS. Earlier handheld OSs by Microsoft are PocketPC and Windows CE. Before you can install additional software, you must verify that the software is compatible both with the PDA's operating system and with the specific PDA model. Some basic models do not allow you to add any software. You also must make sure that the software is compatible with the desktop PC that you want to synchronize with the PDA. Finally, some business organizations will not allow certain PDAs to synchronize with the business network. You will learn more about these issues in this lab, as you research software availability for two different PDA models.

Estimated completion time: **30 minutes**

ACTIVITY

1. Using the manufacturer sites listed in the Tables 12-3 and 12-4, select one Palm OS PDA and one Windows Mobile PDA. Record the name and model number of your choices here:

_____

_____

Table 12-3   Manufacturers of Palm OS PDAs

Manufacturer	Web site
HandEra	*www.handera.com*
Handspring	*www.handspring.com*
IBM	*www.ibm.com*
Palm	*www.palm.com*
Sony	*www.sonystyle.com*

Table 12-4   Manufacturers of Windows Mobile and Pocket PC PDAs

Manufacturer	Web site
Casio	*www.casio.com*
Compaq	*www.hp.com*
Hewlett-Packard	*www.hp.com*
Toshiba	*www.toshiba.com*

2. On the manufacturers' Web sites, search for technical specifications and lists of installed software for the first model you selected. Then answer the following questions for this model. Download and search user manuals if necessary.

- What version of the operating system is installed?

  _____

- What software comes installed on the PDA?

  _____

  _____

  _____

  _____

- Can you install other software? If so, list some available programs.

  _____

  _____

  _____

  _____

  _____

  _____

- Will the applications on the PDA synchronize with common office applications on a desktop PC or notebook? List the applications on the PDA and the applications on the desktop PC or notebook with which they can synchronize.

  _____

  _____

  _____

  _____

  _____

- Does the PDA support upgrades to the OS? Why would you want to have this ability?

  _____

  _____

- What add-on devices are available for the PDA, such as recharger cradles, cameras, and so forth?

  _____

  _____

  _____

12

3. Answer the following questions for the second model PDA:

   - What version of the operating system is installed?

     _____

   - What software comes installed on the PDA?

     _____

     _____

     _____

     _____

■ Can you install other software? If so, list some available programs.

_____

_____

_____

_____

_____

_____

■ Will the applications on the PDA synchronize with common office applications on a desktop PC or notebook? List the applications on the PDA and the applications on the desktop PC or notebook with which they can synchronize.

_____

_____

_____

_____

_____

_____

■ Does the PDA support upgrades to the OS? Why would you want to have this ability?

_____

_____

■ What add-on devices are available for the PDA, such as recharger cradles, cameras, and so forth?

_____

_____

_____

Alternate Activity

If you have access to a PDA, perform the research suggested in this lab for your particular model. Try to locate, download, and install a trial version of an add-on software program for your PDA. Record the necessary steps and the name of the program you installed.

_____

_____

_____

_____

_____

_____

_____

_____

Review Questions

1. Was add-on software available for both of the PDA models you researched?

_____

2. How easy was it to find the information you needed? List the Web sites you visited, ranking them from most user friendly to least user friendly.

_____

_____

_____

_____

3. Which PDA OS appears to support the most PDA applications? Explain your answer.

_____

_____

_____

12

4. Are more software options, or fewer software options, available for the higher priced PDAs? Explain your answer.

_____

_____

_____

_____

5. Would you consider purchasing either of the PDAs you researched in this lab? Why or why not?

_____

_____

_____

_____

6. List three questions you should carefully research about software availability before selecting a PDA.

_____

_____

_____

LAB 12.5 BATTERY CALIBRATION AND POWER MANAGEMENT

Objectives

The goal of this lab is to demonstrate the effect battery calibration has on power management features of a laptop PC. After completing this lab, you will be able to:

➤ Explain the calibration process

➤ Discuss how a battery might drift from calibration

➤ Explain how battery calibration affects some power management features

Materials Required

This lab will require the following:

➤ Windows desktop computer

➤ Windows laptop computer

➤ Internet access

Activity Background

Many factors affect the battery life of a laptop PC. There are two common types of laptop battery: NiMH, or nickel metalhydride, and LiION, or lithium ion. Lithium batteries are the more expensive and longer-lasting type and are more common. A fully charged lithium battery in good condition can provide about 2½ to 3 hours of normal use. By contrast, a healthy, fully charged NiMH battery can provide 1½ to 2 + hours of normal use.

As you might expect, though, "normal use" is a rather subjective term. The actual way you use your laptop can greatly affect battery life. For instance, editing text in a word processor doesn't require much power compared to playing a DVD. The word processor uses only a little processor time and occasionally reads or writes to the hard drive. Playing a DVD is processor intensive and requires powering the laser in the drive, thus requiring even more power than the word processor.

What the laptop does when you stop using it for a time also affects battery life. For instance, if you do not use the laptop for 10 minutes, the laptop might automatically go into hibernation to conserve power. In addition to the many power management features on desktop systems, laptops also employ a few additional features to extend battery life during inactivity and protect data when the battery charge becomes low. Some of these features depend on the laptop being able to accurately judge how much life is left in the battery. If the battery is accurately calibrated, the laptop can make better power-management decisions. In this lab, you will explore how power management and battery life are related.

Estimated completion time: **30 minutes**

ACTIVITY

1. Examine your desktop computer's CMOS setup utility and the Power Management applet in Control Panel. Usually a computer's BIOS offers a greater range of options for defining a power management profile than offered by Windows. Complete Table 12-5 to compare the power-management options offered in BIOS and in Windows.

Table 12-5   Comparing power-management options in BIOS and Windows

Power management options and settings	Found in BIOS	Found in Windows

Although many times the two power management systems might work in conjunction, to avoid possible conflict, Microsoft recommends using the BIOS power management as the preferred method if the BIOS power management conforms to ACPI standards. These standards have been set by a group of manufacturers including Microsoft, Intel, and Compaq.

In addition to the BIOS features you just explored, laptops often have additional features or settings that allow the computer to shut down or suspend activity if the battery is about to run out of power. But how does the computer know when power is about to run out? In many batteries, an EPROM (Electronically Programmable Read-Only Memory) is included in the battery assembly to inform the computer about the remaining battery life. The following steps explain the basic procedure for calibrating a battery's EPROM. For specific steps for your laptop, see your laptop's documentation or search the laptop manufacturer's Web site.

1. Verify that your laptop has a fully charged battery that is attached to AC power.

2. Enter the CMOS setup utility and select the Power Management section.

3. In the Power Management section, disable the Power Savings option(s) so that the computer will not attempt to save power during the calibration process.

4. In the Power Management section, disable any Suspend on Low Battery options to prevent interference with calibration.

5. In the Power Management section, select the Battery Calibration option. A warning message appears, indicating that the calibration should be carried out only with a fully charged battery and prompting you to confirm that you wish to continue.

6. Remove the AC power and then immediately press **Y** or **Enter** to continue. A message appears, indicating the estimated remaining battery life. In a real–life situation, when you actually needed to calibrate your laptop's battery, this information would likely be incorrect.

7. Wait for the battery to drain. It may take much more than an hour to drain the battery.

8. The manufacturer may specify that the battery should be left to cool for a period of time after the battery is drained and the laptop switches off. When appropriate, reattach AC power, boot up, and enter CMOS setup.

9. Enter the Power Management section and select **Battery Reset**. This tells the EPROM that the battery is at (or very near) zero charge and takes you back to the Power Management section of CMOS.

10. Reapply your preferred power management settings and save and exit CMOS setup. The battery is now calibrated so that the related power management and suspend features will work properly.

If you have access to a laptop and the permission of your instructor, do the following to calibrate the battery:

1. Locate documentation (in the user manual or on the Web) that explains how to calibrate the battery. Note below how these steps differ from the ones listed previously.

_____

_____

_____

_____

_____

12

2. Follow the specific steps for your laptop to calibrate the battery. (Do *not* attempt the procedure unless you have the specific steps for your laptop because you might do damage to the laptop or the battery.)

Note that some factors can also prevent power management from functioning as intended. For instance, word processing programs often include an auto-save feature that continually saves changes to a document at specific intervals. This feature is intended to safeguard against lost work but tends to interfere with hard disk power-down settings. Many screen savers cause similar effects and can also prevent a computer from entering or exiting standby or suspend modes.

Review Questions

1. What types of activity do you think might decrease the battery life of a fully charged battery more quickly than reading a document or spreadsheet? Give three examples.

_____

_____

_____

2. In your opinion, is aggressive power management more important on a desktop computer or a laptop computer? Explain why.

_____

_____

_____

3. Should BIOS power management always be used in conjunction with Windows Power Management? Why or why not?

_____

_____

4. What types of program might prevent a hard drive power-down setting from saving power as intended? Why?

_____

_____

_____

_____

5. What are two possible consequences of an improperly calibrated battery? Explain.

_____

_____

_____

_____

SUPPORTING PRINTERS

LAB 13.1 INSTALL AND SHARE A PRINTER

Objectives

The goal of this lab is to help you install and share a printer. After completing this lab, you will be able to:

➤ Install a local printer on a computer

➤ Share that printer with other users on the network

➤ Using another computer on the network, install and use the shared network printer

Materials Required

This lab will require the following:

➤ A printer and its printer drivers

➤ Two or more Windows 9x or Windows 2000/XP computers connected to a network

➤ Windows installation CD or installation files stored in another location

➤ Workgroup of 3–4 students

Activity Background

A printer can be connected to and dedicated to one particular PC (in which case it is called a local printer), or it can be shared with other PCs on the network (in which case it is called a network printer). For a printer to be shared using a Windows operating system, it must be physically connected to and installed on one computer and then shared with others in the same Windows workgroup. The computer that has the printer physically connected to it must have the Microsoft File and Printer Sharing component installed, and the computer on the network that will use this remote printer must have the Client for Microsoft Networks component installed. In most cases, it is easier to install both components on all computers involved. In this lab, you will install and share a printer in a workgroup and then use the shared printer on the network.

Estimated completion time: **45 minutes**

ACTIVITY

You must first install Client for Microsoft Networks and File and Printer Sharing (if they are not already installed). Both of these components are installed on Windows 2000/XP computers by default. Client for Microsoft Networks is installed in Windows 98 by default. To install them on Windows 9x computers (if necessary), use these steps:

1. In the Control Panel, double-click the **Network** applet.

2. The Network dialog box opens. Click **Add**.

3. The Select Network Component Type dialog box opens. In the list box, click **Client** to select it and then click **Add**.

4. The Select Network dialog box opens. Click **Microsoft** on the left and **Client for Microsoft Networks** on the right. Click **OK** and then insert the Windows 98 installation CD. Reboot the PC when prompted.

5. Return to the Network dialog box. Repeat steps 2 and 3, this time selecting **Service** instead of Client.

6. The Select Network Service dialog box opens. Click **File and printer sharing for Microsoft Networks** and then click **OK**. Click **OK** to close the Network dialog box and then insert the Windows 98 installation CD. Reboot the PC when prompted.

7. Return to the Network dialog box and then click **File and Print Sharing**.

8. The File and Print Sharing dialog box opens. Select the **I want to be able to give others access to my files** checkbox and the **I want to be able to allow others to print to my printer(s)** checkbox and then click **OK**. (You will not be practicing file sharing in this lab, but as a general rule you will usually set up files and print sharing at the same time.)

Next, you need to verify that all the computers that need to use the printer are in the same workgroup. Follow these steps:

1. Ask your instructor for the name of the workgroup you are to use for this lab and record the name here:

_____

2. For Windows 98, right-click the **Network Neighborhood** icon on the desktop and select **Properties** from the shortcut menu. The network's Properties window appears. Click the **Identification** tab. (For Windows 2000/XP, right-click **My Computer** and select **Properties** from the shortcut menu. In the System Properties window for Windows 2000, click the **Network Identification** tab and then click the **Properties** button. The Identification Changes window appears.) For Windows XP, click the **Computer Name** tab and then click **Change**.

3. To what workgroup does this computer belong?

_____

4. If necessary, change the workgroup assignment to match the one noted in Step 1.

You are now ready to install and share the printer. On a Windows 2000/XP computer that will be physically connected to the printer, follow these steps. Note that the steps for Windows 98 differ slightly, but you can use these steps as a guide.

1. With the computer off, connect the printer cable to the parallel port or USB port on your computer, turn on the printer, and then boot up the computer.

13

2. If the Add Printer Wizard opens, click **Next** and then skip to step 4.

3. If the wizard does not open for Windows 2000, click **Start** on the taskbar, point to **Settings**, and then click **Printers**. For Windows XP, click **Start** and then click **Printers and Faxes**. The Printers window opens. Double-click **Add Printer**. The Add Printer Wizard opens. Click **Next**.

4. Click **Local printer**, select the **Automatically detect and install my Plug and Play printer** checkbox, and click **Next**.

5. A list of ports is displayed. Select **Use the following port**, select **LPT1** and then click **Next**.

6. A list of manufacturers and printer models is displayed. Select first the manufacturer and then the model from the list. If your printer is not listed and you have the correct printer driver on disk or CD, click **Have Disk**. Keep in mind that drivers designed for one Windows operating system might not work for a later version of Windows, so you need to make sure you have the correct drivers for your computer's version of Windows. (You can download printer driver files from the printer manufacturer's Web site.) If you select a manufacturer and model from the Windows list, a dialog box might appear to allow you to specify the location of the Windows setup files. In that case, insert the Windows setup CD or select another location for the files.

7. The next screen in the Add Printer Wizard asks for a name for the printer. This name will later appear in the list of available printers. Windows provides a default name. Accept the default name or enter your own, and then click **Next** to continue.

8. Click **Share as** to indicate that this printer will be shared with others on a network, and select the operating system that other computers on the network will be using. By selecting the operating system here, you ensure that your computer can communicate with the remote computers when they request access to the printer. Click **Next** to continue.

9. Select **Yes** to print the test page, and then click **Next**.

10. Windows displays the printer settings you selected. Click **Finish** to complete the installation.

Once the printer is installed, you need to make it possible for other computers in the network to access it. Follow these directions to share the printer with other computers in the workgroup:

1. On the computer that has the printer installed locally, for Windows 2000, click **Start** on the taskbar, point to **Settings**, and click **Printers**. For Windows XP, click **Start** and then click **Printers and Faxes**.

2. The Printers window opens, showing the printer you just installed. Right-click the printer and select **Sharing** in the shortcut menu.

3. The Properties window for the printer opens with the Sharing tab selected. Click the **Shared as** option button, type a share name for the printer, and then click **OK**.

4. For Windows 2000/XP computers, click **Additional Drivers**, select the operating systems used by the remote computers and then click **OK**. Windows can then provide the remote computers with the necessary driver files when they first attempt to connect to the shared printer. (Windows 98 does not provide this service.)

The printer is now listed in the Network Neighborhood window (or, for Windows 2000/XP, in the My Network Places window) on all the other computers on the network. However, before the printer can be used by a remote computer, printer drivers must be installed on that computer.

There are two approaches to installing a shared network printer on a remote PC. You can perform the installation using the printer drivers installed on the host PC, or you can perform the installation using the drivers on CD (either the Windows CD or printer manufacturer's CD). If you need to install the printer on several remote PCs, it is faster to use the drivers installed on the host PC. The disadvantage of using this method is that you must share the C:\Windows folder on the host PC, an action that is considered a security risk. For this reason, as soon as the printer is installed on all the remote PCs, you should unshare the C:\Windows folder on the host PC to protect that critical folder.

Follow these steps to install the shared printer on the other PCs:

1. On the computer that has the printer connected locally, share the **C:\Windows** folder so that the drivers in this folder will be available to the other computers. To do this, right-click the **C:\Windows** folder in Explorer, click **Properties** in the shortcut menu, click the **Sharing** tab, and select the option **Shared as** to share the folder. Do not require a password to access the folder. Click **OK**.

2. On the remote PCs, open My Network Places or Network Neighborhood and find the printer. Right-click the printer and click **Install** (for Windows 98) or **Connect** (for Windows 2000/XP) on the shortcut menu.

3. Enter a name for the printer and print a test page to complete the installation.

4. After all remote computers have installed the printer, remove the shared option on the C:\Windows folder of the local computer to protect this important folder. To do this, right-click the folder in Explorer, click **Properties**, click the **Sharing** tab, and select **Not Shared**. Click **OK**.

13

Review Questions

1. What two Windows components must be installed before you can share a printer in a workgroup?

_____

_____

2. What would happen if the C:\Windows folder on the host PC were not shared when you tried to install the printer on the remote PCs? How could you have installed the printer on a remote computer if you did not have access to the C:\Windows folder on the host computer?

_____

_____

3. Name an advantage of installing file sharing at the same time you install printer sharing.

_____

_____

4. Suppose you want to stop others on the network from using a shared printer, but you still want the printer to be available to the computer on which it is locally installed. What is the easiest way to accomplish this?

_____

_____

LAB 13.2 INSTALL A NETWORK PRINTER

In Lab 13.1, you installed a printer as a local printer and as a network printer. This lab gives you further practice in installing local and network printers, showing you an alternate way to install a network printer.

Objectives

The goal of this lab is to give you practice installing a local printer on a computer, sharing it, and then installing it on a remote computer on the network. After completing this lab, you will be able to:

➤ Install a local printer

➤ Install a network printer

➤ Test the printer across the network

Materials Required

This lab will require the following:

➤ Windows 98, Windows 2000, or Windows XP operating system

➤ Printer, printer cable, and printer driver files

➤ Functioning network

➤ Workgroup of 2–4 students

Activity Background

A local printer is one that is connected to a PC by way of a serial, parallel infrared, or USB connection. A local printer is not usually available to the network for general printing jobs, but in some cases it may be useful to allow other computers to print from your local printer. (For example, suppose you have an expensive photo-quality printer installed locally on your computer. You might sometimes want to let users who need to print photos access your printer through the network.) In this lab you will install a local printer and a network printer. Instructions in this lab are written for Windows 98 but work the same for Windows 2000 or Windows XP if you substitute My Network Places for Network Neighborhood.

Estimated completion time: **30 minutes**

ACTIVITY

The following steps describe the default method for installing a printer in Windows. However, printer manufacturers often provide specialized steps for installing their devices. In that case, you should follow the steps prescribed by the manufacturer of your printer rather than the steps provided here.

1. With the computer off, attach the printer cable to the computer and the printer. Attach the power cable to the printer and then plug it in. Turn on the printer and then the computer. After the computer starts up, insert the installation disk if you have one.

2. Click **Start** on the taskbar, point to **Settings**, and then click **Printers**. The Printers window opens, displaying any installed printers as well as the Add Printers icon.

3. Double-click the **Add Printers** icon to open the Add Printer wizard.

4. In the Add Printer wizard, click **Next** to begin the installation process.

5. What two options do you see in the Add Printer Wizard?

6. In the Add Printer Wizard, select the **Local Printer** option and then click **Next** to continue.

7. In the right pane of the Add Printers Wizard, select the manufacturer of your printer. A list of printers for that manufacturer is displayed in the left pane. Scroll down the list in the left pane to locate your printer.

13

8. If you can locate your printer, click it in the left pane of the Add Printer Wizard, click **Next**, and then skip to step 11. If you cannot locate your printer in the list, click **Have Disk**. The Install From Disk dialog box opens.

9. In the Install From Disk dialog box, click **Browse**. Then locate and select the installation file for your operating system. This file will have an .inf file extension and most likely will be found in a folder that is named according to your operating system (such as \Win98\install.inf or \Windows98\oem.inf or something similar). Click **OK** to tell the wizard to use the selected file.

10. Click **OK** in the Install From Disk dialog box to close it. The Add Printer Wizard identifies your printer. Click **Next** to continue.

11. The Add Printer Wizard asks you to select the port you will use for the printer. In the Available Ports list box, select **LPT1: Printer Port**. This indicates that your printer is attached to the parallel port. Click **Next** to continue.

12. In the Printer name text box type a name for the printer (replacing the model name, which appears by default).

13. You are asked if you want this printer to be your Windows default printer. Click **Yes** and then click **Next**. When asked if you would like to print a test page, click **No** and then click **Finish**. The necessary files are copied to your computer, and in some cases (if the printer has fax capabilities, for instance) a new wizard launches. If this occurs, complete the wizard or follow instructions supplied by your instructor. When the installation process is complete, an icon for the newly installed printer appears in the Printers window.

Follow these steps to test the printer:

1. In the Printers window, right-click the icon for your printer and select **Properties** from the shortcut menu. The printer's Properties dialog box opens.

2. Click the **General** tab and then click **Print Test Page**. A test print job is sent to the printer, and a dialog box opens asking you whether the page printed correctly.

3. Verify that your test page printed correctly (without any gibberish), then click **OK** to close the dialog box.

4. Open Windows Explorer and arrange it so that you can still see your printer's icon in the Printer's window. Using Windows Explorer, locate a .txt file or .bat file and drag the file onto the printer's icon. What happens?

_____

_____

Now that you have tested your printer, share your printer (using Lab 13.1 as a guide). After you have shared your printer, go to the other computer and follow these steps to install a network printer:

1. Open the Printers window and launch the **Add Printer Wizard** as you did previously.

2. Click **Next**.

3. Select **Network Printer** and click **Next** to continue.

4. Click **Browse** to locate the printer that you will install. The Browse for Printer dialog box opens.

5. The Browse for Printer dialog box displays the network in a similar way to Windows Explorer. Locate your printer by expanding the computer on which you installed and shared it. When you have found the correct printer, click it (to select it) and then click **OK** to close the Browse for Printer dialog box.

6. In the Add Printer Wizard, verify that the path displayed is correct and click **Next** to continue.

7. In the Add Printer Wizard, as before, select the manufacturer and model or **Have Disk**, as appropriate for your particular printer.

8. Complete the Add Printer Wizard.

9. Test your printer.

Review Questions

1. A printer is connected to the parallel port on computer A but is shared on the network. Computer B installs the shared computer and connects to it. Computer A considers it a _____ printer and computer B considers it a _____ printer.

2. If a manufacturer's prescribed method for installing its printer differs from the default Windows method, which method should you use?

   _____

3. When installing a local printer that is attached through a parallel cable, what port should you specify?

   _____

13

4. Is it possible for a single printer to be both a local and a network printer? Why or why not?

_____

_____

_____

5. Explain how to print a document without opening it.

_____

_____

LAB 13.3 UPDATE PRINTER DRIVERS

Objectives

The goal of this lab is to give you experience upgrading printer drivers. After completing this lab, you will be able to:

➤ Identify driver information

➤ Locate new drivers

➤ Install new drivers

➤ Test the printer drivers for functionality

Materials Required

➤ Windows 9x, Windows 2000, or Windows XP

➤ Windows installation CD or installation files stored at another location

➤ Administrator account and password, if applicable

➤ File compression tool (optional)

➤ Internet access

➤ Local printer

Activity Background

Printer manufacturers often release new drivers for their existing printers to fix problems with earlier drivers, add new functions, support new applications, and accommodate new operating system features. A PC support technician needs to know how to update printer drivers as they become available. The process of updating printer drivers is similar to that for other devices. You must gather information about the device and the currently installed drivers, download the new drivers, and install them. Like other devices, after the drivers are installed, you should test the printer to be certain it is functioning correctly before turning it over to the end user. Unlike many other devices, it is easy to verify that a printer is working correctly. You will also find that the process of updating printer drivers is similar across various Windows platforms and printer manufacturers. This lab gives you general instructions for updating printer drivers. Modify these instructions to fit your particular situation and printer.

Estimated completion time: **30 minutes**

ACTIVITY

The first step to updating printer drivers is to gather information about your current printer and drivers. Research and list the following information:

1. How is your printer generally used (for example, text, photographs, or graphics)?

   _____

2. What operating system are you using?

   _____

3. Who is the printer manufacturer?

   _____

4. What is the model of the printer?

   _____

5. What is the printer interface (parallel, USB, other)?

   _____

6. Printers typically have many setup options that deal with print quality and paper handling. Right-click the printer and select **Properties** from the shortcut menu. Note any important settings, because it is likely that you will need to reapply them after the driver is updated.

   _____

   _____

   _____

When using Windows 9x, follow these instructions to view driver details:

1. Open Device Manager.

2. In Device Manager, locate your printer and click to highlight it.

13

3. With the device selected, click **Properties** to display the device information. If you see a dialog box with only a General tab, close the dialog box and in Device Manager, click the plus sign + next to the printer to expand the heading and then select the appropriate printer from the displayed printer list. Then click **Properties**. A dialog box with both General and Driver tabs should appear.

4. Select the **Driver** tab and then click the **Driver File Details** button to display the Driver File Details dialog box as shown in Figure 13-1. List all drivers listed in the dialog box under "Driver files."

Figure 13-1   Windows 98 driver file details for a local printer

In addition to the previous information, list all driver information shown in the dialog box that will later help you identify the current driver. Include the Provider, File Version, and Copyright information. This will give you a starting point in locating new drivers for your printer.

When using Windows 2000/XP, follow these instructions to identify the printer driver:

1. Open the Printers window.

2. Right-click the **printer** icon and select **Properties** from the shortcut menu. The printer properties dialog box appears.

3. Click the **Advanced** tab (see Figure 13-2). Note that tabs might differ from one printer to another.

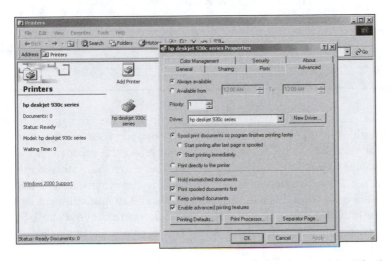

Figure 13-2   Use the printer Properties dialog box to identify the printer driver

4. What is the name of the driver listed under Driver?

_____

Follow these general directions to locate any available driver updates:

1. Go to the printer manufacturer's Web site and locate the driver download section. Use the following table to help you locate the Web site. What is the URL of the driver download page?

_____

Printer manufacturer	Web site
Brother	www.brother.com
Canon	usa.canon.com
Hewlett-Packard	www.hp.com
IBM	www.ibm.com
Lexmark	www.lexmark.com
Okidata	www.okidata.com
SATO	www.satoamerica.com
Seiko Epson	www.epson.com
Tally	www.tally.com
Xerox	www.xerox.com

2. When you search for the correct driver on the Web site, you might be presented with more than one driver that will work for your printer, operating system, or application. In most cases, you should select the most recent version that matches your printer and operating system. There are exceptions to this. For instance, if a driver is listed as BETA, it is still in development and has been released for evaluation. Usually, but not always, the manufacturer will have most of the kinks worked out. To be on the safe side, don't download a BETA release driver. List all drivers, with brief descriptions, for your particular printer and operating system.

_____

_____

_____

3. What is the driver that you have selected to download?

_____

4. Identify and list any special installation instructions the manufacturer recommends.

_____

5. Create a folder on your hard drive named C:\Download and then create a subfolder named by the manufacturer, for example, C:\Download\Lexmark. What is your folder name?

_____

6. Download the driver you intend to install to that folder.

With any device, it is best to follow the manufacturer's recommended method of installation rather than the Windows approach. A good manufacturer will have tested the driver as well as the installation process. The exception is when you have several printers installed on a system and you think that one set of drivers might overwrite files needed by another printer. In this case, use Windows to update the drivers. Do the following to install the new driver using the manufacturer's installation process:

1. As a document or digital picture, print an example of the main use of the printer. This printout verifies that your printer is working before you make any changes and will be used for comparison later to verify that the new drivers are working.

2. Using Windows Explorer, double-click the file you downloaded. If it is a compressed file, it will self-extract files or use file compression software on your PC to extract the files. If an installation wizard automatically launches, exit it.

3. Were any files extracted? List them here:

_____

4. Locate any ReadMe text files for late-breaking information about installation.

5. Double-click the setup or install program. Document the process you used to install the new drivers.

_____

_____

_____

13

Do the following to test the printer and new drivers:

1. Open the Printers window.

2. Right-click the printer and select **Properties** from the shortcut menu. Click the **Print Test Page** button and verify that the test page is legible.

3. Apply the correct printer settings that you recorded.

4. Reprint the typical document or photograph and compare it to the one printed prior to the driver update. List any differences that you see.

_____

Review Questions

1. List four reasons why you might want to update a printer's drivers.

_____

_____

2. List four things you should know before you start searching the Web for updated drivers.

_____

_____

_____

_____

3. What does a driver being in BETA release indicate about that driver?

_____

4. List the steps to print a Windows test page.

_____

_____

LAB 13.4 PRINTER MAINTENANCE AND TROUBLESHOOTING

Objectives

The goal of this lab is to give you experience supporting printers. After completing this lab, you will be able to:

➤ Use the Web to help with printer maintenance

➤ Correct common printer problems

Materials Required

➤ Internet access

➤ Printer

Activity Background

Printers require more maintenance than most peripherals. Paper gets jammed, the ink cartridge or toner runs out, and the image or document quality is degraded by dust and misalignment. Most manufacturers and many models have specific instructions for maintaining ink and toner cartridges that apply exclusively to that printer. You must rely on the printer manufacturer for instructions when maintaining a particular printer. In this lab, you will investigate maintenance and troubleshooting instructions for several types of printer.

Estimated completion time: **30 minutes**

ACTIVITY

Use the Internet to research how to solve the following problems. The printer is a high-end laser printer by Hewlett-Packard (*www.hp.com*), the LaserJet 8100. Answer these questions about routine maintenance for this printer:

1. Everything needed for routine maintenance of the LaserJet 8100 can be purchased in a printer maintenance kit. List the printer components included in this kit:

   _____

   _____

   _____

2. On the HP Web site, find the instructions for using the kit to perform the routine maintenance. What should you wear while you do the maintenance?

   _____

3. How many pages can be printed before maintenance should be performed?

The next printer is an inkjet printer, the HP Deskjet 930c. Answer these questions:

1. Your computer displays the message to replace the ink cartridge. You replace the cartridge, but the message is still displayed. Also, you notice the Resume light on the printer is blinking. Search the HP Web site and locate the troubleshooting steps to solve the problem.

2. What is the first thing HP suggests you do when you see these errors?

   _____

3. The second thing HP suggests is that you clean the cartridge contacts. List the steps:

   _____

   _____

   _____

   _____

4. If the problem does not disappear, HP suggests you reclean the cartridge contacts, this time using a cotton swab dipped in _____.

Now you will investigate how to perform routine maintenance or troubleshoot problems on your local printer. Do the following:

1. List the following information to identify your local printer:

   ■ Printer manufacturer: _____

   ■ Printer model: _____

   ■ Printer interface (parallel, USB, other): _____

13

2. Search the manufacturer's Web site for troubleshooting and maintenance procedures and answer the following questions:

- What types of problem can you find addressed for your printer?

  _____

  _____

  _____

- Does the manufacturer offer a printer maintenance kit? If so, what components are included and how much does the kit cost?

  _____

  _____

  _____

- What maintenance tips for your printer can you find on the Web site?

  _____

  _____

Review Questions

1. When a printer is not working correctly, what are two ways the problem can be communicated to the user?

   _____

   _____

2. What is the purpose of a printer maintenance kit?

   _____

3. How often should you perform printer maintenance using a printer maintenance kit purchased from the printer manufacturer?

   _____

4. After replacing an ink cartridge in an inkjet printer, an error message is displayed. What is the first thing you should do?

   _____

LAB 13.5 CRITICAL THINKING: SABOTAGE AND REPAIR A NETWORK PRINTER

Objectives

The goal of this lab is to learn to troubleshoot problems with a network printer.

Materials Required

This lab will require the following:

➤ Two or more computers connected to a network, one with a local printer attached

➤ Access to the Windows installation CD or installation files stored in another location

➤ Workgroup of 2–4 students

Activity Background

Problems with a network printer are common, and a PC support technician is often called on to solve them. This lab will give you practice solving these types of problem.

Estimated completion time: **45 minutes**

ACTIVITY

1. Using the steps provided in Lab 13.1, verify that each computer in a workgroup is able to print to a network printer, locally installed on one of the computers in the workgroup.

2. Trade systems with another group and sabotage the other group's system while they sabotage your system. Do one or more things that will prevent one or more computers in the workgroup from using the network printer. The following list has some sabotage suggestions. Do something in this list, or think of another option.

   ■ On the host computer, remove the sharing option for the printer

   ■ Uninstall the printer on a remote computer

   ■ Pause printing on one or more computers

   ■ Turn the printer off or offline

   ■ Disconnect the printer cable from the host computer

   ■ Remove paper from the printer

   ■ Introduce an error in the printer configuration on the host computer or a remote computer

3. What did you do to sabotage the other team's system?

   _____

   _____

   _____

4. Return to your system and troubleshoot it.

13

5. Describe the problem as a user would describe it if you were at a help desk.

_____

_____

6. What is your first guess as to the source of the problem?

_____

7. List the steps you took in the troubleshooting process.

_____

_____

_____

_____

8. How did you solve the problem and return the printing system to working order?

_____

_____

Review Questions

1. What would you do differently the next time you encounter the same symptoms?

_____

2. What are three easy things you could ask a user to check that do not require experience with Windows?

_____

_____

3. What might cause this problem to happen? List three possible causes.

_____

_____

_____

ALL ABOUT SCSI

LAB 14.1 COMPARE SCSI TO COMPETING TECHNOLOGIES

Objectives

The goal of this lab is to compare the price of a SCSI system to a similar system without SCSI. After completing this lab, you will be able to:

> ➤ Recognize the cost of SCSI components

> ➤ Explain how SCSI components can improve performance

Materials Required

This lab will require the following:

> ➤ Internet access

Activity Background

SCSI components, in general, cost significantly more than non-SCSI components but offer similar basic functionality. At one time SCSI performance and capabilities far exceeded those of other devices. Due to the emergence of new technologies and the refinement of other technologies, this is not necessarily true today. In this lab you will compare the cost and performance of SCSI components to similar non-SCSI components.

Estimated completion time: **30 minutes**

ACTIVITY

1. Most motherboards come with embedded EIDE controllers. Generally speaking, they do not come with embedded SCSI controllers or FireWire ports. Use *www.pricewatch.com* and various manufacturers' Web sites to compare controllers for each technology. For each technology, select one mid-priced device and record the information for that device in the table.

	SCSI host adapter	EIDE adapter	FireWire adapter
Model and manufacturer			
Cost			
Number of devices supported			

2. Use *www.pricewatch.com* to compare hard drives that use SCSI, IDE, and FireWire. Decide on a drive capacity to use for your comparisons (for example 50 GB). Try to use drives that are within approximately 5 GB of each other. Also, when comparing drives, try to compare drives with similar rotation speed. For each technology, pick one mid-priced drive, and complete the following tables. For EIDE, use the most common speed, 7200 rpm. Use manufacturer Web sites for any information not available on *www.pricewatch.com*:

	SCSI Drive	EIDE Drive	FireWire Drive
Model and manufacturer			
Capacity (GB)			
Cost			
Rotation speed (rpm)		7200 rpm	
Avg. access time (ms)			
Max. transfer speed (ms)			

3. Use Pricewatch.com and manufacturer Web sites to compare CD-RW drives. Pick one mid-price drive for each technology and complete the following table:

	SCSI CD-RW	EIDE CD-RW	FireWire CD-RW
Model and manufacturer			
Cost			
Read speed			
Write speed			
Rewrite speed			
Avg. access time (ms)			
Max. transfer speed (ms)			

Review Questions

1. What advantages does SCSI hold over EIDE?

_____

_____

2. What advantage over EIDE do SCSI and FireWire share?

_____

3. What are two advantages EIDE has over SCSI?

_____

_____

4. What technology is appropriate for an office PC that would need only one hard drive and would be used mainly for word processing? Explain your answer.

_____

_____

_____

5. What technology is appropriate for a video editing workstation requiring 200 GB of disk space, a high-speed CD-RW drive, and a DVD drive? Assume that the workstation would play video files directly from the hard drives. Explain your answer.

_____

_____

_____

LAB 14.2 COMPARE SCSI STANDARDS

Objectives

The goal of this lab is to familiarize you with the various SCSI standards. After completing this lab, you will be able to:

➤ Identify key specifications of various SCSI standards

Materials Required

This lab will require the following:

➤ Internet access

Activity Background

SCSI standards are a clear illustration of the principle that every improvement to a particular technology complicates the official standard for that technology. For example, the SCSI-1 standards (introduced in 1986) were relatively straightforward because they were established before refinements to SCSI technology had been introduced. However, SCSI-2 (introduced in 1994) was more complicated, reflecting various improvements to SCSI technology. At this stage, you shouldn't expect to be an expert on everything related to SCSI technology. For that, you'll need to investigate one of the many books devoted to the topic. In this lab you will concentrate instead on the basic differences in SCSI specifications.

Estimated completion time: **30 minutes**

ACTIVITY

1. Use the textbook *A+ Guide to Hardware* or the textbook *A+ Guide to Managing and Maintaining Your PC* and the Web site *www.pcguide.com* to complete Tables 14-1, 14-2, and 14-3:

Table 14-1   SCSI-1

Date introduced	ANSI standard	Bus width	Max # of devices	Max transfer rate

Table 14-2   SCSI-2

Version	Date introduced	ANSI standard	Bus width	Max # of devices	Max transfer rate
Fast					
Wide					
Fast/Wide					

Table 14-3   SCSI-3

Version	Date published	ANSI standard	Bus width	Max # of devices	Max transfer rate	Cable length Single ended	Cable length Differential
Fast							
Wide							
Fast/Wide							

Use the textbook *A+ Guide to Hardware* or the textbook *A+ Guide to Managing and Maintaining Your PC* and the Web site *www.pcguide.com* to answer the following questions:

1. What organization actually researches and develops SCSI standards?

_____

2. What signaling specification is used with Ultra 160 SCSI?

_____

3. What does the symbol in Figure 14-1 mean?

_____

14

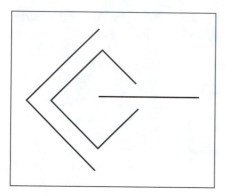

Figure 14-1   Identifying a figure

4. What is the most popular name for the latest SCSI standard that is officially known as SCSI-3 Parallel Interface 4 or SPI-4?

_____

Review Questions

1. What does SCSI stand for?

_____

2. Can SCSI devices built to differing standards be used on the same bus? Explain.

_____

3. Define the term "active termination."

_____

4. What are four organizations that govern SCSI standards?

_____

5. What SCSI standard has a maximum transfer rate of 80 MBps?

_____

LAB 14.3 INSTALL A HOST ADAPTER AND HARD DRIVE

Objectives

The goal of this lab is to familiarize you with the process of installing SCSI devices. After completing this lab, you will be able to:

➤ Install and configure a SCSI host adapter

➤ Install and configure a SCSI hard drive

Materials Required

➤ Windows 9x or Windows 2000/XP operating system

➤ SCSI host adapter and documentation

➤ Drivers, cables, and terminators

➤ SCSI hard drive and documentation

➤ PC toolkit with ground strap

➤ Workgroup of 2-4 students

Activity Background

A basic SCSI subsystem consists of one or more SCSI devices attached to a SCSI host adapter. The device can be attached either internally or outside the computer case. Recall that if you have more than one SCSI device on a SCSI subsystem, the devices are daisy-chained together, with a terminator at each end of the chain. In this lab, you will learn how to set up a basic SCSI subsystem.

Estimated completion time: **45 minutes**

ACTIVITY

Follow these steps to install a SCSI host adapter and hard drive:

1. Remove the case cover and determine which expansion slot will be used for the host adapter.

2. Consult the host adapter documentation and then configure the host adapter to SCSI ID 7. Enable any onboard termination.

3. Install the host adapter in the expansion slot and secure it with a screw.

4. Consult the hard drive documentation and set the jumper on the drive to assign the hard drive as SCSI ID 6.

5. Physically install the SCSI hard drive in the case. If you think you might want to add a second SCSI drive later, place the drive in a bay that is next to a vacant bay.

6. Attach one terminator to one end of the cable.

7. Attach the cable to the host adapter using the connector closest to the terminator.

8. Attach the SCSI data cable to the hard drive.

9. Attach the terminator to the connector that is closest to the hard drive. Note that the terminator should not be placed between the drive and host adapter (even if that's where the closest connector happens to be located).

10. Attach a power cable to the hard drive.

11. Use rubber bands or cable ties to secure the ends of the SCSI data cable so that it does not fall into other components.

14

12. Boot the PC and follow the manufacturer's instructions to install drivers for the SCSI host adapter.

13. When the installation process is complete, reboot the PC.

14. Observe the boot process and notice that before Windows loads, the SCSI host adapter initializes, scans the bus, and reports devices found.

15. Partition and format the hard drive using the same methods that you would use to partition and format an EIDE hard drive.

16. Verify that Windows recognizes the drive and that you can read from and write to it.

17. If asked to do so by your instructor, remove the SCSI components.

Review Questions

1. What SCSI ID should be assigned to the host adapter?

   _____

2. Why didn't you need to use the CMOS setup to identify the hard drive?

   _____

3. In what situation would you need to adjust the CMOS setup to use the newly installed hard drive?

   _____

4. Where should terminators not be placed? Why?

   _____

5. According to the documentation, how many devices will the host adapter support?

   _____

LAB 14.4 INSTALL AN EXTERNAL DRIVE

Objectives

The goal of this lab is to give you experience configuring an external SCSI drive. After completing this lab, you will be able to:

➤ Identify the advantages of an external drive

➤ Install the drive in the external chassis

➤ Connect the drive to the system

Materials Required

This lab will require the following:

- ➤ Windows 9x or Windows 2000/XP operating system
- ➤ External chassis and drive with documentation
- ➤ Drivers, if necessary
- ➤ External cable and terminator
- ➤ PC toolkit with ground strap
- ➤ Workgroup of 2-4 students

Activity Background

Suppose you need to add a drive to your SCSI-equipped PC, but have no free drive bays in the case. One option is to upgrade the case, which involves disassembling and reassembling the PC, plus the cost of the case and drive. The simpler, and often cheaper, option is to install an external SCSI drive. This is usually accomplished by installing an internal SCSI component in an external chassis, including its own power supply (eliminating the need for the PC's power supply to power the device). In addition to the external chassis and SCSI drive, you will also need an external SCSI cable and a terminator. The cost of these components is about the same or less than a new case and eliminates the need to rebuild the system. Another advantage of using an external drive is that it can be moved to any compatible SCSI system with little effort. In this lab you will assemble, configure and install an external SCSI drive.

Before you begin, note that the external chassis design varies from one manufacturer to the next. Review the documentation for your external chassis, and look for any steps not included here. Be sure to perform those additional steps when assembling your external SCSI drive.

Note that in a real-world situation, you would first have to decide which SCSI standard to follow. Then you would have to decide which components and adapters (if any) you needed. Then you would have to purchase the components. This lab assumes that your instructor has selected compatible standards for each component and that you have the necessary devices on hand.

14

Estimated completion time: **45 minutes**

ACTIVITY

To install the internal drive in the external chassis, follow these steps (as well as any additional steps specified in your documentation):

1. Determine what SCSI IDs are available on the bus, and, if necessary, disable termination on the host adapter so you can use the external connector.

2. Consult the drive documentation, and then set the jumper on the new drive to assign the SCSI ID.

3. Open the external chassis and examine the cabling. Decide which cable to attach first and whether to secure the drive in the chassis or attach the cabling first. It is usually best to connect the data cable, followed by the power cable, before securing the drive in the chassis.

4. Install and secure the drive in the chassis.

5. Close and secure the external chassis.

6. Attach the SCSI cable to the chassis.

7. Attach the terminator to the chassis.

Note that many SCSI devices now have internal termination available. This feature is usually activated and deactivated by a jumper setting. In general, using an actual terminator is considered more reliable than internal termination.

8. Attach the power cable to the chassis and to a power source.

Follow these steps to set up the drive and verify that it is functioning:

1. Switch on power to the external drive assembly.

2. Boot the PC and observe the boot process. Did the host adapter detect the new drive?

_____

3. As necessary, partition and format the new hard drive or follow the manufacturer's instructions to install drivers for the drive.

4. When the drive is fully configured, verify that you can read from and write to the drive.

5. If instructed, remove and disassemble the external assembly.

Review Questions

1. What are some advantages of using an external SCSI drive?

_____

_____

2. What should you do before you purchase SCSI components?

_____

_____

3. Did you find it easier to connect cabling before securing the drive in the chassis or after securing the drive?

_____

4. Is it preferable to use internal or external termination?

_____

5. Does the process of partitioning a SCSI hard drive differ from partitioning an IDE hard drive? Why or why not?

_____

_____

LAB 14.5 CRITICAL THINKING: PLAN A SCSI SYSTEM

Objectives

The goal of this lab is to use your knowledge to plan a SCSI-based system. After completing this lab, you will be able to:

➤ Identify and select the best components to meet your performance requirements

➤ Plan the configuration of the system

➤ Estimate the cost of the system

Materials Required

This lab will require the following:

➤ Internet access

Activity Background

Often a customer will give a technician a set of performance requirements and explain that she wants to upgrade her PC to meet those requirements. The technician has to design a configuration to meet the requirements and estimate the cost of the upgrade. You'll practice that in this lab.

Estimated completion time: **45 minutes**

ACTIVITY

1. Review the following information about the customer's existing system:

   ■ Windows 2000 Professional

   ■ Pentium 4 1.8 GHz with 256 MB Rambus RAM

   ■ Mini ATX motherboard with AGP, 3 PCI slots, no embedded SCSI adapter

   ■ Standard 3.5-inch floppy and internal EIDE Zip drive

   ■ Internal 40 GB EIDE hard drive, DVD-ROM drive, CD-RW drive

14

- Mid-tower case with 350 Watt power supply, three 5-inch drive bays, and three 3.5-inch drive bays
- AGP video adapter, PCI MPEG card, and PCI Ethernet NIC
- USB mouse and Microsoft keyboard

2. Review this list summarizing the customer's upgrade requirements:

- Two identical 50 GB SCSI hard drives
- Transfer rate of at least 40 Mbps
- Compatibility with a SCSI 10-disk array that will eventually be installed in a server room that is 20 feet away

3. Design an upgrade configuration compatible with the customer's existing system. Explain your configuration on a piece of paper. You may, if necessary, remove one (but only one) component of the existing system. In your design notes, report the physical and logical configuration, including termination and ID assignments. Also include an estimated cost of parts. Use the textbook *A+ Guide to Hardware* or the textbook *A+ Guide to Managing and Maintaining Your PC* and the Internet for research. Print documentation that supports your final configuration.

Review Questions

1. How did you determine on which SCSI standard to base your upgrade?

   _____

   _____

2. Did you decide to remove any existing components? Why or why not?

   _____

   _____

3. How did you determine if your host adapter was compatible with Windows 2000?

   _____

   _____

4. How many IRQs would the SCSI system use with a total of one host adapter and three SCSI devices?

   _____

5. How many devices will your selected host adapter support?

   _____

CHAPTER FIFTEEN

PURCHASING A PC OR BUILDING YOUR OWN

Labs included in this chapter

➤ Lab 15.1 Choose a System
➤ Lab 15.2 Determine System Requirements
➤ Lab 15.3 Compare What You Need with What You Can Afford
➤ Lab 15.4 Check System Compatibility
➤ Lab 15.5 Evaluate an Upgrade

LAB 15.1 CHOOSE A SYSTEM

Objectives

The goal of this lab is to help you determine what system you might purchase or build to meet your needs and desires. After completing this lab, you will be able to:

➤ List applications you want to run on your system

➤ Determine the type of system required for several types of application

Materials Required

This lab will require the following:

➤ Workgroup of 2–4 students

Activity Background

The goal of this chapter is to help you learn how to plan and build a new system from scratch. The first four labs in this chapter explore the various stages of creating a new system, and each lab builds on the one before it.

One of the first steps in planning and constructing your own PC is deciding what you're going to use it for and what applications you will be running on it. After you make these decisions, you can decide what components are required to meet your needs. In this lab, you will describe and discuss the kind of system you would build for particular uses. Most of the labs in this chapter will require research, but in this case, all you need to do is discuss issues with your workgroup partners.

Estimated completion time: **20 minutes**

ACTIVITY

In the following steps, you will plan four different systems. Each member of the workgroup should work separately, with each member planning four systems. Follow these steps:

1. Plan a system that will be used for gaming and Web surfing. Complete the following:

   ■ Applications that you are likely to install:

   _____

   _____

   ■ Hardware needed:

   _____

   _____

- Most important hardware component(s) needed for gaming and Web surfing:

   _____

2. Plan a system that will be used for programming. Complete the following:
   - Applications that you are likely to install:

      _____

      _____

   - Hardware needed:

      _____

      _____

   - Most important hardware component(s) needed for programming:

      _____

3. Plan a system that will be used for office applications. Complete the following:
   - Applications that you are likely to install:

      _____

      _____

   - Hardware needed:

      _____

      _____

   - Most important hardware component(s) needed for office applications:

      _____

4. Plan a system that will be used for a company file server. Complete the following:
   - Applications that you are likely to install:

      _____

      _____

   - Hardware needed:

      _____

      _____

   - Most important hardware component(s) needed for a company file server:

      _____

15

5. For each type of system, discuss the differences in the systems planned by each member of your group. List the major differences here:

_____

_____

_____

_____

6. As a group, agree on a set of specifications for each system. How do the specifications agreed on by your group differ from your original specifications?

_____

_____

_____

_____

7. Assign one type of system to each member of the group. List the assignments for each group member. In Lab 15.2 and Lab 15.3, each member of the group will continue planning the type of system assigned here:

_____

_____

_____

_____

Review Questions

1. What type of system was assigned to you?

_____

2. What resources will you need to produce a detailed design for this system?

_____

_____

3. Did you find the process of discussing the different types of systems helpful? Why or why not?

_____

_____

4. On which type of system was there the most disagreement on requirements?

_____

_____

5. If you had a budget crunch, where would you sacrifice on your system? Justify your reasoning.

_____

_____

_____

LAB 15.2 DETERMINE SYSTEM REQUIREMENTS

Objectives

The goal of this lab is to help you determine the specific requirements for the system you plan to build. After completing this lab, you will be able to:

➤ List minimum software and hardware components required for a particular type of system

Materials Required

This lab will require the following:

➤ Internet access

➤ Workgroup of 2–4 students (different people than in Lab 15.1)

Activity Background

In the previous lab, you were assigned a type of system to build and you made some preliminary plans for it. In this lab, you will make more specific decisions regarding the required software and hardware components. For now, we will ignore budget constraints and address those issues in Lab 15.3.

Estimated completion time: **30 minutes**

ACTIVITY

1. Working from the preliminary requirements you formed in Lab 15.1, use the Internet to research system requirements for your assigned type of system. Complete the following list of requirements:

■ CPU speed _____

■ Memory _____

■ Hard drive size _____

15

- Case _____
- Motherboard _____
- Monitor size and resolution _____
- Type of printer _____
- Expansion cards _____

_____

_____

_____

_____

- Other peripheral hardware (such as keyboard, mouse, PC camera, speakers, etc.)

_____

_____

_____

_____

- Drives needed (for example, hard drives, CD or DVD, tape backup, Zip, or floppy)

_____

_____

_____

_____

- Operating system

_____

- Applications

_____

_____

_____

_____

- Any other requirements

_____

_____

_____

_____

2. Use the Internet or your local computer store to learn more about each component. List the description and cost of each component. If you are doing your research on the Internet, print the Web page describing each component. (The Web page you print should include the component's price.) If you are conducting your research at a computer store, take careful notes, and be sure to note a price for each component. At this point, you are interested in evaluating your options for each component, so collect information on more than one possibility. For example, for a motherboard, gather information for two or three different motherboards that all satisfy your system requirements. Although you need to list the price for each component, do not be concerned about total cost at this point in your research. The following Internet resources might be helpful in your search, although you can use others as well:

- *www.cnet.com*
- *www.tomshardware.com*
- *www.motherboards.com*
- *www.pricewatch.com*
- *www.dirtcheapdrives.com*

3. After you have finished gathering system requirements, find another student from another group who planned the same type of system you did. Compare your plans and note the differences.

_____

_____

_____

_____

15

Review Questions

1. What sites did you use for your research besides the previously listed ones?

_____

_____

2. Did you add any components to your list or remove any from it after researching the type of system you want to build? Explain.

_____

_____

_____

3. What processor manufacturer, model, and speed did you select? Why? How
much would the same speed processor from another manufacturer cost?

_____

_____

4. What amount of memory and hard drive size do you plan to use? How did
you make your choices?

_____

_____

_____

5. What components did you decide to use in your system other than the ones
listed in the lab? What purpose will they serve in the new system?

_____

_____

_____

6. List any differences between your plans and the other student's plans for the
same type of system.

_____

_____

_____

LAB 15.3 COMPARE WHAT YOU NEED WITH WHAT YOU CAN AFFORD

Objectives

The goal of this lab is to help you determine the cost of building your own PC. After completing this lab, you will be able to:

➤ Research and compare component prices

➤ Determine how to build a system within your budget

Materials Required

This lab will require the following:

➤ Internet access

➤ Workgroup of 2–4 students

Activity Background

When planning a system, it is important to consider the cost of the components that you want to include. You might not be able to afford everything that you'd like to have in the system, or you might have to buy less expensive versions of some components to get what you want in another area. In this lab, you will develop several versions of a budget for the system you want to build. You will begin without a budget—that is, by figuring out what your dream system would cost. Then you will prioritize your list of components, and determine ways to reduce the system's total cost.

Estimated completion time: **30 minutes**

ACTIVITY

1. Use the information regarding specific hardware components that you compiled in Lab 15.2 to complete Table 15-1. List the price of each component in your dream system in Table 15-1. (Note that you might not use all of the rows in the table.) At the bottom of the table, list the total cost for your dream system.

15

Table 15-1   Dream system

Component	Manufacturer and model	Cost
Processor		
Memory		
Hard drive		
Case		
Motherboard		
Monitor		
Printer		
Expansion card 1		
Expansion card 2		
Expansion card 3		
Expansion card 4		
Keyboard		
Mouse		
Speakers		
CD or DVD drive		
Tape drive		
Zip drive		
Floppy drive		
Other drive		
Operating system		
Application 1		
Application 2		
Application 3		
Application 4		
Other		
Other		
Other		
Total cost of the system		

2. Review your list of components in Table 15-1 and prioritize them. In Table 15-2, list the components in order of importance. In the Notes column of Table 15-2, make notes regarding how much you need each component and whether you can use a lower-cost version or eliminate it altogether. Indicate which (if any) components you are most willing to sacrifice to be able to afford a better component in another area of the system.

Table 15-2 Priority of system components

Component	Notes

3. Pare down your list to the absolute minimum for the type of system you are building: the lowest amount of memory and hard drive space, the cheapest monitor, and so on. In Table 15-3, list the lowest prices available for each component, and calculate the total cost of your bare-bones system.

15

Table 15-3 Bare-bones system

Component	Manufacturer and model	Cost
Processor		
Memory		
Hard drive		
Case		
Motherboard		
Monitor		
Printer		
Expansion card 1		
Expansion card 2		
Expansion card 3		
Expansion card 4		
Keyboard		
Mouse		
Speakers		
CD or DVD drive		
Tape drive		
Zip drive		
Floppy drive		
Other drive		
Operating system		
Application 1		
Application 2		
Application 3		
Application 4		
Other		
Other		
Other		
Total cost of the system		

4. In Table 15-4, list the components of a system that is a reasonable compromise between the dream system and the bare-bones system. This midrange system is the one you will work with in the next lab.

Table 15-4   Midrange system

Component	Manufacturer and model	Cost
Processor		
Memory		
Hard drive		
Case		
Motherboard		
Monitor		
Printer		
Expansion card 1		
Expansion card 2		
Expansion card 3		
Expansion card 4		
Keyboard		
Mouse		
Speakers		
CD or DVD drive		
Tape drive		
Zip drive		
Floppy drive		
Other drive		
Operating system		
Application 1		
Application 2		
Application 3		
Application 4		
Other		
Other		
Other		
Total cost of the system		

15

5. Compare your results from steps 1–4 with the results of another student who is planning the same type of system. Compare cost estimates and note differences in the components you both planned to include. Note how you arrived at your calculation.

_____

_____

_____

_____

6. Repeat step 5 with at least one student who is planning a different type of system.

_____

_____

_____

_____

Review Questions

1. What was the cost difference between your dream system and the bare-bones version?

_____

2. On which components were you willing to compromise and why?

_____

_____

3. On which components were you *not* willing to compromise and why?

_____

_____

4. How would the performance of your midrange system compare to the dream system? How would the performance of the midrange system compare to the bare-bones system? How would the performance of the dream system compare to the bare-bones system?

_____

_____

_____

LAB 15.4 CHECK SYSTEM COMPATIBILITY

Objectives

The goal of this lab is to help you verify that the components in a proposed system are compatible. After completing this lab, you will be able to:

➤ Find incompatibilities between components in a proposed system

➤ Suggest an alternative system of approximately the same price

Materials Required

This lab will require the following:

➤ Internet access

➤ Workgroup of 2–4 students

Activity Background

No matter how much time you spend planning and building a PC, the system won't work correctly unless the system components are compatible. You will save yourself a lot of trouble by attempting to discover incompatibilities before you begin to build a system. In this lab you will figure out which components in your proposed system are incompatible and suggest compatible components so that the cost of building the system remains approximately the same.

> Estimated completion time: **40 minutes**

ACTIVITY

1. Alter your plan for your midrange system (from Lab 15.3) by introducing component incompatibilities. Write this altered version on a separate piece of paper or develop a new plan that incorporates incompatible components. Incompatibilities are suggested below, but you can introduce a problem not listed here:

   - A processor not supported by the motherboard
   - Not enough space in your case for all of your drives (hard drive, CD-ROM, Zip drive)
   - Power supply not powerful enough
   - Too much RAM for your motherboard
   - An incompatible mix of SCSI and IDE devices
   - A type of memory not supported on the motherboard
   - Five parallel ATA IDE devices on a system
   - A video card that uses the wrong kind of AGP slot for the motherboard
   - Expansion cards included with a motherboard that already has built-in logic

15

2. Calculate and record the total cost of the components in the system:

_____

3. Trade revised PC plans with another student in your group. Ask the other student to find the incompatible components in your plan and suggest replacement components while keeping the price about the same. Do the same with the plan you receive, recording the incompatibilities you find, the original cost of the system, replacement components, and the final cost of the altered system.

_____

_____

_____

_____

4. With the group, discuss the incompatibilities found in the plans and how you fixed them. Make note of incompatibilities that were introduced but not found.

_____

_____

_____

Review Questions

1. Did you, or the other students in your group, introduce incompatibilities not suggested in step 1? If so, list them here:

_____

_____

_____

2. Were all the incompatibilities introduced in the plans discovered? If not, which ones were not, and why might these have been more difficult to find?

_____

_____

_____

3. List the incompatibility problems you located in the other student's plan and explain how you solved them.

_____

_____

_____

_____

4. Did the students in your group have different ways of solving the same incompatibility problems? Explain.

_____

_____

_____

_____

5. For the plan that you reviewed and revised, what was the difference in the original cost and the cost after you incorporated your solutions?

_____

_____

LAB 15.5 EVALUATE AN UPGRADE

Objectives

The goal of this lab is to help you determine the ease and cost of upgrading a PC. After completing this lab, you will be able to:

➤ Determine whether a system needs to be upgraded

➤ Explain why a system needs to be upgraded

➤ List components necessary to upgrade a system

Materials Required

This lab will require the following:

➤ Lab computer

➤ Documentation for computer components, if available

➤ Internet access

15

Activity Background

An important factor to consider when purchasing or building a PC is how easy it will be to upgrade the system. You might upgrade an existing system rather than replacing it with a new system. Factors that affect the ease of upgrading include the processors supported by the motherboard, the size of the case, and the number and type of ports and expansion slots on the motherboard. In this lab, you will examine a system to determine whether you can make upgrades to it and then evaluate how practical the upgrades are.

Estimated completion time: **45 minutes**

ACTIVITY

Follow these steps to determine whether your system can be upgraded:

1. In Table 15-5, list the components currently installed on your system. Useful sources of information include Device Manager, the Control Panel, and the Properties windows for various drives and devices.

Table 15-5   Current system components

Device	Description
Motherboard (make and model)	
BIOS type	
Memory (type and size)	
Hard drive (type and size)	
Other drives installed (floppy, Zip, CD-ROM, etc.)	
Monitor (type and size)	
Printer	
Sound card	
Modem (or other Internet connection)	
NIC	
Other devices	
Operating system (including version number)	
Applications (including version number)	

2. Using the Internet and available documentation, select three components to upgrade. Determine the following for each component and record the information:

   Component 1:_____

■ Replacement component:

_____

_____

■ Cost of the upgrade:

_____

■ Are there other components that must also be upgraded for this upgrade to work? If so, what are they?

_____

_____

Component 2: _____

■ Replacement component:

_____

_____

■ Cost of the upgrade:

_____

■ Are there other components that must also be upgraded for this upgrade to work? If so, what are they?

_____

_____

Component 3: _____

■ Replacement component:

_____

_____

■ Cost of the upgrade:

_____

■ Are there other components that must also be upgraded for this upgrade to work? If so, what are they?

_____

_____

15

3. Print a Web page showing the specifications and cost of each new component. What is the total cost of the upgrades?

_____

4. Suppose you had to sell the system in its current state (without the upgrades). What would be a reasonable price?

_____

5. When upgrading an existing system, the cost of the upgrade should not exceed half the value of the existing system. Will your proposed upgrade exceed that limit?

_____

6. Using *www.cnet.com* (or another Web site where you can compare systems), locate a notebook computer with specifications similar to your lab PC. Compare the cost of upgrading the memory, the processor, and the CD-ROM drive on each. (Substitute another component if your computer does not have a CD-ROM drive.) In Table 15-6, compare the cost of upgrading your lab PC to that of a similar upgrade for a notebook computer.

Table 15-6   PC upgrade versus notebook upgrade

Component	Cost of upgrading on PC	Cost of upgrading on notebook
Processor		
Memory		
CD-ROM drive		

Review Questions

1. What components did you choose to upgrade and why?

_____

_____

_____

2. Which would be cheapest to upgrade, your lab PC or a comparable notebook? Explain your answer.

_____

_____

_____

3. What other resources, besides the ones you used in the lab, do you think might be helpful in planning an upgrade?

_____

_____

4. Among the components you selected, which upgrade was the most expensive?

_____

_____

5. If you were actually performing these upgrades, is there any component or any system that you would *not* choose to upgrade? Explain your answer.

_____

_____

_____

6. Which component is the most popular to upgrade? The easiest? The hardest?

_____

_____

_____

15

TROUBLESHOOTING AND MAINTENANCE FUNDAMENTALS

LAB 16.1 RESEARCH DATA RECOVERY SERVICES

Objectives

The goal of this lab is to help you research data recovery services. After completing this lab, you will be able to:

➤ Find tips on how to make recovery services less necessary

➤ Explain how to minimize data loss

➤ Describe some recovery options

Materials Required

This lab will require the following:

➤ Internet access

Activity Background

You've probably experienced the feeling that comes with accidentally deleting or overwriting an important file. To make matters worse, you probably couldn't replace the file unless you had backed it up previously. Now imagine if the lost file consisted of financial information that could affect the success or failure of a business employing 100 employees or the lost file contained a creative work that took months to produce. You would certainly try to recover the data yourself, but if you were unable to, you might decide to seek the help of a professional data recovery service. In this lab, you will research sites offering such services.

> Estimated completion time: **45 minutes**

ACTIVITY

Use your favorite search engine to research data recovery services. Alternatively, search these Web sites and answer the following questions:

➤ www.datarecoveryclinic.com

➤ www.savemyfiles.com

➤ www.drivesavers.com

➤ www.adv-data.com

➤ www.atl-datarecovery.com

1. Name two Web sites that offer a do-it-yourself data recovery option in addition to professional recovery services.

   _____

   _____

2. Give an example of a service that offers recovery of data in a Linux operating environment.

   _____

3. Give two examples of services that recover data from striped sets or volume sets.

   _____

   _____

4. From what type or types of media can files be recovered? Circle the correct answer(s):

   a. Tape

   b. CD-ROM

   c. Zip disk

   d. Floppy disk

   e. Hard disk

5. Give two examples of companies that will not charge you if they are unable to recover your important data.

   _____

   _____

6. List two general levels of turn-around time for data recovery.

   _____

   _____

7. What measures are taken when recovering ultrasensitive (secure) data?

   _____

   _____

   _____

16

8. Besides natural disaster and mechanical failure, what are four other common causes of data loss?

_____

_____

_____

_____

9. If you learn that you have lost data on drive D, what things should you absolutely not do? Circle the correct answer(s):

a. Install recovery software on drive C

b. Defragment drive D

c. Restore objects in the Recycle Bin

d. Install recovery software on drive D

10. Give two examples of services designed to proactively prevent data loss.

_____

_____

11. List some reasons why it might be impossible to recover some data.

_____

_____

_____

12. Will you always be able to recover all the data that you lose? Why or why not?

_____

_____

_____

13. Why is it important to perform hard drive data recovery in a clean room?

_____

_____

_____

14. What class of clean room should be used for data recovery?

_____

15. In what ways can your recovered data be returned to you?

_____

_____

_____

16. Give one example of a company that specializes in recovery from optical media.

_____

17. What Web site (or sites) includes a "museum" of interesting recovery projects they have undertaken?

_____

_____

18. What circumstances might require that the data recovery service perform a recovery attempt at your site?

_____

_____

19. List two companies that recover data from Flash cards or memory sticks.

_____

_____

20. Pick two of the companies you researched and list some of the other services and products they offer.

_____

_____

16

Review Questions

1. Based on your research, what impression do you get about how expensive data recovery services are? Explain your answer.

   _____

   _____

2. Based on your research, do you think individuals or companies would be more interested in using data recovery services? Why?

   _____

   _____

3. In general, do companies specialize in recovery from specific types of media or do they tend to provide data recovery for all types of media?

   _____

   _____

4. Based on your research, what three factors would affect the price you might pay for recovery services from a specific provider?

   _____

   _____

LAB 16.2 PRODUCE HELP DESK PROCEDURES

Objectives

The goal of this lab is to demonstrate the process of setting up help desk troubleshooting procedures. After completing this lab, you will be able to:

➤ Identify problems that would prevent users from browsing the network

➤ Decide which problems can be solved over the telephone

➤ Decide which problems require administrative intervention

➤ Create a support matrix for telephone instruction

Materials Required

This lab will require the following:

➤ Windows 9x or Windows 2000/XP operating system

➤ PC connected to a working TCP/IP network

➤ Two workgroups with 2–4 students in each group

Activity Background

When a company sets up a help desk for computer users, it establishes a set of procedures to address common troubleshooting situations. These procedures should include instructions that the average user can be expected to carry out with telephone support. In this lab, you will design and create help desk procedures for one common problem: the inability to connect to a network. In this lab, assume that you are working at the company help desk. Assume that if you cannot solve the problem, you will escalate the problem to the network administrator or to another technician who will actually go to the computer that has the problem.

Estimated completion time: **60 minutes**

ACTIVITY

1. Assume that your company network is designed according to the following parameters. (Note that your instructor might alter these parameters so they more closely resemble the parameters of your working network.)

   ■ Ethernet LAN is using only a single subnet

   ■ TCP/IP is the only protocol

   ■ Workgroup name is ATLGA

   ■ DHCP server assigns IP information

2. Assume that all users on your company network use computers with the following parameters. (Note that your instructor might alter these parameters so they more closely resemble your PC.)

   ■ Pentium III 750 MHz

   ■ Windows XP operating system

   ■ Internal NIC

   ■ Category 5 cabling with RJ-45 connectors

16

3. As a group, discuss the various reasons a user might not be able to connect to the network, and then make a list of the four most common reasons. List the source of these problems below. Consider both hardware and software problems. In your list, include at least one problem that is difficult to solve over the phone by talking to the user, requiring, instead, that the network administrator or another technician actually go to the computer to solve the problem. Order the four problems from the least difficult to solve to the most difficult to solve. List the one problem that requires administrator intervention at the bottom of the list.

- Source of Problem 1:

  _____

- Source of Problem 2:

  _____

- Source of Problem 3:

  _____

- Source of Problem 4 (requires administrator or another technician to get involved):

  _____

For each problem, describe the symptoms as a user would describe them:

- Symptoms of Problem 1:

  _____

  _____

- Symptoms of Problem 2:

  _____

  _____

- Symptoms of Problem 3:

  _____

  _____

- Symptoms of Problem 4 (requires administrator or another technician intervention):

  _____

  _____

As a group, decide how to solve each of the problems. On separate pieces of paper, list the steps required to verify and resolve the problems. (Such a list of steps is sometimes referred to as a procedure, support matrix, or job aid.) Double-check the steps by testing them on your computer. (In real life, you would actually test your steps using a computer attached to the network you are supporting.) When making your list of steps, allow for alternatives, based on how the user responds to your questions. For example, you might include one list of steps for situations in which the user says others on the network are visible in My Network Places and another list of steps for situations in which the user says no remote computers can be seen in My Network Places. Well-written help desk procedures ensure that the help desk worker knows exactly what steps to perform; this in turn results in quicker and more confident user support. For any problem that cannot be solved by the procedure, the last step should be for the help desk personnel to notify the administrator. In your procedure, include questions to the user where appropriate. As you work, you might find it helpful to use a diagram or flowchart of the questions asked and decisions made.

An example of one step that involves a question is:

➤ **Question:** Is your computer on?

➤ **Answer:** Yes, go to step 3; No, go to step 2

Now test your help desk procedures by using them on another workgroup. Follow these steps:

1. Introduce one of your four problems to a PC connected to a network.

2. Have someone from another workgroup sit at your PC. The remainder of these steps refer to this person as "the user."

3. Sit with your back to this person so you cannot see what he or she is doing. Place your step-by-step procedures in front of you, either on paper or on screen. (It's helpful if you can sit at a PC that is connected to the network, so that you can perform the same steps you ask the user to perform. But make sure you cannot see the other PC or see what the user is doing.)

4. The user should attempt to access the network and then "call" your help desk for assistance.

5. Follow your procedure to solve the problem.

6. Revise your procedure as necessary.

7. Test all four help desk procedures.

Review Questions

1. Can all users' computer problems be resolved with help desk support? Explain.

_____

_____

2. After you first design and write your help desk procedures to resolve problems, what should you do next?

_____

_____

3. How should help desk procedures address complex problems that require administrative intervention?

_____

_____

_____

4. How should you alter your procedures based on the technical experience of your users? Explain.

_____

_____

_____

_____

5. Why do you need to consider what the network and computer are like when creating your procedures?

_____

_____

_____

6. What has been your experience when calling a help desk? How well did the technician walk you through the process of solving your problem?

_____

_____

Lab 16.3 Flash BIOS

Objectives

The goal of this lab is to help you examine the process of flashing BIOS. After completing this lab, you will be able to:

➤ Gather motherboard information

➤ Gather BIOS string information

➤ Research correct BIOS update information

➤ Record current BIOS settings

➤ Flash your BIOS, if permitted by your instructor

Materials Required

This lab will require the following:

➤ Windows 9x or Windows 2000/XP operating system

➤ Motherboard documentation or SANDRA software installed in Lab 1.3

➤ Internet access

➤ Blank floppy disk

Activity Background

The BIOS on a motherboard controls many of the basic input/output functions of the system. The BIOS programming can be updated by downloading the latest update from the BIOS or motherboard manufacturer's Web site and then following specific procedures to update (or flash) the BIOS. Flashing a computer's BIOS is necessary when troubleshooting an unstable motherboard. You may also need to flash a computer's BIOS to provide support for new hardware (such as a processor, hard drive, or CD-ROM drive) or an operating system that you are about to install. For example, before upgrading your operating system to Windows 2000/XP Professional, you could update your BIOS to add support for ACPI power management. In this lab you will gather information about your system, including what BIOS you are using and how to flash the BIOS. If you instructor permits, you will also flash your BIOS.

16

Estimated completion time: **45 minutes**

Activity

Before making hardware, software, or BIOS changes to a system, it's important to know your starting point so that, if problems occur, you will know whether the problems already existed or you created them by what you did to the system. Do the following:

1. Verify that your computer can successfully boot to a Windows desktop with no errors.

2. Does the PC boot without errors?

_____

It's critical that when flashing the BIOS you use the correct BIOS update. Using the wrong BIOS update can render your system inoperable. Follow these steps to gather information on the motherboard chip set and BIOS:

1. Use motherboard documentation or SANDRA to find and record the following:

- Motherboard manufacturer:

_____

- Motherboard model number and version/revision:

_____

- Chip set manufacturer:

_____

- Chip set model number and version/revision:

_____

2. Next, you need to record the BIOS string and manufacturer information that are displayed during the boot process. To make it possible to record this information, for an older PC, turn off the PC, unplug your keyboard and then turn on the PC. In most cases, the very first screen will contain video BIOS information from the video card and will be identified by "VGA BIOS" or "Video BIOS." Ignore this screen and wait for the next screen, which indicates the start of POST. At this point, because you unplugged the keyboard, POST will stop and report the error about a missing keyboard. This freezes the screen so you can read the BIOS information. For a newer PC, turn off the PC and then turn on the PC while pressing the Pause/Break key, which causes POST to halt.

3. The BIOS manufacturer and version can usually be found at the top left of the POST screen. You may also see a release date, which is useful in determining whether newer versions of the BIOS are available. The motherboard identifica-

tion string will usually be located at the bottom left of the screen and usually contains dozens of characters. It is important to verify that this string is correct so that the exact BIOS update is obtained. Record your information below.

- BIOS manufacturer and version:

  _____

- BIOS release date, if provided:

  _____

- Motherboard identification string:

  _____

If you have a name-brand PC that does not identify BIOS information during the boot process, you should be able to locate BIOS information on the manufacturer's Web site by computer model number and serial number. Also, some newer computers will not halt the boot process if the keyboard is missing. Alternatively, you can go to CMOS setup and look for the BIOS identifying information on the CMOS main menu screen.

Using the information you gathered, you can search the Web to determine what files you will need to update your BIOS.

1. First, search the motherboard manufacturer's Web site and then the BIOS manufacturer's Web site's support section for information on updating your BIOS. Alternatively, search by motherboard model number or BIOS version number. Download the files required to update your BIOS or, if your computer is running the latest version of the BIOS, download the files required to refresh your existing BIOS. Answer the following questions:

   - Did you download files to update or refresh your BIOS?

     _____

   - Which manufacturer provided the BIOS: the BIOS manufacturer or motherboard manufacturer?

     _____

   - What is the name of the file you downloaded?

     _____

   - What is the release date of the latest version?

     _____

2. Search the manufacturer's Web site for the steps required to flash your BIOS. Print this procedure so you can use it during the upgrade. Does the procedure call for an additional BIOS utility or Flash utility? If so, download this utility as well. Research Flash utilities on *www.wimsbios.com*. Wim's BIOS is an excellent

16

Web site for researching BIOS information in general. Print information on what BIOS utilities are available.

3. The next step is to record any changes you have previously made to CMOS settings. Generally, when BIOS is updated, settings are returned to their default state, so you will probably need to return the settings to their present state after you have flashed BIOS. In addition, you might need to manually input settings for all hard drives (or allow these settings to be detected automatically). Record any settings that you know you changed, as well as any hard drive settings that might have to be reconfigured after you update the BIOS. Also, record any additional settings specified by your instructor.

- Hard drive information:

_____

_____

- Settings you have changed:

_____

_____

_____

_____

- Settings specified by your instructor:

_____

_____

_____

_____

4. At this point, if your update procedures require the use of a bootable floppy, verify that the boot order allows you to boot from drive A before drive C.

5. Prepare to update your BIOS. Decompress any files, double-check procedures, read any readme.txt files included in the upgrade files (which often contain last-minute adjustments to the procedure), and create the upgrade boot disk, if necessary.

6. If your instructor permits, follow the BIOS update procedure to update your BIOS. During the procedure, if you are given the opportunity to save your old BIOS, do so. This will make it possible to return to the previous BIOS version if you encounter problems with the new BIOS.

7. Reboot, verify CMOS settings, and verify that the computer will boot to a Windows desktop successfully.

Review Questions

1. At what point in the boot process is BIOS information displayed?

   _____

2. How can you freeze the screen during POST so that you can read the BIOS information?

   _____

   _____

3. Why is it so important to record BIOS and motherboard information correctly?

   _____

   _____

4. What files might contain last-minute changes to the upgrade procedures?

   _____

5. In what state are CMOS settings usually placed after a BIOS update?

   _____

6. If given the opportunity during the update, what should you always do and why?

   _____

   _____

16

LAB 16.4 TROUBLESHOOT GENERAL COMPUTER PROBLEMS

Objectives

The goal of this lab is to troubleshoot and remedy general computer problems. After completing this lab, you will be able to:

➤ Diagnose and solve problems with various hardware devices

➤ Document the troubleshooting process

Materials Required

This lab will require the following:

➤ Windows 98 or Windows 2000/XP operating system

➤ Windows 98 or Windows 2000/XP installation CD or installation files stored in another location

➤ Drivers for all devices

➤ PC toolkit with ground strap

➤ Workgroup partner

Activity Background

In previous labs, you have learned to troubleshoot problems in specific subsystems of a PC. This lab takes a comprehensive approach to troubleshooting an entire system, where the problem might relate to any subsystem. Troubleshooting a general problem is no different from troubleshooting a specific subsystem. You simply apply your troubleshooting techniques to a larger range of possibilities.

> Estimated completion time: **120 minutes**

ACTIVITY

1. Verify that your computer and your partner's computers are working by verifying that the system runs smoothly and that all drives are accessible. Browse the network and connect to a Web site.

2. Randomly pick one of the following problems and introduce it to your PC:

   ▪ For PCs that have SIMMs installed, move the RAM to a different SIMM slot.

   ▪ Change the boot sequence to boot from a nonexistent device.

   ▪ If both the mouse and the keyboard have PS/2 connectors, switch the connectors at the case.

   ▪ Using Add/Remove Hardware, install a nonexisting device.

   ▪ Remove the data cable from the primary master hard drive.

   ▪ Change the display settings to two colors that are hard to read.

   ▪ Install the wrong type SIMM or DIMM or the wrong number of SIMMs or DIMMs on the motherboard. Or, for a system that uses SIMMs, remove one SIMM. Be sure to store all memory modules in an anti-static bag while they are outside the case.

- Unplug the monitor from the video adapter.
- Add drive B in BIOS, but do not install a second floppy drive.
- In BIOS, manually add information for a fictitious hard disk drive.
- Unplug the network cable from the wall or hub.
- Connect the floppy drive to the drive B connector on the data cable (the one without the twist).

3. Troubleshoot your partner's PC while your partner troubleshoots your computer. Verify that you can accomplish all the tasks that you could before the computer was sabotaged.

4. On a separate sheet of paper, answer these questions:

- What is the initial symptom of a problem as a user would describe it?

   _____

   _____

- How did you discover the source of the problem?

   _____

   _____

   _____

- How did you resolve the problem?

   _____

   _____

   _____

- If you were working at a help desk and someone called with this problem, could the problem have been solved over the phone or would it have required a visit from a technician? Explain your answer.

   _____

   _____

16

5. Return to your computer and repeat steps 2 through 4. Continue until you have solved all the problems listed in step 2. For each problem, make sure to answer the questions listed in step 4.

Review Questions

1. Which problems caused the computer to halt during the boot process?

_____

_____

_____

2. What problem was the most difficult to repair? Why?

_____

_____

_____

3. Of those problems that *allowed* the computer to boot, which problem was easiest to detect? Why?

_____

_____

_____

4. Of those problems that *prevented* the computer from booting, which problem was easiest to detect? Why?

_____

_____

_____

LAB 16.5 TROUBLESHOOT HYPOTHETICAL SITUATIONS

Objectives

The goal of this lab is to help you think through the troubleshooting process using hypothetical situations. After completing this lab, you will be able to:

➤ Evaluate a troubleshooting situation

➤ Determine a likely source of a problem

➤ Explain how to verify the source of a problem

➤ Briefly explain a problem and the procedure required to remedy it

Materials Required

This lab will require the following:

➤ Workgroup of 2–4 students

Activity Background

One way to sharpen your troubleshooting skill is to think through the process of solving hypothetical problems. This lab will present situations that, while common, should present a challenge for your workgroup.

To complete this lab, imagine that you are in charge of repairs at a small computer shop. As part of your job, you first need to describe the symptoms of the problem on the repair work order and explain your initial guess or opinion as to the source of the problem. You must then write a short summary on the work order explaining what you did to repair the computer. The explanations you write on the work order should be as clear and precise as possible. Customers who know something about computers will appreciate your careful explanations. And even if the customer does not fully understand, a detailed work order will help assure the customer that you did a thorough job.

16

Estimated completion time: **30 minutes**

ACTIVITY

1. A customer installed a new 20 GB hard drive and complains that it will not work. He claims that he called the manufacturer's technical support, who walked him through BIOS setup. When he rebooted, POST did recognize the hard drive but Windows still did not. The customer then became frustrated and decided to bring the computer to you.

- What are the possible sources of the problem?

  _____

  _____

  _____

  _____

- What would you do to find out how to resolve the problem?

  _____

  _____

  _____

  _____

2. A customer brings in a computer and says that when she turns on the computer it will not boot. She says that a screen appears with an error message regarding something about the operating system. The customer claims that she has never modified the system, but that she does have children who use the computer and may have changed something inadvertently.

   When you boot the system, you get an invalid system disk error and you can hear the hard drive spin up when power is applied. You suspect that the BIOS settings are incorrect and that the hard drive is not being recognized. You successfully detect the hard drive using the BIOS autodetection feature. In standard CMOS setup you notice that the date and time are also incorrect, so you reset them. You save your changes and reboot. The system reboots to Windows. You test the system for 10 minutes, leave it on and come back to it after an hour, and it is still functioning correctly. You call the customer and tell her that you have fixed the situation and she can come and pick it up the next day. Then you shut the system off and eventually leave work.

   The next day the customer comes in, and when you demonstrate that you have fixed the problem, you see the invalid system disk message again.

   - What do you suspect the problem is?

     _____

   - How long will it probably take you to fix it?

     _____

     _____

3. A customer brings in a computer. The customer was trying to install a new U. S. Robotics modem, but the modem will not work, even after trying several different ways to install the drivers for the new modem. When you boot and check Device Manager, you see two instances of U.S. Robotics modems, neither of which are functioning correctly. You also see one instance of a modem made by Creative Labs, which is reportedly functioning correctly. When you physically check the modem card, only the U.S. Robotics modem is present in the computer.

- What is the source of the problem?

  _____

  _____

- What steps would you take to install the U.S. Robotics modem?

  _____

  _____

  _____

  _____

  _____

4. A customer brings in a computer with a new external modem and says that the computer is working fine but that the modem does not work. The customer wants you to get the modem to work with his computer. The customer says he tried attaching the external modem on both serial ports but to no avail. You decide to test the modem on a separate system and you find that it functions correctly. On the customer's computer, you check the Ports Group in Device Manager and only the parallel port is present.

- What is likely the problem?

  _____

- What will you do to correct it?

  _____

  _____

16

5. A customer brings in a system and claims that it does not work after a thunderstorm. You open the case and immediately notice a burning smell. You test each component in a test system and find no functional components. You call and report the sad news to the customer. The customer is upset about the system but even more upset about the loss of important information on the hard drive for which he has no backup.

- What information or recommendation can you give the customer about what he can do now and what he should do in the future to safeguard important data?

  _____

  _____

  _____

  _____

- What advice can you give the customer about protecting his hardware?

  _____

  _____

  _____

6. A customer wanted to upgrade his processor to a faster one. He checked with the motherboard manufacturer and discovered that his motherboard supports a faster processor. When the client installed the new processor, the system booted and the POST reported that the processor is only running at two-thirds of its potential. Windows works and the computer functions normally but at a slower clock speed.

- What is the likely problem?

  _____

- How would you solve the problem?

  _____

Review Questions

1. How could a properly functioning hard drive, which is recognized by BIOS, fail to show up in Windows?

  _____

  _____

2. What device maintains CMOS settings even if the computer is totally unplugged from AC power?

_____

3. What Control Panel applet will let the inexperienced user forcibly install an incorrect device or non-existent device? What Windows feature will let you remove devices?

_____

_____

4. Suppose that the COM ports were enabled in BIOS. How could they be disabled in Windows, thereby preventing a modem from using a COM port?

_____

_____

_____

5. How, besides coming in through the roof and directly striking the computer, might lightning destroy a computer?

_____

Lab 16.6 Critical Thinking: Update Motherboard Drivers

Objectives

The goal of this lab is to help you update the drivers for motherboard components. After completing this lab, you will be able to:

➤ Identify a motherboard and its embedded devices

➤ Search a motherboard's manufacturer's Web site for updated drivers

➤ Download all applicable drivers for a motherboard

➤ Install drivers

➤ Document the process of updating motherboard drivers

16

Materials Required

This lab will require the following:

- ➤ Windows 98 or Windows 2000/XP operating system
- ➤ Motherboard documentation or SANDRA software installed in Lab 1.3
- ➤ Internet access
- ➤ PC toolkit with ground strap (if necessary)
- ➤ Blank floppy disk (if necessary)

Activity Background

Like other devices, components on the motherboard use drivers to interact with the operating system. These drivers may be updated from time to time to resolve newly discovered bugs or to conform to newly implemented industry standards. However, know that if the motherboard is working properly and performance is acceptable, you should not update the drivers because, when doing so, you might introduce new problems. In this lab, you will use your experience researching and installing drivers to install all available drivers for the components embedded on your motherboard.

Estimated completion time: **90 minutes**

Activity

1. Using procedures learned in previous labs, provide information below:

   - Motherboard manufacturer:

   _____

   - Motherboard model:

   _____

2. Using procedures learned in previous labs, identify the components on your motherboard and record the information in Table 16-1. In the Included? column, enter Yes or No for whether a component is included on the motherboard. Enter the version number of each component, if you have that information.

Table 16-1   Identifying components

Component	Included?	Version number (if available)
CPU type		
Chip set		
IDE controller		
AGP controller		
Embedded audio		
Embedded NIC/LAN		
Embedded modem		
Embedded video		
Other		
Other		

3. Research the motherboard manufacturer's Web site for driver updates and doc-umentation for performing the updates.

4. Download any necessary files, including any documentation. List the files you downloaded and the purpose of each file in Table 16-2.

Table 16-2   Identifying downloaded files

Downloaded file	Purpose of the file

5. Print any documentation describing how to perform the updates.

6. Update the drivers.

7. Briefly explain how you updated the drivers.

_____

_____

_____

_____

_____

16

Review Questions

1. What is an embedded device?

   _____

   _____

2. If your motherboard documentation covers different models of motherboards, some with more embedded components than others, how can you definitely determine which model is installed in your computer?

   _____

   _____

3. What embedded device controls non-SCSI hard drives?

   _____

4. If you connect your monitor to a PCI video card in an expansion slot, would downloading and installing drivers for embedded video or for an AGP controller likely resolve any problems related to video performance? Explain.

   _____

   _____

   _____

5. Why would you want to update motherboard drivers? Give two reasons.

   _____

   _____

6. When would you not want to update the motherboard drivers?

   _____

   _____

GLOSSARY

This glossary defines the key terms listed at the end of each chapter and other terms related to managing and maintaining a personal computer.

100BaseFX — A variation of 100BaseT that supports fiber optic cable.

100BaseT — An Ethernet standard that operates at 100 Mbps and uses STP cabling. Also called Fast Ethernet. Variations of 100BaseT are 100BaseTX and 100BaseFX.

10Base2 — An Ethernet standard that operates at 10 Mbps and uses small coaxial cable up to 200 meters long. Also called ThinNet.

10Base5 — An Ethernet standard that operates at 10 Mbps and uses thick coaxial cable up to 500 meters long. Also called ThickNet.

1394.3 — *See* IEEE 1394.3.

3-D RAM — Special video RAM designed to improve 3-D graphics simulation.

80 conductor IDE cable — An IDE cable that has 40 pins but uses 80 wires, 40 of which are ground wires designed to reduce crosstalk on the cable. The cable is used by ATA/66, ATA/100, and ATA/133 IDE drives.

Accelerated Graphics Port (AGP) — A slot on a motherboard for a video card that transfers video data from the CPU and runs at a frequency synchronized with the system bus.

active backplane — A type of backplane system in which there is some circuitry, including bus connectors, buffers, and driver circuits, on the backplane.

active matrix — A type of video display that amplifies the signal at every intersection in the grid of electrodes, which enhances the pixel quality over that of a dual-scan passive matrix display.

active partition — The primary partition on the hard drive that boots the OS. Windows NT/2000 /XP calls the active partition the system partition.

active terminator — A type of terminator for single-ended SCSI cables that includes voltage regulators in addition to the simple resistors used with passive termination.

adapter address — *See* MAC address.

adapter card — A small circuit board inserted in an expansion slot and used to communicate between the system bus and a peripheral device. Also called an interface card.

address bus — Lines on the system bus used by the CPU to communicate memory addresses and I/O addresses to the memory controller and I/O devices.

Advanced Transfer Cache (ATC) — A type of L2 cache contained within the Pentium processor housing that is embedded on the same core processor die as the CPU itself.

alternating current (AC) — Current that cycles back and forth rather than traveling in only one direction. In the U.S., the AC voltage from a standard wall outlet is normally between 110 and 115 V AC. In Europe, the standard AC voltage from a wall outlet is 220 V AC.

ammeter — A meter that measures electrical current in amps.

ampere or amp (A) — A unit of measurement for electrical current. One volt across a resistance of one ohm will produce a flow of one amp.

amplifier repeater — A repeater that does not distinguish between noise and signal; it amplifies both.

ANSI (American National Standards Institute) — A nonprofit organization dedicated to creating trade and communications standards.

ASCII (American Standard Code for Information Interchange) — A popular standard for writing letters and other characters in binary code. Originally, ASCII characters were 7 bits, so there were 127 possible values. ASCII has been expanded to an 8-bit version, allowing 128 additional values.

ASPI (Advanced SCSI Programming Interface) — A popular device driver that enables operating systems to communicate with a SCSI host adapter. The "A" originally stood for Adaptec before that company licensed the technology to others.

asynchronous SRAM — Static RAM that does not work in step with the CPU clock and is, therefore, slower than synchronous SRAM.

AT — A form factor, generally no longer produced, in which the motherboard requires a full-size case. Because of their dimensions and configuration, AT systems are difficult to install, service, and upgrade. Also called full AT.

AT command set — A set of commands that a PC uses to control a modem and that a user can enter to troubleshoot the modem.

ATAPI (Advanced Technology Attachment Packet Interface) — An interface standard — part of the IDE/ATA standards — that allows tape drives, CD-ROM drives, and other drives to be treated like an IDE hard drive by the system.

attenuation — Signal degeneration over distance. The problem caused by attenuation is solved on a network by adding repeaters to the network.

ATX — The most common form factor for PC systems presently in use, originally introduced by Intel in 1995. ATX motherboards and cases make better use of space and resources than did the AT form factor.

audio/modem riser (AMR) — A specification for a small slot on a motherboard to accommodate an audio or modem riser card. A controller on the motherboard contains some of the logic for the audio or modem functionality.

autodetection — A feature on newer system BIOS and hard drives that automatically identifies and configures a new drive in the CMOS setup.

Autoexec.bat — A startup text file that was once used by DOS and is used by Windows 9x/Me to provide backward compatibility. It tells the computer what commands or programs to execute automatically during boot and is used to create a 16-bit environment.

Automatic Private IP Address (APIPA) — An IP address in the address range 169.254.x.x, used by a computer when it cannot successfully lease an IP address from a DHCP server.

autorange meter — A multimeter that senses the quantity of input and sets the range accordingly.

Baby AT — An improved and more flexible version of the AT form factor. Baby AT was the industry standard from approximately 1993 to 1997 and can fit into some ATX cases.

back side bus — The bus between the CPU and the L2 cache inside the CPU housing.

backplane system — A form factor in which there is no true motherboard. Instead, motherboard components are included on an adapter card plugged into a slot on a board called the backplane.

backup — An extra copy of a file, used in the event that the original becomes damaged or destroyed.

bandwidth — In relation to analog communication, the range of frequencies that a communications channel or cable can carry. In general use, the term refers to the volume of data that can travel on a bus or over a cable stated in bits per second (bps), kilobits per second (Kbps), or megabits per second (Mbps). Also called data throughput or line speed.

bank — An area on the motherboard that contains slots for memory modules (typically labeled bank 0, 1, 2, and 3).

baud rate — A measure of line speed between two devices such as a computer and a printer or a modem. This speed is measured in the number of times a signal changes in one second. *See also* bps.

beam detect mirror — Detects the initial presence of a laser printer's laser beam by reflecting the beam to an optical fiber.

binary number system — The number system used by computers; it has only two numbers, 0 and 1, called binary digits, or bits.

binding — The process by which a protocol is associated with a network card or a modem card.

BIOS (basic input/output system) — Firmware that can control much of a computer's input/output functions, such as communication with the floppy drive and the monitor. Also called ROM BIOS.

bit (binary digit) — A 0 or 1 used by the binary number system.

bits per second (bps) — A measure of data transmission speed. For example, a common modem speed is 56,000 bps, or 56 Kbps.

block mode — A method of data transfer between hard drive and memory that allows multiple data transfers on a single software interrupt.

Bluetooth — A standard for wireless communication and data synchronization between devices, developed by a group of electronics manufacturers and overseen by the Bluetooth Special Interest Group. Bluetooth uses the same frequency range as 802.11b, but does not have as wide a range.

BNC connector — A connector used with thin coaxial cable. Some BNC connectors are T-shaped and called T-connectors. One end of the T connects to the NIC, and the two other ends can connect to cables or end a bus formation with a terminator.

boot record — The first sector of a floppy disk or logical drive in a partition; it contains information about the disk or logical drive. On a hard drive, if the boot record is in the active partition, then it is used to boot the OS. Also called boot sector.

boot sector — *See* boot record.

boot sector virus — An infectious program that can replace the boot program with a modified, infected version of the boot command utilities, often causing boot and data retrieval problems.

booting — The process that a computer goes through when it is first turned on, preparing the computer to receive commands.

bootstrap loader — A small program at the end of the boot record that can be used to boot an OS from the disk or logical drive.

break code — A code produced when a key on a computer keyboard is released.

bridge — A device used to connect two or more network segments. It can make decisions about allowing a packet to pass based on the packet's destination MAC address.

broadband — A transmission technique that carries more than one type of transmission on the same medium, such as cable modem or DSL.

broadcast — Process by which a message is sent from a single host to all hosts on the network, without regard to the kind of data being sent or the destination of the data.

brouter — A device that functions as both a bridge and a router. A brouter acts as a router when handling packets using routable protocols such as TCP/IP and IPX/SPX. It acts as a bridge when handling packets using nonroutable protocols such as NetBEUI.

brownouts — Temporary reductions in voltage, which can sometimes cause data loss. Also called sags.

BTX (Balanced Technology Extended) — The latest form factor expected to replace ATX. It has higher quality fans, is designed for better air flow, and has improved structural support for the motherboard.

burst EDO (BEDO) — A refined version of EDO memory that significantly improved access time over EDO. BEDO was not widely used because Intel chose not to support it. BEDO memory is stored on 168-pin DIMM modules.

burst SRAM — Memory that is more expensive and slightly faster than pipelined burst SRAM. Data is sent in a two-step process; the data address is sent, and then the data itself is sent without interruption.

bus — The paths, or lines, on the motherboard on which data, instructions, and electrical power move from component to component.

bus mastering — A device other than the CPU controlling a bus on the motherboard in order to access memory or another device.

bus mouse — A mouse that plugs into a bus adapter card and has a round, 9-pin mini-DIN connector.

bus riser — *See* riser card.

bus speed — The speed, or frequency, at which the data on the motherboard is moving.

bus topology — A LAN architecture in which all the devices are connected to a bus, or one communication line. Bus topology does not have a central connection point.

byte — A collection of eight bits that is equivalent to a single character. When referring to system memory, an additional error-checking bit might be added, making the total nine bits.

C-RIMM (Continuity RIMM) — A placeholder RIMM module that provides continuity so that every RIMM slot is filled.

cable modem — A technology that uses cable TV lines for data transmission requiring a modem at each end. From the modem, a network cable connects to a NIC in the user's PC.

cache memory — A kind of fast RAM that is used to speed up memory access because it does not need to be continuously refreshed.

CAM (Common Access Method) — A standard adapter driver used by SCSI.

capacitor — An electronic device that can maintain an electrical charge for a period of time and is used to smooth out the flow of electrical current. Capacitors are often found in computer power supplies.

CardBus — The latest PCMCIA specification. It improves I/O speed, increases the bus width to 32 bits, and supports lower-voltage PC Cards, while maintaining backward compatibility with earlier standards.

cards — Adapter boards or interface cards placed into expansion slots to expand the functions of a computer, allowing it to communicate with external devices such as monitors or speakers.

carrier — A signal used to activate a phone line to confirm a continuous frequency; used to indicate that two computers are ready to receive or transmit data via modems.

CAS Latency (CL) — A feature of memory that reflects the number of clock cycles that pass while data is written to memory.

CAU (Controlled-Access Unit) — See MAU.

CCITT (Comité Consultatif International Télégraphique et Téléphonique) — An international organization that was responsible for developing standards for international communications. This organization has been incorporated into the ITU. See also ITU.

CDFS (Compact Disc File System) — The 32-bit file system for CD discs and some CD-R and CD-RW discs that replaced the older 16-bit mscdex file system used by DOS. See also UDF.

CD-R (CD-recordable) — A CD drive that can record or write data to a CD. The drive may or may not be multisession, but the data cannot be erased once it is written.

CD-RW (CD-rewritable) — A CD drive that can record or write data to a CD. The data can be erased and overwritten. The drive may or may not be multisession.

central processing unit (CPU) — Also called a microprocessor or processor. The heart and brain of the computer, which receives data input, processes information, and executes instructions.

chain — A group of clusters used to hold a single file.

checksum — A method of error checking transmitted data, whereby the digits are added up and their sum compared to an expected sum.

chip creep — A condition in which chips loosen because of thermal changes.

chip set — A group of chips on the motherboard that controls the timing and flow of data and instructions to and from the CPU.

CISC (complex instruction set computing) — An earlier type of instruction set used by CPUs that has a large number of instructions.

CHS (cylinder, head, sector) mode — The traditional method by which BIOS reads from and writes to hard drives by addressing the correct cylinder, head, and sector. Also called normal mode.

circuit board — A computer component, such as the main motherboard or an adapter board, that has electronic circuits and chips.

clamping voltage — The maximum voltage allowed through a surge suppressor, such as 175 or 330 volts.

clock speed — The speed, or frequency, expressed in MHz, that controls activity on the motherboard and is generated by a crystal or oscillator located somewhere on the motherboard.

clone — A computer that is a no-name Intel- and Microsoft-compatible PC.

cluster — One or more sectors that constitute the smallest unit of space on a disk for storing data (also referred to as a file allocation unit). Files are written to a disk as groups of whole clusters.

cluster chain — A series of clusters used to hold a single file.

CMOS (complementary metal-oxide semiconductor) — The technology used to manufacture microchips. CMOS chips require less electricity, hold data longer after the electricity is turned off, are slower, and produce less heat than earlier technologies. The configuration, or setup, chip is a CMOS chip.

CMOS configuration chip — A chip on the motherboard that contains a very small amount of memory, or RAM — enough to hold configuration, or setup, information about the computer. The chip is powered by a battery when the PC is turned off. Also called CMOS setup chip or CMOS RAM chip.

CMOS setup — (1) The CMOS configuration chip. (2) The program in system BIOS that can change the values in the CMOS RAM.

CMOS setup chip — *See* CMOS configuration chip.

COAST (cache on a stick) — Memory modules that hold memory used as a memory cache. *See* cache memory.

coaxial cable — Networking cable used with 10Mbps Ethernet ThinNet or ThickNet.

cold boot — *See* hard boot.

collision — Conflict that occurs when two computers send a signal on the same channel at the same time.

color depth — The number of possible colors used by a monitor. Determines the number of bits used to compose one pixel and affects the amount of data sent to the video card to build one screen.

combo card — An Ethernet card that contains more than one transceiver, each with a different port on the back of the card, in order to accommodate different cabling media.

communication and networking riser (CNR) — A specification for a small expansion slot on a motherboard that accommodates a small audio, modem, or network riser card.

compact case — A type of case used in low-end desktop systems. Compact cases, also called low-pro-file or slimline cases, follow either the NLX, LPX, or Mini LPX form factor. They are likely to have fewer drive bays, but they generally still provide for some expansion.

constant angular velocity (CAV) — A technology used by hard drives and newer CD-ROM drives whereby the disk rotates at a constant speed.

constant linear velocity (CLV) — A CD-ROM format in which the spacing of data is consistent on the CD, but the speed of the disc varies depending on whether the data being read is near the center or the edge of the disc.

continuity — A continuous, unbroken path for the flow of electricity. A continuity test can determine whether or not internal wiring is still intact, or whether a fuse is good or bad.

control blade — A laser printer component that prevents too much toner from sticking to the cylinder surface.

control bus — The lines on the system bus used to send control signals to manage communication on the motherboard.

cooler — A combination cooling fan and heat sink mounted on the top or side of a processor to keep it cool.

CRC (cyclical redundancy check) — A process in which calculations are performed on bytes of data before and after they are transmitted to check for corruption during transmission.

credit card memory — A type of memory used on older notebooks that could upgrade existing memory by way of a specialized memory slot.

cross-linked clusters — Errors caused when more than one file points to a cluster, and the files appear to share the same disk space, according to the file allocation table.

crossover cable — A cable used to connect two PCs into the simplest network possible. Also used to connect two hubs.

CSMA/CA (Carrier Sense Multiple Access with Collision Avoidance) — A method to control collisions on a network, whereby each computer signals its intent to send data before sending it. This method is used on wireless LANs.

CSMA/CD (Carrier Sense Multiple Access with Collision Detection) — A method that Ethernet networks use to monitor the network to determine if the line is free before sending a transmission.

data bus — The lines on the system bus that the CPU uses to send and receive data.

data cartridge — A type of tape medium typically used for backups. Full-sized data cartridges are $4 \times 6 \times \frac{5}{8}$ inches in size. A minicartridge is only $3\frac{1}{4} \times 2\frac{1}{2} \times \frac{5}{8}$ inches in size.

datagram — *See* packet.

data line protector — A surge protector designed to work with the telephone line to a modem.

data path size — The number of lines on a bus that can hold data, for example, 8, 16, 32, and 64 lines, which can accommodate 8, 16, 32, and 64 bits at a time.

data throughput — *See* bandwidth.

DC controller — A card inside a notebook that converts voltage to CPU voltage. Some notebook manufacturers consider the card to be a FRU.

DCE (Data Communications Equipment) — The hardware, usually a dial-up modem, that provides the connection between a data terminal and a communications line. *See also* DTE.

DDR SDRAM — *See* Double Data Rate SDRAM

DDR2 SDRAM — A version of SDRAM that is faster than DDR and uses less power.

de facto standard — A standard that does not have official backing but is considered a standard because of widespread use and acceptance by the industry.

default printer — The printer Windows prints to unless another printer is selected.

defragment — To "optimize" or rewrite a file to a disk in one contiguous chain of clusters, thus speeding up data retrieval.

demodulation — The process by which digital data that has been converted to analog data is converted back to digital data. *See* modulation.

device driver — A small program stored on the hard drive that tells the computer how to communicate with an input/output device such as a printer or modem.

diagnostic cards — Adapter cards designed to discover and report computer errors and conflicts at POST time (before the computer boots up), often by displaying a number on the card.

diagnostic software — Utility programs that help troubleshoot computer systems. Some Windows diagnostic utilities are CHKDSK and SCANDISK. PC-Technician is an example of a third-party diagnostic program.

differential — A signaling method for SCSI cables in which a signal is carried on two wires, each carrying voltage, and the signal is the difference between the two. Differential signaling provides for error checking and greater data integrity. Compare to single-ended.

DIMM (dual inline memory module) — A miniature circuit board used in newer computers to hold memory. DIMMs can hold up to 2 GB of RAM on a single module.

diode — An electronic device that allows electricity to flow in only one direction. Used in a rectifier circuit.

DIP (dual inline package) switch — A switch on a circuit board or other device that can be set on or off to hold configuration or setup information.

direct current (DC) — Current that travels in only one direction (the type of electricity provided by batteries). Computer power supplies transform AC to low DC.

Direct Rambus DRAM — A memory technology by Rambus and Intel that uses a narrow, very fast network-type system bus. Memory is stored on a RIMM module. Also called RDRAM or Direct RDRAM.

Direct RDRAM — *See* Direct Rambus DRAM.

discrete L2 cache — A type of L2 cache contained within the Pentium processor housing, but on a different die, with a cache bus between the processor and the cache.

disk mirroring — A strategy whereby the same data is written to two hard drives in a computer to safeguard against hard drive failure. Disk mirroring uses only a single controller for two drives.

disk striping — Treating multiple hard drives as a single volume. Data is written across the multiple drives in small segments, in order to increase performance and logical disk volume. When parity is used, disk striping also provides logical fault tolerance. RAID 5 is disk striping with parity information distributed over all drives in the array.

Display Power Management Signaling (DPMS) — Energy Star standard specifications that allow for the video card and monitor to go into sleep mode simultaneously. *See also* Energy Star systems.

DMA (direct memory access) channel — A number identifying a channel whereby a device can pass data to memory without involving the CPU. Think of a DMA channel as a shortcut for data moving to/from the device and memory.

DMA transfer mode — A transfer mode used by devices, including the hard drive, to transfer data to memory without involving the CPU.

docking station — A device that receives a notebook so that it can provide additional secondary storage and easily connect to peripheral devices.

dot pitch — The distance between the dots that the electronic beam hits on a monitor screen.

Double Data Rate SDRAM (DDR SDRAM) — A type of memory technology used on DIMMs that runs at twice the speed of the system clock.

doze time — The time before an Energy Star or "Green" system will reduce 80 percent of its activity.

drop height — The height from which a manufacturer states that its drive can be dropped without making the drive unusable.

DSL (Digital Subscriber Line) — A telephone line that carries digital data from end to end, and can be leased from the telephone company for individual use. DSL lines are rated at 5 Mbps, about 50 times faster than regular telephone lines.

DTE (Data Terminal Equipment) — Both the computer and a remote terminal or other computer to which it is attached. *See also* DCE.

dual channel — A motherboard feature that improves memory performance by providing two 64-bit channels between memory and the chipset. DDR and DDR2 memory can use dual channels.

dual porting — Allows the video chip set (input) and the RAM DAC (output) to access video memory at the same time. A special kind of video RAM is required.

dual-scan passive matrix — A type of video display that is less expensive than an active-matrix display and does not provide as high-quality an image. With dual-scan display, two columns of electrodes are activated at the same time.

dual-voltage CPU — A CPU that requires two different voltages, one for internal processing and the other for I/O processing.

duplexing — An improvement of disk mirroring in which each hard drive had its own adapter card.

DVD (digital video disc or digital versatile disk) — A faster, larger CD format that can read older CDs, store over 8 GB of data, and hold full-length motion picture videos.

dye-sublimation printer — A type of printer with photo-lab-quality results that uses transparent dyed film. The film is heated, which causes the dye to vaporize onto glossy paper.

dynamic RAM (DRAM) — The most common type of system memory, it requires refreshing every few milliseconds.

ECC (error-correcting code) — A chip set feature on a motherboard that checks the integrity of data stored on DIMMs or RIMMs and can correct single-bit errors in a byte. More advanced ECC schemas can detect, but not correct, double-bit errors in a byte.

ECHS (extended CHS) mode — *See* large mode.

ECP (Extended Capabilities Port) — A bidirectional parallel port mode that uses a DMA channel to speed up data flow.

EDO (extended data out) — A type of RAM that may be 10 to 20 percent faster than conventional RAM because it eliminates the delay before it issues the next memory address.

EEPROM (electrically erasable programmable ROM) — A type of chip in which higher voltage may be applied to one of the pins to erase its previous memory before a new instruction set is electronically written.

EISA (Extended ISA) bus — A 32-bit bus that can transfer 4 bytes at a time at a speed of about 20 MHz.

EMI (electromagnetic interference) — A magnetic field produced as a side effect from the flow of electricity. EMI can cause corrupted data in data lines that are not properly shielded.

Energy Star systems — "Green" systems that satisfy the EPA requirements to decrease the overall consumption of electricity. *See also* Green Standards.

enhanced BIOS — A system BIOS that has been written to accommodate large-capacity drives (over 504 MB, usually in the gigabyte range).

Enhanced IDE (EIDE) — A standard for managing the interface between secondary storage devices and a computer system. A system can support up to six serial ATA and parallel ATA IDE devices or up to four parallel ATA IDE devices such as hard drives, CD drives, and DVD drives.

EPIC (explicitly parallel instruction computing) — The CPU architecture used by the Intel Itanium that bundles programming instructions with instructions as to how to use multiprocessing abilities to do two instructions in parallel.

EPP (Enhanced Parallel Port) — A parallel port that allows data to flow in both directions (bidirectional port) and is faster than original parallel ports on PCs that only allowed communication in one direction.

EPROM (erasable programmable ROM) — A type of chip with a special window that allows the current memory contents to be erased with special ultraviolet light so that the chip can be reprogrammed. Many BIOS chips are EPROMs.

error correction — The ability of a modem to identify transmission errors and then automatically request another transmission.

ESD (electrostatic discharge) — Another name for static electricity, which can damage chips and destroy motherboards, even though it might not be felt or seen with the naked eye.

Ethernet — The most popular LAN architecture that can run at 10 Mbps (ThinNet or ThickNet), 100 Mbps (Fast Ethernet), or 1 Gbps (Gigabit Ethernet).

Execution Trace Cache — A type of Level 1 Cache used by some CPUs to hold decoded operations waiting to be executed.

expansion bus — A bus that does not run in sync with the system clock.

expansion card — A circuit board inserted into a slot on the motherboard to enhance the capability of the computer.

expansion slot — A narrow slot on the motherboard where an expansion card can be inserted. Expansion slots connect to a bus on the motherboard.

extended partition — The only partition on a hard drive that can contain more than one logical drive.

external bus — *See* system bus.

external cache — Static cache memory, stored on the motherboard or inside CPU housing, that is not part of the CPU (also called L2 or L3 cache).

faceplate — A metal plate that comes with the motherboard and fits over the ports to create a well-fitted enclosure around them.

Fast Ethernet — *See* 100BaseT.

FAT12 — The 12-bit wide, one-column file allocation table for a floppy disk, containing information about how each cluster or file allocation unit on the disk is currently used.

fault tolerance — The degree to which a system can tolerate failures. Adding redundant components, such as disk mirroring or disk duplexing, is a way to build in fault tolerance.

FDDI (Fiber Distributed Data Interface) — A ring-based network that does not require a centralized hub and can transfer data at a rate of 100 Mbps.

field replaceable unit (FRU) — A component in a computer or device that can be replaced with a new component without sending the computer or device back to the manufacturer. Examples: power supply, DIMM, motherboard, floppy disk drive.

file allocation table (FAT) — A table on a disk that tracks the clusters used to contain a file.

file allocation unit — *See* cluster.

FireWire — An expansion bus that can also be configured to work as a local bus. It is expected to replace the SCSI bus, providing an easy method to install and configure fast I/O devices. Also called IEEE 1394 and i.Link.

firmware — Software that is permanently stored in a chip. The BIOS on a motherboard is an example of firmware.

flash memory — A type of RAM that can electronically hold memory even when the power is off.

flash ROM — ROM that can be reprogrammed or changed without replacing chips.

flat panel monitor — A desktop monitor that uses an LCD panel.

FlexATX — A version of the ATX form factor that allows for maximum flexibility in the size and shape of cases and motherboards. FlexATX is ideal for custom systems.

flow control — When using modems, a method of controlling the flow of data to adjust for problems with data transmission. Xon/Xoff is an example of a flow control protocol.

forced perfect terminator (FPT) — A type of SCSI active terminator that includes a mechanism to force signal termination to the correct voltage, eliminating most signal echoes and interference.

formatting — Preparing a hard drive volume or floppy disk for use by placing tracks and sectors on its surface to store information (for example, FORMAT A:).

form factor — A set of specifications on the size, shape, and configuration of a computer hardware component such as a case, power supply, or motherboard.

FPM (fast page mode) — A memory mode used before the introduction of EDO memory. FPM improved on earlier memory types by sending the row address just once for many accesses to memory near that row.

fragmentation — On a hard drive, the distribution of data files such that they are stored in noncontiguous clusters.

fragmented file — A file that has been written to different portions of the disk so that it is not in contiguous clusters.

frame — The header and trailer information added to data to form a data packet to be sent over a network.

front side bus (FSB) — *See* system bus.

full AT — *See* AT.

full-duplex — Communication that happens in two directions at the same time.

General Protection Fault (GPF) — A Windows error that occurs when a program attempts to access a memory address that is not available or is no longer assigned to it.

Gigabit Ethernet — The newest version of Ethernet supports rates of data transfer up to 1 gigabit per second.

gigahertz (GHz) — One thousand MHz, or one billion cycles per second.

graphics accelerator — A type of video card that has an on-board processor that can substantially increase speed and boost graphical and video performance.

graphics DDR (G-DDR), graphics DDR2, graphics DDR3 — Types of DDR, DDR2, and DDR3 memory specifically designed to be used in graphics cards.

Green Standards — A computer or device that conforms to these standards can go into sleep or doze mode when not in use, thus saving energy and helping the environment. Devices that carry the Green Star or Energy Star comply with these standards.

ground bracelet — A strap you wear around your wrist that is attached to the computer case, ground mat, or another ground so that ESD is discharged from your body before you touch sensitive components inside a computer. Also called static strap, ground strap, ESD bracelet.

guard tone — A tone that an answering modem sends when it first answers the phone, to tell the calling modem that a modem is on the other end of the line.

half-duplex — Communication between two devices whereby transmission takes place in only one direction at a time.

half-life — The time it takes for a medium storing data to weaken to half of its strength. Magnetic media, including traditional hard drives and floppy disks, have a half-life of five to seven years.

handshaking — When two modems begin to communicate, the initial agreement made as to how to send and receive data.

hard boot — Restarting the computer by turning off the power or by pressing the Reset button. Also called cold boot.

hard copy — Output from a printer to paper.

hard-disk loading — The illegal practice of installing unauthorized software on computers for sale. Hard-disk loading can typically be identified by the absence of original disks in the original system's shipment.

hard drive — The main secondary storage device of a PC, a small case that contains magnetic coated platters that rotate at high speed.

hard drive controller — The firmware that controls access to a hard drive contained on a circuit board mounted on or inside the hard drive housing. Older hard drives used firmware on a controller card that connected to the drive by way of two cables, one for data and one for control.

hard drive standby time — The amount of time before a hard drive will shut down to conserve energy.

hardware — The physical components that constitute the computer system, such as the monitor, the keyboard, the motherboard, and the printer.

hardware interrupt — An event caused by a hardware device signaling the CPU that it requires service.

head — The top or bottom surface of one platter on a hard drive. Each platter has two heads.

heat sink — A piece of metal, with cooling fins, that can be attached to or mounted on an integrated chip (such as the CPU) to dissipate heat.

hertz (Hz) — Unit of measurement for frequency, calculated in terms of vibrations, or cycles per second. For example, for 16-bit stereo sound, a frequency of 44,000 Hz is used. *See also* megahertz.

hexadecimal notation (hex) — A numbering system that uses sixteen digits, the numerals 0–9 and the letters A–F. Hexadecimal notation is often used to display memory addresses.

hibernation — A notebook OS feature that conserves power by using a small trickle of electricity. Before the notebook begins to hibernate, everything currently stored in memory is saved to the hard drive. When the notebook is brought out of hibernation, open applications and their data are returned to the state before hibernation.

hidden file — A file that is not displayed in a directory list. Whether to hide or display a file is one of the file's attributes kept by the OS.

high-level formatting — Formatting performed by means of the DOS or Windows Format program (for example, FORMAT C:/S creates the boot record, FAT, and root directory on drive C and makes the drive bootable). Also called OS formatting.

host — Any computer or other device on a network that has been assigned an IP address. Also called node.

host adapter — The circuit board that controls a SCSI bus supporting as many as seven or fifteen separate devices. The host adapter controls communication between the SCSI bus and the PC.

host bus — *See* memory bus or system bus.

hot-pluggable — *See* hot-swappable.

hot-swappable — A device that can be plugged into a computer while it is turned on and the computer will sense the device and configure it without rebooting, or the device can be removed without an OS error. Also called hot-pluggable.

hub — A network device or box that provides a central location to connect cables.

HVD (High Voltage Differential) — A type of SCSI differential signaling requiring more expensive hardware to handle the higher voltage. HVD became obsolete with the introduction of SCSI-3.

IBM-compatible PC — A computer that uses an Intel (or compatible) processor and can run DOS and Windows.

IBM Data Connector — *See* IDC.

IDC (IBM Data Connector) — A connector used with STP cable on a Token Ring network. Also called a *UDC (Universal Data Connector)*.

IEEE (Institute of Electrical and Electronics Engineers) — A nonprofit organization that develops standards for the computer and electronics industries.

IEEE 1284 — A standard for parallel ports and cables developed by the Institute for Electrical and Electronics Engineers and supported by many hardware manufacturers.

IEEE 1394 — A new standard, developed by the 1394 Trade Association, that is designed for peer-to-peer data transmission and allows imaging devices to send images and photos directly to printers without involving a computer.

IEEE 802.11a/b/g — IEEE specifications for wireless communication and data synchronization. Also known as Wi-Fi. Apple Computer's versions of 802.11b/g are called AirPort and Airport Extreme.

i.Link — *See* FireWire.

in-band signaling — In modem communication, the name of the signaling used by software flow control, which pauses transmission by sending a special control character in the same channel (or band) that data is sent in.

infrared transceiver — A wireless transceiver that uses infrared technology to support some wireless devices such as keyboards, mice, and printers. A motherboard might have an embedded infrared transceiver, or the transceiver might plug into a USB or serial port. The technology is defined by the Infrared Data Association (IrDA). Also called an *IrDA transceiver* or *infrared port*.

inkjet printer — A type of ink dispersion printer that uses cartridges of ink. The ink is heated to a boiling point and then ejected onto the paper through tiny nozzles.

instruction set — The set of instructions, on the CPU chip, that the computer can perform directly (such as ADD and MOVE).

IDE (Integrated Drive Electronics or Integrated Device Electronics) — A hard drive whose disk controller is integrated into the drive, eliminating the need for a controller cable and thus increasing speed, as well as reducing price. *See also* EIDE.

intelligent UPS — A UPS connected to a computer by way of a USB or serial cable so that software on the computer can monitor and control the UPS. Also called *smart UPS*.

interlaced — A type of display in which the electronic beam of a monitor draws every other line with each pass, which lessens the overall effect of a lower refresh rate.

internal bus — The bus inside the CPU that is used for communication between the CPU's internal components.

internal cache — Memory cache that is faster than external cache, and is contained inside CPU chips (also referred to as primary, Level 1, or L1 cache).

interrupt handler — A program (either BIOS or a device driver) that is used by the CPU to process a hardware interrupt. Also called a request handler.

I/O addresses — Numbers that are used by devices and the CPU to manage communication between them. Also called ports or port addresses.

I/O controller card — An older card that can contain serial, parallel, and game ports and floppy drive and IDE connectors.

IP address (Internet Protocol address) — A 32-bit address consisting of four numbers separated by periods, used to uniquely identify a device on a network that uses TCP/IP protocols. The first numbers identify the network; the last numbers identify the host, or the device. An example of an IP address is 206.96.103.114.

IPX/SPX (Internetwork Packet Exchange/ Sequenced Packet Exchange) — A networking protocol first used by Novell NetWare, which corresponds to the TCP/IP protocols.

IrDA transceiver — *See* infrared transceiver.

IRQ (interrupt request) line — A line on a bus that is assigned to a device and is used to signal the CPU for servicing. These lines are assigned a reference number (for example, the normal IRQ for a printer is IRQ 7).

ISA (Industry Standard Architecture) slot — An older slot on the motherboard used for slower I/O devices, which can support an 8-bit or a 16-bit data path. ISA slots are mostly replaced by PCI slots.

ISA bus — An 8-bit industry standard architecture bus used on the original 8088 PC. Sixteen-bit ISA buses were designed for the 286 AT, and are still used in some Pentium motherboards for devices such as modems.

ISDN (Integrated Services Digital Network) — A digital telephone line that can carry data at about five times the speed of regular telephone lines. Two channels (telephone numbers) share a single pair of wires.

isochronous data transfer — A method used by IEEE 1394 to transfer data continuously without breaks.

ITU (International Telecommunications Union) — The international organization responsible for developing international standards of communication. Formerly CCITT.

JPEG (Joint Photographic Experts Group) — A graphical compression scheme that allows the user to control the amount of data that is averaged and sacrificed as file size is reduced. It is a common Internet file format. Most JPEG files have a .jpg extension.

jumper — Two wires that stick up side by side on the motherboard that are used to hold configuration information. The jumper is considered closed if a cover is over the wires, and open if the cover is missing.

keyboard — A common input device through which data and instructions may be typed into computer memory.

LAN (local area network) — A computer network that covers only a small area, usually within one building.

lands — Microscopic flat areas on the surface of a CD or DVD that separate pits. Lands and pits are used to represent data on the disk.

laptop computer — *See* notebook.

large-capacity drive — A hard drive larger than 504 MB.

large mode — A mode of addressing information on hard drives that range from 504 MB to 8.4 GB, addressing information on a hard drive by translating cylinder, head, and sector information in order to break the 528-MB hard drive barrier. Also called ECHS mode.

laser printer — A type of printer that uses a laser beam to control how toner is placed on the page and then uses heat to fuse the toner to the page.

LBA (logical block addressing) mode — A mode of addressing information on hard drives in which the BIOS and operating system view the drive as one long linear list of LBAs or addressable sectors, permitting drives to be larger than 8.4 GB (LBA 0 is cylinder 0, head 0, and sector 1).

Level 1 (L1) cache — *See* internal cache.

Level 2 (L2) cache — *See* external cache.

Level 3 (L3) cache — *See* external cache.

line conditioner — A device that regulates, or conditions, power, providing continuous voltage during brownouts and spikes.

line-interactive UPS — A variation of a standby UPS that shortens switching time by always keeping the inverter that converts AC to DC working, so that there is no charge-up time for the inverter.

line speed — *See* bandwidth.

local bus — A bus that operates at a speed synchronized with the CPU frequency. The system bus is a local bus.

local I/O bus — A local bus that provides I/O devices with fast access to the CPU. The PCI bus is a local I/O bus.

logical drive — A portion or all of a hard drive partition that is treated by the operating system as though it were a physical drive. Each logical drive is assigned a drive letter, such as drive C, and contains a file system. Also called a volume.

logical geometry — The number of heads, tracks, and sectors that the BIOS on the hard drive controller presents to the system BIOS and the OS. The logical geometry does not consist of the same values as the physical geometry, although calculations of drive capacity yield the same results.

lost allocation units — *See* lost clusters.

lost clusters — File fragments that, according to the file allocation table, contain data that does not belong to any file. The command CHKDSK/F can free these fragments. Also called lost allocation units.

low insertion force (LIF) socket — A socket that requires the installer to manually apply an even force over the microchip when inserting the chip into the socket.

low-level formatting — A process (usually performed at the factory) that electronically creates the hard drive tracks and sectors and tests for bad spots on the disk surface.

low-profile case — *See* compact case.

LPX — A form factor in which expansion cards are mounted on a riser card that plugs into a motherboard. The expansion cards in LPX systems are mounted parallel to the motherboard, rather than perpendicular to it as in AT and ATX systems.

LUN (Logical Unit Number) — A number assigned to a logical device (such as a tray in a CD changer) that is part of a physical SCSI device, which is assigned a SCSI ID.

LVD (Low Voltage Differential) — A type of differential signaling that uses lower voltage than does HVD, is less expensive, and can be compatible with single-ended signaling on the same SCSI bus.

MAC (Media Access Control) address — A 6-byte hexadecimal hardware address unique to each NIC card and assigned by the manufacturer. The address is often printed on the adapter. An example is 00 00 0C 08 2F 35. Also called a physical address, an adapter address, or a hardware address.

main board — *See* motherboard.

make code — A code produced by pressing a key on a computer keyboard.

Master Boot Record (MBR) — The first sector on a hard drive, which contains the partition table and a program the BIOS uses to boot an OS from the drive.

material safety data sheet (MSDS) — A document that explains how to properly handle substances such as chemical solvents; it includes information such as physical data, toxicity, health effects, first aid, storage, disposal, and spill procedures.

MAU (Multistation Access Unit) — A centralized hub used in Token Ring networks to connect stations. Also called CAU or MSAU.

MDRAM (multibank DRAM) — A special kind of RAM used on video cards that is able to use a full 128-bit bus path without requiring the full 4 MB of RAM.

megahertz (MHz) — One million Hz, or one million cycles per second. *See* hertz (Hz).

memory — Physical microchips that can hold data and programming, located on the motherboard or expansion cards.

memory address — A number assigned to each byte in memory. The CPU can use memory addresses to track where information is stored in RAM. Memory addresses are usually displayed as hexadecimal numbers in segment/offset form.

memory bus — *See* system bus.

memory cache — A small amount of faster RAM that stores recently retrieved data, in anticipation of what the CPU will request next, thus speeding up access. *See also* system bus.

microATX — A recent version of the ATX form factor. MicroATX addresses some new technologies that have been developed since the original introduction of ATX.

Micro Channel Architecture (MCA) bus — A proprietary IBM PS/2 bus, seldom seen today, with a width of 16 or 32 bits and multiple master control, which allowed for multitasking.

MicroDIMM — A type of memory module used on sub-notebooks that has 144 pins and uses a 64-bit data path.

microprocessor — *See* central processing unit (CPU).

Mini-ATX — A smaller ATX board that can be used with regular ATX cases and power supplies.

minicartridge — A tape drive cartridge that is only 3¼ × 2½ × ⅜ inches. It is small enough to allow two drives to fit into a standard 5½-inch drive bay of a PC case.

Mini-LPX — A smaller version of the LPX motherboard.

Mini PCI — The PCI industry standard for desktop computer expansion cards, applied to a much smaller form factor for notebook expansion cards.

MMX (Multimedia Extensions) — Multimedia instructions built into Intel processors to add functionality such as better processing of multimedia, SIMD support, and increased cache.

modem — From MOdulate/DEModulate. A device that modulates digital data from a computer to an analog format that can be sent over telephone lines, then demodulates it back into digital form.

modem eliminator — *See* null modem cable.

modem riser card — A small modem card that uses an AMR or CNR slot. Part of the modem logic is contained in a controller on the motherboard.

modem speed — The speed at which a modem can transmit data along a phone line, measured in bits per second (bps). Also called line speed.

modulation — Converting binary or digital data into an analog signal that can be sent over standard telephone lines.

monitor — The most commonly used output device for displaying text and graphics on a computer.

motherboard — The main board in the computer, also called the system board. The CPU, ROM chips, SIMMs, DIMMs, RIMMs, and interface cards are plugged into the motherboard.

motherboard bus — *See* system bus.

motherboard mouse — *See* PS/2-compatible mouse.

mouse — A pointing and input device that allows the user to move a cursor around a screen and select programs with the click of a button.

MP3 — A method to compress audio files that uses MPEG level 1. It can reduce sound files as low as a 1:24 ratio without losing much sound quality.

MPEG (Moving Pictures Experts Group) — A process-ing-intensive standard for data compression for motion pictures that tracks movement from one frame to the next and only stores the data that has changed.

MSAU — *See* MAU.

MultiBank DRAM (MDRAM) — A type of video memory that is faster than VRAM or WRAM, but can be more economical because it can be installed on a video card in smaller increments.

multimedia — A type of computer presentation that combines text, graphics, animation, photos, sound, and/or full-motion video.

multimeter — A device used to measure the various components of an electrical circuit. The most common measurements are voltage, current, and resistance.

multiplier — The factor by which the bus speed or frequency is multiplied to get the CPU clock speed.

multiscan monitor — A monitor that can work within a range of frequencies and thus can work with different standards and video cards. It offers a variety of refresh rates.

multisession — A feature that allows data to be read from or written to a CD during more than one session. This is important if the disk was only partially filled during the first write.

narrow SCSI — One of the two main SCSI specifications. Narrow SCSI has an 8-bit data bus. The word narrow is not usually included in the names of narrow SCSI devices.

NetBEUI (NetBIOS Extended User Interface) — A fast, proprietary Microsoft networking protocol used only by Windows-based systems, and limited to LANs because it does not support routing.

network adapter — *See* network interface card.

network interface card (NIC) — A expansion card that plugs into a computer's motherboard and provides a port on the back of the card to connect a PC to a network. Also called a network adapter.

NLX — A low-end form factor that is similar to LPX but provides greater support for current and emerging processor technologies. NLX was designed for flexibility and efficiency of space.

node — *See* host.

noise — An extraneous, unwanted signal, often over an analog phone line, that can cause communication interference or transmission errors. Possible sources are fluorescent lighting, radios, TVs, lightning, or bad wiring.

noninterlaced — A type of display in which the electronic beam of a monitor draws every line on the screen with each pass.

nonparity memory — Eight-bit memory without error checking. A SIMM part number with a 32 in it (4 × 8 bits) is nonparity.

nonvolatile — Refers to a kind of RAM that is stable and can hold data as long as electricity is powering the memory.

normal mode — *See* CHS mode.

North Bridge — That portion of the chip set hub that connects faster I/O buses (for example, AGP bus) to the system bus. Compare to South Bridge.

notebook — A portable computer that is designed for travel and mobility. Notebooks use the same technology as desktop PCs, with modifications for conserving voltage, taking up less space, and operating while on the move. Also called a laptop computer.

null modem cable — A cable that allows two data terminal equipment (DTE) devices to communicate in which the transmit and receive wires are cross-connected and no modems are necessary.

ohm (Ω) — The standard unit of measurement for electrical resistance. Resistors are rated in ohms.

on-board ports — Ports that are directly on the motherboard, such as a built-in keyboard port or on-board serial port.

operating system (OS) — Software that controls a computer. An OS controls how system resources are used and provides a user interface, a way of managing hardware and software, and ways to work with files.

operating system formatting — *See* high-level formatting.

overclocking — Running a motherboard at a frequency that is not recommended or guaranteed by CPU or chip set manufacturers.

P1 connector — Power connection on an ATX motherboard.

P8 connector — One of two power connectors on an AT motherboard.

P9 connector — One of two power connectors on an AT motherboard.

packet — Segment of network data that also includes header, destination address, and trailer information that is sent as a unit. Also called data packet or datagram.

parallel ATA (PATA) — An older IDE cabling method that uses a 40-pin flat data cable or an 80 conductor cable and a 40-pin IDE connector. *Also see* serial ATA.

parallel port — A female 25-pin port on a computer that can transmit data in parallel, 8 bits at a time, and is usually used with a printer. The names for parallel ports are LPT1 and LPT2.

parity — An error-checking scheme in which a ninth, or "parity," bit is added. The value of the parity bit is set to either 0 or 1 to provide an even number of ones for even parity and an odd number of ones for odd parity.

parity error — An error that occurs when the number of 1s in the byte is not in agreement with the expected number.

parity memory — Nine-bit memory in which the ninth bit is used for error checking. A SIMM part number with a 36 in it (4 × 9 bits) is parity. Older PCs almost always use parity chips.

partition — A division of a hard drive that can be used to hold logical drives.

partition table — A table at the beginning of the hard drive that contains information about each partition on the drive. The partition table is contained in the Master Boot Record.

passive backplane — A type of backplane system in which the backplane contains no circuitry at all. Passive backplanes locate all circuitry on a mothercard plugged into a backplane.

passive terminator — A type of terminator for single-ended SCSI cables. Simple resistors are used to provide termination of a signal. Passive termination is not reliable over long distances and should only be used with narrow SCSI.

patch cable — A network cable that is used to connect a PC to a hub.

PC Card — A credit-card-sized adapter card that can be slid into a slot in the side of many notebook computers and is used for connecting to modems, networks, and CD-ROM drives. Also called PCMCIA Card.

PC Card slot — An expansion slot on a notebook computer, into which a PC Card is inserted. Also called a PCMCIA Card slot.

PCI (Peripheral Component Interconnect) bus — A bus common on Pentium computers that runs at speeds of up to 33 MHz or 66 MHz, with a 32-bit-wide or 64-bit-wide data path. PCI-X, released in September 1999, enables PCI to run at 133 MHz. For some chip sets, it serves as the middle layer between the memory bus and expansion buses.

PCI bus IRQ steering — A feature that makes it possible for PCI devices to share an IRQ. System BIOS and the OS must both support this feature.

PCMCIA (Personal Computer Memory Card International Association) Card — *See* PC Card.

PCMCIA Card slot — *See* PC Card slot.

PDA (Personal Digital Assistant) — A small, handheld computer that has its own operating system and applications.

peripheral devices — Devices that communicate with the CPU but are not located directly on the motherboard, such as the monitor, floppy drive, printer, and mouse.

physical address — *See* MAC address.

physical geometry — The actual layout of heads, tracks, and sectors on a hard drive. Refer also to logical geometry.

pin array cartridge (PAC) — The cartridge that houses the Intel Itanium processor.

Ping (Packet Internet Groper) — A Windows and Unix command used to troubleshoot network connections. It verifies that the host can communicate with another host on the network.

pin grid array (PGA) — A feature of a CPU socket whereby the pins are aligned in uniform rows around the socket.

pinout — A description of how each pin on a bus, connection, plug, slot, or socket is used.

PIO (Programmed I/O) transfer mode — A transfer mode that uses the CPU to transfer data from the hard drive to memory. PIO mode is slower than DMA mode.

pipelined burst SRAM — A less expensive SRAM that uses more clock cycles per transfer than non-pipelined burst but does not significantly slowdown the process.

pits — Recessed areas on the surface of a CD or DVD, separating lands, or flat areas. Lands and pits are used to represent data on a disc.

pixel — A small spot on a fine horizontal scan line. Pixels are illuminated to create an image on the monitor.

Plug and Play (PnP) — A standard designed to make the installation of new hardware devices easier by automatically configuring devices to eliminate system resource conflicts (such as IRQ or I/O address conflicts). PnP is supported by Windows 9x/Me, Windows 2000, and Windows XP.

polling — A process by which the CPU checks the status of connected devices to determine if they are ready to send or receive data.

port — (1) Another name for an I/O address. *See also* I/O address. (2) A physical connector, usually at the back of a computer, that allows a cable from a peripheral device, such as a printer, mouse, or modem, to be attached.

port address — *See* I/O address.

port replicator — A device designed to connect to a notebook computer in order to make it easy to connect the notebook to peripheral devices.

port settings — The configuration parameters of communications devices such as COM1, COM2, or COM3, including IRQ settings.

port speed — The communication speed between a DTE (computer) and a DCE (modem). As a general rule, the port speed should be at least four times as fast as the modem speed.

power conditioner — A line conditioner that regulates, or conditions, power, providing continuous voltage during brownouts.

power on password — A password that a computer uses to control access during the boot process.

power-on self test (POST) — A self-diagnostic program used to perform a simple test of the CPU, RAM, and various I/O devices. The POST is performed by startup BIOS when the computer is first turned on, and is stored in ROM-BIOS.

power supply — A box inside the computer case that supplies power to the motherboard and other installed devices. Power supplies provide 3.3, 5, and 12 volts DC.

primary cache — *See* internal cache.

primary partition — A partition on a hard drive that can contain only a single logical drive.

primary storage — Temporary storage or memory on the motherboard, used by the CPU to process data and instructions. Memory is considered primary storage.

printer — A peripheral output device that produces printed output to paper. Different types include dot matrix, ink-jet, and laser printers.

printer maintenance kit — A kit purchased from a printer manufacturer that contains parts, tools, and instructions needed to perform routine printer maintenance.

processor — *See* central processing unit (CPU).

processor speed — The speed, or frequency, at which the CPU operates. Usually expressed in GHz.

program — A set of step-by-step instructions to a computer. Some are burned directly into chips, while others are stored as program files. Programs are written in languages such as BASIC and C++.

protocol — A set of rules and standards that two entities use for communication.

PS/2-compatible mouse — A mouse that plugs into a round mouse PS/2 port on the motherboard. Sometimes called a motherboard mouse.

Quarter-Inch Committee or quarter-inch cartridge (QIC) — A name of a standardized method used to write data to tape. These backup files have a .qic extension.

RAID (redundant array of inexpansive disks or redundant array of independent disks) — Several methods of configuring multiple hard drives to store data to increase logical volume size, improve performance, or ensure that if one hard drive fails, the data is still available from another hard drive.

RAM drive — An area of memory that is treated as though it were a hard drive, but works much faster than a hard drive. The Windows 9x/Me startup disk uses a RAM drive. Compare to virtual memory.

RAM (random access memory) — Memory modules on the motherboard containing microchips used to temporarily hold data and programs while the CPU processes both. Information in RAM is lost when the PC is turned off.

RDRAM — *See* Direct Rambus DRAM.

read/write head — A sealed, magnetic coil device that moves across the surface of a disk either reading data from or writing data to the disk.

rectifier — An electrical device that converts AC to DC. A PC power supply contains a rectifier.

refresh — The process of periodically rewriting data, such as on dynamic RAM.

refresh rate — As applied to monitors, the number of times in one second an electronic beam can fill the screen with lines from top to bottom. Also called vertical scan rate.

re-marked chips — Chips that have been used and returned to the factory, marked again, and resold. The surface of the chips may be dull or scratched.

repeater — A device that amplifies signals on a network so they can be transmitted further down the line.

request handler — *See* interrupt handler.

resistance — The degree to which a device opposes or resists the flow of electricity. As the electrical resistance increases, the current decreases. *See* ohm and resistor.

resistor — An electronic device that resists or opposes the flow of electricity. A resistor can be used to reduce the amount of electricity being supplied to an electronic component.

resolution — The number of pixels on a monitor screen that are addressable by software (example: 1024 × 768 pixels).

REt (Resolution Enhancement technology) — The term used by Hewlett-Packard to describe the way a laser printer varies the size of the dots used to create an image. This technology partly accounts for the sharp, clear image created by a laser printer.

RIMM — A type of memory module developed by Rambus, Inc.

ring topology — A network topology in which the nodes in a network form a ring. Each node is connected only to two other nodes, and a centralized hub is not required.

RISC (Reduced Instruction Set Computing) chips — Chips that incorporate only the most frequently used instructions, so that the computer operates faster (for example, the PowerPC uses RISC chips).

riser card — A card that plugs into a motherboard and allows for expansion cards to be mounted parallel to the motherboard. Expansion cards are plugged into slots on the riser card.

RJ-11 — A phone line connection found on modems, telephones, and house phone outlets.

RJ-45 connector — A connector used with twisted-pair cable that connects the cable to the NIC.

ROM (read-only memory) — Chips that contain programming code and cannot be erased.

ROM BIOS — *See* BIOS.

routable protocol — A protocol that can be routed to interconnected networks on the basis of a network address. TCP/IP is a routable protocol, but NetBEUI is not.

router — A device that connects networks and makes decisions as to the best routes to use when forwarding packets.

sags — *See* brownouts.

sampling rate — The rate of samples taken of an analog signal over a period of time, usually expressed as samples per second, or hertz.

scanning mirror — A component of a laser printer consisting of an octagonal mirror that can be directed in a sweeping motion to cover the entire length of a laser printer drum.

SCSI (Small Computer System Interface) — A fast interface between a host adapter and the CPU that can daisy chain as many as 7 or 15 devices on a single bus.

SCSI ID — A number from 0 to 15 assigned to each SCSI device attached to the daisy chain.

SDRAM II — *See* Double Data Rate SDRAM (DDR SDRAM).

secondary storage — Storage that is remote to the CPU and permanently holds data, even when the PC is turned off, such as a hard drive.

sector — On a disk surface, one segment of a track, which almost always contains 512 bytes of data.

sequential access — A method of data access used by tape drives, whereby data is written or read sequentially from the beginning to the end of the tape or until the desired data is found.

serial ATA (SATA) — An ATAPI cabling method that uses a narrower and more reliable cable than the 80-conductor cable. *Also see* parallel ATA.

serial ATA cable — An IDE cable that is narrower and has fewer pins than the parallel IDE 80-con-ductor cable.

serial mouse — A mouse that uses a serial port and has a female 9-pin DB-9 connector.

serial port — Male 9-pin or 25-pin ports on the computer used for transmitting data serially, one bit at a time. Serial ports are sometimes configured as COM1, COM2, COM3, or COM4.

SGRAM (synchronous graphics RAM) — Memory designed especially for video card processing that can synchronize itself with the CPU bus clock.

shadow RAM or shadowing ROM — ROM programming code copied into RAM to speed up the system operation, because of the faster access speed of RAM.

shielded twisted-pair (STP) cable — A cable that is made of one or more twisted pairs of wires and is surrounded by a metal shield.

signal-regenerating repeater — A repeater that is able to distinguish between noise and signal. It reads the signal and retransmits it without the accompanying noise.

SIMD (single instruction, multiple data) — A process that allows the CPU to execute a single instruction simultaneously on multiple pieces of data, rather than by repetitive looping.

SIMM (single inline memory module) — A miniature circuit board used in older computers to hold RAM. SIMMs hold 8, 16, 32, or 64 MB on a single module.

single-ended (SE) — A type of SCSI signaling in which two wires are used to carry a signal, one of which carries the signal itself and the other is a ground for the signal.

single-voltage CPU — A CPU that requires one voltage for both internal and I/O operations.

slack — Wasted space on a hard drive caused by not using all available space at the end of clusters.

sleep mode — A mode used in many "Green" systems that allows them to be configured through CMOS to suspend the monitor or even the drive, if the keyboard and/or CPU have been inactive for a set number of minutes. *See also* Green Standards.

slimline case — *See* compact case.

smart UPS — *See* intelligent UPS.

SMAU (Smart Multistation Access Unit) — *See* MAU.

SO-DIMM (small outline DIMM) — A type of memory module used in notebook computers that uses DIMM technology and can have either 72 pins or 144 pins.

SO-RIMM (small outline RIMM) — A 160-pin memory module used in notebooks that uses Rambus technology.

soft boot — To restart a PC without turning off the power, for example, in Windows XP, by clicking Start, Turn Off Computer, and Restart. Also called warm boot.

soft power — *See* soft switch.

soft switch — A feature on an ATX system that allows an OS to power down the system and allows for activity such as a keystroke or network activity to power up the system. Also called soft power.

software — Computer programs, or instructions to perform a specific task. Software may be BIOS, OSs, or applications software such as a word-processing or spreadsheet program.

software interrupt — An event caused when a program currently being executed by the CPU signals the CPU that it requires the use of a hardware device.

solid ink printer — A type of printer that uses sticks or blocks of solid ink. The ink is melted and then jetted onto the paper as the paper passes by on a drum.

South Bridge — That portion of the chip set hub that connects slower I/O buses (for example, ISA bus) to the system bus. Compare to North Bridge.

spacers — *See* standoffs.

SPI (SCSI Parallel Interface) — The part of the SCSI-3 standard that specifies how SCSI devices are connected.

spikes — Temporary surges in voltage, which can damage electrical components. Also called swells.

SSE (Streaming SIMD Extension) — A technology used the Intel Pentium III and later CPUs designed to improve performance of multimedia software.

staggered pin grid array (SPGA) — A feature of a CPU socket whereby the pins are staggered over the socket in order to squeeze more pins into a small space.

standby time — The time before a "Green" system will reduce 92 percent of its activity. *See also* Green Standards.

standoffs — Round plastic or metal pegs that separate the motherboard from the case, so that components on the back of the motherboard do not touch the case.

star bus topology — A LAN that uses a logical bus design, but with all devices connected to a central hub, making a physical star.

star ring topology — A topology that is physically arranged in a star formation but is logically a ring because of the way information travels on it. Token Ring is the primary example.

star topology — A LAN in which all the devices are connected to a central hub.

startup BIOS — Part of system BIOS that is responsible for controlling the PC when it is first turned on. Startup BIOS gives control over to the OS once it is loaded.

startup password — *See* power on password.

stateless — Term for a device or process that manages data or some activity without regard to all the details of the data or activity.

static electricity — *See* ESD.

static RAM (SRAM) — RAM chips that retain information without the need for refreshing, as long as the computer's power is on. They are more expensive than traditional DRAM.

streaming audio — Downloading audio data from the Internet in a continuous stream of data without first downloading an entire audio file.

surge suppressor or surge protector — A device or power strip designed to protect electronic equipment from power surges and spikes.

suspend time — The time before a green system will reduce 99 percent of its activity. After this time, the system needs a warmup time so that the CPU, monitor, and hard drive can reach full activity.

swap file — A file on the hard drive that is used by the OS for virtual memory. Also called page file.

swells — *See* spikes.

switch — A device used to segment a network. It can decide which network segment is to receive a packet, on the basis of the packet's destination MAC address.

synchronization — The process by which files and programs are transferred between PDAs and PCs.

synchronous DRAM (SDRAM) — A type of memory stored on DIMMs that runs in sync with the system clock, running at the same speed as the motherboard.

synchronous SRAM — SRAM that is faster and more expensive than asynchronous SRAM. It requires a clock signal to validate its control signals, enabling the cache to run in step with the CPU.

SyncLink DRAM (SLDRAM) — A type of DRAM developed by a consortium of 12 DRAM manufactures. It improved on regular SDRAM but is now obsolete.

system BIOS — BIOS located on the motherboard.

system board — *See* motherboard.

system bus — The bus between the CPU and memory on the motherboard. The bus frequency in the documentation is called the system speed, such as 400 MHz. Also called memory bus, motherboard bus, host bus, external bus, or front side bus.

system clock — A line on a bus that is dedicated to timing the activities of components connected to it. The system clock provides a continuous pulse that other devices use to time themselves.

system resource — A channel, line, or address on the motherboard that can be used by the CPU or a device for communication. The four system resources are IRQ, I/O address, DMA channel, and memory address.

TAPI (Telephony Application Programming Interface) — A standard developed by Intel and Micro-soft that can be used by 32-bit Windows communications programs for communicating over phone lines.

TCP/IP (Transmission Control Protocol/Internet Protocol) — The suite of protocols that supports communication on the Internet. TCP is responsible for error checking, and IP is responsible for routing.

telephony — A term describing the technology of converting sound to signals that can travel over telephone lines.

terminating resistor — The resistor added at the end of a SCSI chain to dampen the voltage at the end of the chain.

termination — A process necessary to prevent an echo effect of power at the end of a SCSI chain, resulting in interference with the data transmission.

thermal printer — A type of line printer that uses wax-based ink, which is heated by heat pins that melt the ink onto paper.

ThickNet — *See* 10Base5 Ethernet.

ThinNet — *See* 10Base2 Ethernet.

throughput performance — Also called data throughput. Throughput performance is a measure of the actual data transmitted by the bus, not including error-checking bits or redundant data.

token — A small packet used on token ring networks to send data from one station to the next.

touch screen — An input device that uses a monitor or LCD panel as a backdrop for user options. Touch screens can be embedded in a monitor or LCD panel or installed as an add-on device.

tower case — The largest type of personal computer case. Tower cases stand vertically upright and can be as much as two feet tall. They have more drive bays and are a good choice for computer users who anticipate making significant upgrades.

trace — A wire on a circuit board that connects two components or devices.

tracks — The concentric circles into which the surface of a disk is divided.

training — *See* handshaking.

transceiver — The component on a NIC that is responsible for signal conversion. Combines the words transmitter and receiver.

transformer — A device that changes the ratio of current to voltage. A computer power supply is basically a transformer and a rectifier.

transistor — An electronic device that can regulate electricity and act as a logical gate or switch for an electrical signal.

translation — A technique used by system BIOS and hard drive controller BIOS to break the 504-MB hard drive barrier, whereby a different set of drive

parameters are communicated to the OS and other software than that used by the hard drive controller BIOS.

TSR (terminate-and-stay-resident) — A program that is loaded into memory but is not immediately executed, such as a screen saver or a memory-resident antivirus program.

UART (universal asynchronous receiver-transmitter) chip — A chip that controls serial ports. It sets protocol and converts parallel data bits received from the system bus into serial bits.

UDC (Universal Data Connector) — *See* IDC (IBM Data Connector).

UDF (Universal Disk Format) — A file system for optical media used by all DVD discs and some CD-R and CD-RW discs.

unshielded twisted-pair (UTP) cable — A cable that is made of one or more twisted pairs of wires and is not surrounded by a metal shield.

UPS (uninterruptible power supply) — A device designed to provide a backup power supply during a power failure. Basically, a UPS is a battery backup system with an ultrafast sensing device.

USB host controller — Manages the USB bus. If the motherboard contains on-board USB ports, the USB host controller is part of the chipset. The USB uses only a single set of resources for all devices on the bus.

USB (universal serial bus) port — A type of port designed to make installation and configuration of I/O devices easy, providing room for as many as 127 devices daisy-chained together.

V.92 — The latest standard for data transmission over phone lines that can attain a speed of 56 Kbps.

vertical scan rate — *See* refresh rate.

VESA (Video Electronics Standards Association) VL bus — An outdated local bus used on 80486 computers for connecting 32-bit adapters directly to the local processor bus.

video card — An interface card installed in the computer to control visual output on a monitor. Also called display adapter.

virtual file allocation table (VFAT) — A variation of the original DOS 16-bit FAT that allows for long filenames and 32-bit disk access.

virtual memory — A method whereby the OS uses the hard drive as though it were RAM. Compare to RAM drive.

volatile — Refers to a kind of RAM that is temporary, cannot hold data very long, and must be frequently refreshed.

volt (V) — A measure of potential difference in an electrical circuit. A computer ATX power supply usually provides five separate voltages: +12V, –12V, +5V, –5V, and +3.3V.

voltage — Electrical differential that causes current to flow, measured in volts. *See* volt.

voltage regulator module (VRM) — A device embedded or installed on the motherboard that regulates voltage to the processor.

voltmeter — A device for measuring electrical AC or DC voltage.

volume — *See* logical drive.

VRAM (video RAM) — RAM on video cards that holds the data that is being passed from the computer to the monitor and can be accessed by two devices simultaneously. Higher resolutions often require more video memory.

wait state — A clock tick in which nothing happens, used to ensure that the microprocessor isn't getting ahead of slower components. A 0-wait state is preferable to a 1-wait state. Too many wait states can slow a system down.

warm boot — *See* soft boot.

watt (W) — The unit used to measure power. A typical computer may use a power supply that provides 200W.

wattage — Electrical power measured in watts.

wide SCSI — One of the two main SCSI specifications. Wide SCSI has a 16-bit data bus. *Also see* narrow SCSI.

wireless LAN (WLAN) — A type of LAN that does not use wires or cables to create connections, but instead transmits data over radio or infrared waves.

WRAM (window RAM) — Dual-ported video RAM that is faster and less expensive than VRAM. It has its own internal bus on the chip, with a data path that is 256 bits wide.

zero insertion force (ZIF) socket — A socket that uses a small lever to apply even force when you install the microchip into the socket.

zone bit recording — A method of storing data on a hard drive whereby the drive can have more sectors per track near the outside of the platter.